The Ten Commandments and the Beatitudes

The Ten Commandments and the Beatitudes

Biblical Studies and Ethics for Real Life

Yiu Sing Lúcás Chan

Foreword by Daniel J. Harrington, S.J., and James F. Keenan, S.J.

A SHEED & WARD BOOK

ROWMAN & LITTLEFIELD PUBLISHERS, INC.
Lanham • Boulder • New York • Toronto • Plymouth, UK

A Sheed & Ward Book

Published by Rowman & Littlefield Publishers, Inc.
A wholly owned subsidiary of The Rowman & Littlefield Publishing Group, Inc.
4501 Forbes Boulevard, Suite 200, Lanham, Maryland 20706
www.rowman.com

10 Thornbury Road, Plymouth PL6 7PY, United Kingdom

British Library Cataloguing in Publication Information Available

Library of Congress Cataloging-in-Publication Data

Chan, Yiu Sing Lúcás, 1968–
The Ten commandments and the Beatitudes : biblical studies and ethics for real life / Yiu Sing Lúcás
Chan ; foreword by Daniel J. Harrington and James F. Keenan.
p. cm.
"A Sheed & Ward book."
ISBN 978-1-4422-1553-5 (cloth : alk. paper) — ISBN 978-1-4422-1554-2 (pbk. : alk. paper) —
ISBN 978-1-4422-1555-9 (electronic)
1. Ten commandments—Criticism, interpretation, etc. 2. Beatitudes—Criticism, interpretation, etc. 3.
Christian ethics—Biblical teaching. I. Title.
BV4655.C43 2012
241.5—dc23
2012018744

The paper used in this publication meets the minimum requirements of American
National Standard for Information Sciences Permanence of Paper for Printed Library
Materials, ANSI/NISO Z39.48-1992.

Printed in the United States of America

To Ms. Mary Yung Wong-hei (RIP), my beloved grandmother

who adopted my mother unconditionally,
raised me and my siblings wholeheartedly,
and brought Christian faith to our family devotedly.

Contents

Foreword

One of the most widely quoted directives from the Second Vatican Council (1962–1965) was the hope that Catholic moral theology "should draw more fully on the teaching of Holy Scripture" (*Optatam totius* 16). We believe that the work of our former student and friend, Yiu Sing Lúcás Chan, represents a milestone toward the fulfillment of that hope. He has immersed himself both in the best of modern biblical scholarship relevant to ethics and in the virtue ethics approach to Christian moral theology. And he has applied his method concretely to two of the most important texts in the Christian Bible. Of course, Chan's *The Ten Commandments and the Beatitudes: Biblical Studies and Ethics for Real Life* is very ecumenical in its indebtedness and engagement of Protestant biblical theologians and theological ethicists, and rightly so. The Catholic participation in the field of biblical ethics is a fairly recent development. In fact, one could say that Catholic involvement in this scholarship began nearly one hundred years ago almost to the day.

The story was told ten years ago on the occasion of the one hundredth anniversary of the Pontifical Biblical Commission, by then Cardinal Joseph Ratzinger.[1] It states that on June 29, 1912, a Vatican congregation issued a decree condemning a claim by a biblical theologian, Friedrich Wilhelm Maier, who had written an essay on the synoptic gospels in which he sustained the so-called two-source theory. The essay appeared in a commentary edited by Fritz Tillmann, a successful and influential biblical theologian who had written three biblical studies dealing with Jesus's own self-understanding and his future coming.

The decree ordered that the commentary be banned and that both Maier *and* Tillmann be forbidden to work ever again as biblical theologians. They were, however, given the option of changing theological disciplines: Maier became a prison chaplain, Tillmann a moral theologian.

Tillmann's first book in theological ethics appeared seven years later; it was on the community in the preaching of Jesus. His most significant academic achievement was published in 1934 on the notion of the disciple of Christ. The book was a tremendous success: the concept of discipleship in Catholic theological ethics was completely new and it was quickly appropriated. In 1937 he published a more accessible text for laypeople, *Die Meister Ruft*. This work had an even greater impact on theological discourse. It used the triple love command and developed a virtue-based ethics for living out the biblical charge to love God, self, and neighbor. In 1961, the book was translated into English: *The Master Calls*.

A second Catholic breakthrough into biblically based theological ethics happened about thirty years ago when the theological ethicist William C. Spohn penned a very popular handbook: *What Are They Saying about Scripture and Ethics?* (1984). It highlighted how more and more theologians applied biblical scholarship to practical living.

In his study, Spohn noticed that theologians were working with different presuppositions, and so he articulated six different models that outlined these different approaches to applying the Bible to ordinary ethical life. The first was the robust Protestant Divine Command, reminiscent of the work of Karl Barth and Dietrich Bonhoeffer, while the second was a barely relevant Scripture as a reminder, which reflected Karl Rahner's and Bruno Schüller's use of the Bible. The third was the fairly recent liberationist approach, made famous by Gustavo Gutiérrez and appropriated by feminists like Letty Russell and Phyllis Trible. The fourth was a response to God's revelation that focused, as H. Richard Niebuhr did, on what God does in the world. Ironically, the fifth, a call to discipleship, made no reference to Tillmann but reflected on the initiatives of Stanley Hauerwas, Sallie McFague, and John Howard Yoder. The last one captured Spohn's own preference, a Gospel response to love and an ordering of the affections.

Spohn's lack of familiarity with Tillmann is noteworthy, since Tillmann brought together the last two models, discipleship and love, by using the virtues. This omission becomes even more interesting when considering that Spohn put the two together in his own remarkable book, *Go and Do Likewise: Jesus and Ethics* (1999). There Spohn argues that virtue ethics is the most promising interpretive key for receiving the Scriptures, hearing the call of discipleship, and living out the love command.

Spohn's initiatives led to other developments—notably, a greater frequency of teaching collaboration between biblical theologians and theological ethicists. Practicing what he preached, Spohn taught a biblical ethics course with the exegete John Donahue. Similarly, we began teaching together, arguing the need for the two competencies of biblical exegesis and ethical interpretation, while agreeing to rely on virtue ethics as the appropriate hermeneutics of interpretation. In one of those courses, Yiu Sing Lúcás Chan agreed to be our teaching assistant.

Chan's book, we think, marks the third major breakthrough by a Catholic contributor to the field of biblical ethics. Chan takes the work of Spohn and Donahue, together with ours, and makes it normative. But he also weaves in the proposal by the Protestant theologian Allen Verhey, a trained exegete and ethicist, who frames these claims throughout his writings arguing that the work of blending exegesis and ethical interpretation is something of a performance.

What makes Chan's work so foundational is its two achievements. First, despite the claims of Spohn, Donahue, and Verhey, the majority of people writing in biblical ethics ignore the twofold tasks: in most instances, ethicists do not do exegesis when they attempt biblical ethics, and Scripture scholars have little or no hermeneutics to their ethical application. Each side assumes or ignores the competency that they lack. Chan raises these scholars up and demonstrates that without exegesis and ethical interpretation, these scholars' works fall quite short of the true demands of biblical ethics. His work is thus a manifesto for the double competencies of a biblically based ethics.

Second, he not only makes the argument, he also performs it! By linking the Ten Commandments with the Beatitudes, Chan takes the most fundamental ethical texts of each Testament and subjects them to the same analytic method. Inasmuch as the Decalogue embodies the norms for moral action in light of our created nature and the Beatitudes embody those traits for disciples in the light of Jesus Christ, Chan provides us with a fairly comprehensive "performance" of the moral expectations of the Christian Scriptures.

In these hundred years since the condemnation of Maier and Tillmann, we have come a long way. Now, as we begin the next centenary of our work, Yiu Sing Lúcás Chan provides us with a foundation as well as a tangible exposé of what we need as we go forward in our study of the Scriptures and in our application of those texts for an ethics of real life.

Daniel J. Harrington, S.J.
James F. Keenan, S.J.
Boston College

NOTE

1. Pope Benedict VI, *Relationship between Magisterium and Exegetes*, May 10, 2003, http://www.vatican.va/roman_curia/congregations/cfaith/pcb_documents/rc_con_cfaith_doc_20030510_ratzinger-comm-bible_en.html.

Abbreviations

A	*Analects*
CCC	*Catechism of the Catholic Church*
DM	*Doctrine of the Mean*
GL	*Great Learning*
ICR	*Institutes of the Christian Religion*
LC	*The Large Catechism*
M	The book of *Mencius*
ST	*Summa Theologiae*

Prologue

Ten to Eight

For centuries the use of Scripture[1] in Christian ethics has differentiated Protestants from Catholics. The Reformers turned to Scripture as the primary source of moral wisdom; Catholics reiterated, instead, their dependency on tradition. The Second Vatican Council, however, admonished Catholic moral theologians to turn to Scripture: "Special care should be given to the perfecting of moral theology. Its scientific presentation should draw more fully on the teaching of Holy Scripture."[2]

In the second half of the twentieth century, the Roman Catholic Church began to catch up. Given that Catholic ethics now turns favorably to the Bible for its sources, where should we turn concretely in the Bible for moral guidance? What specific scriptural texts are foundational to our Christian moral living nowadays?

Within the Catholic tradition, the 1993 encyclical on the Christian moral life, *Veritatis Splendor*, established the Decalogue and the Sermon on the Mount as the two pillars of Christian morality: the former is central to every other precept, while the latter is "the *magna carta* of Gospel morality" (##12, 13, 15).[3] Eberhard Schockenhoff adopts these claims of the encyclical and turns to these two texts for his own argument on the relevance of natural law as a methodological approach in theological ethics.[4]

The most recent document from the Vatican's Pontifical Biblical Commission, *The Bible and Morality: Biblical Roots of Christian Conduct*, aims to situate Christian morality in the larger context of biblical morality and shows how the Bible provides criteria for moral progress. It again specifies the Decalogue in Exodus 20:2–17 and the Beatitudes in Matthew 5:3–12 in the Sermon on the Mount as the two biblical texts that best illustrate the fundamental criteria for judging moral actions. They are convinced that these two texts are the characteristic expressions of biblical morality found in the Hebrew Bible[5] and the New Testament, respectively; they add that the latter radicalizes the values promoted by the former.[6]

While welcoming their claims, I note that there are other important reasons for turning to these two specific texts for moral guidance.

THE TEN COMMANDMENTS

Without any doubt, one of the Bible's most widely known texts is the Ten Commandments.[7] Surveys show that most movie viewers in North America would associate the phrase "Ten Commandments" with Cecil DeMille's 1956 classic of the same name.[8] Across the world, Polish director Krzysztof Kieślowski's *Decalogue* of the mid-1980s has drawn even greater attention. Many film critics and moral theologians alike comment that the success of the series "has also aroused a new interest in the Ten Commandments."[9]

Apart from its familiarity in the contemporary Western world, the text has actually been known to other cultures for many centuries already. For example, the first Roman Catholic catechism published in China, 天主教要理 [*Catholic Doctrine*], written by the Italian Jesuit missionary Mateo Ricci in the early seventeenth century, attends to the Ten Commandments. The efforts of Jesuit missionaries coupled with the moral chaos of that period (the late Ming and early Qing dynasties) helped make the Decalogue known and needed by Chinese society.[10]

The Ten Commandments not only enjoy global popularity and familiarity, they also have a special place in most societies. In the contemporary United States, for instance, the Decalogue is sometimes perceived as a "*cultural* icon."[11]

Still, the Ten Commandments occupy an even more significant place throughout the history of Judaism and Christianity. In the first place, the Decalogue has a unique character among all the Hebrew Scriptures:[12] it is the only law in the Torah (the first five books of the Hebrew Bible) that seems to be the direct address of YHWH to the people and was kept in the Ark of the Covenant. It is separated from the rest of the law and does not prescribe any concrete penalties as other laws do. The text is repeated twice, and parallels can be found elsewhere in the Torah. Moreover, the terse form of the text encourages memorization and calls for appropriation.

This call for appropriation leads into a second point concerning the Decalogue's religious and moral significance for Judaism.[13] According to the *Mishnah* (the first written Rabbinic redaction of the oral traditions), the Decalogue was read with the *Shema* (Deuteronomy 6:4–9) in the temple during worship. Later, the people of Israel celebrated the "feast of Giving the Torah" in which they renewed the oath to keep the Ten Commandments. Additionally, the first-century Jewish philosopher Philo of Alexandria claimed that all of the laws are simply detailed elaborations of the Decalogue. Indeed, the Ten Commandments played a special role in the moral life of the law-binding ancient Jewish people by claiming a superior status among other *mitzvot* (biblical laws/commandments).

For various reasons, the Decalogue lost its uniqueness and moral significance in subsequent generations.[14] Nonetheless, many pious Jews to this day include the Ten Commandments in their morning prayer.

The Decalogue has become a crucial part in the life of Christians for many centuries, particularly in catechetical instruction and guiding moral living.[15] As early as the second century, the Decalogue was employed in catechetical work along with excerpts from the Sermon on the Mount to form a code of ethics. The early Church Fathers like Tertullian perceived the Decalogue as a kind of universal moral law for all humankind.

During the Middle Ages, Thomas Aquinas compiled a lengthy collection of his catechetical instructions on the Decalogue. The fifteenth-century Catholic theologian Jean de Charlier de Gerson also named the Ten Commandments "the rock of Christian Ethics." On the eve of and during the Reformation period, the Decalogue replaced the seven deadly sins (and the penitential manuals) to become the most important instrument for moral teaching. Martin Luther and John Calvin made the Ten Commandments the foundation of their moral instruction. Among Catholics the Council of Trent similarly incorporated into its catechism the Decalogue as the core basis of moral instruction.

In modern times, the Ten Commandments were inscribed on the walls of the apse in many nineteenth-century Episcopal churches as a reminder of God's exhortation to the congregation. They were to be read once a month during the prayer service in these churches.

Contemporary Christian theology similarly privileges the Decalogue. For example, the *Catechism of the Catholic Church* dedicates more than half of the entire morals section to the Ten Commandments (*CCC* ##2052–2557). It states clearly that "the Ten Commandments have occupied a predominant place in the catechesis of baptismal candidates and the faithful" (*CCC* #2065). Within the discipline of biblical studies, many point out that the above-mentioned unique characters of the Decalogue add weight to its significance as a moral foundation in general and in the study of biblical ethics in particular. The Decalogue is "a comprehensive framework and ground for the ethics of the Old Testament or indeed of the Bible as a whole."[16] The Pontifical Biblical Commission similarly claims that the Ten Commandments possess a foundational character on both the literary and theological levels that best serves to illustrate the conformity of moral reflection with the

Bible. On the part of Christian ethicists, some even stress that "the recovery of the commandments is crucial for our survival as a people called Christian in the face of today's challenges."[17]

THE BEATITUDES

The Beatitudes[18] likewise enjoys popularity, although more so within Christian traditions than without.[19] This popularity derives from its being a part of the Sermon on the Mount, the first of the great Matthean discourses, and a compilation of a series of Jesus's sayings arranged topically and edited by the Evangelist. Matthew 5–7 has been "continually the subject of re-interpretation by Christians throughout the ages . . . [and] one can even speak of a 'history of interpretation' of the Sermon."[20] Hans Dieter Betz even claims that neither a complete history of interpretation nor a complete bibliography on Matthew 5–7 is possible. Daniel Harrington, in a similar way, comments that this history of interpretation of the Sermon is a miniature history of Christianity.

The Beatitudes is "historically the best-known and most-valued portion of the Sermon."[21] Many theologians have produced their own commentaries on the text:[22] Gregory of Nyssa in the fourth century interpreted the eight beatitudes as "stages in the ascent of the soul . . . constituting the steps of the mystical ladder."[23] Later, John Chrysostom understood the text (and the overall Sermon on the Mount) "as the foundational speech . . . that constitutes the life of all Christians" and provides the building blocks for a life of virtue.[24] Among the scholastics, Aquinas also perceived it as "the touchstone of Christ's teaching in the Sermon on the Mount," just as the Decalogue contains "the essence of the moral precepts of the Mosaic Law."[25]

Such interest in the Beatitudes is not limited to the theologians of the past, though. Many modern Christian theologians, from Richard Niebuhr to Bernard Häring, from liberationist to feminist theologians, and from Catholic to Protestant scholars, have either employed the text in their writings or actually examined the teaching of the text.

The popularity of and interest in this text points to another reason for choosing the Beatitudes—that is, the importance of Matthew 5:3–12 in contemporary Christian theology.[26] For example, Häring is convinced that the Christian life is in essence a manifestation of the Beatitudes and thus invites readers to meditate and reflect on the personal and social implications of the text. Indeed, more and more theologians turn to the Beatitudes for inspiration in writings related to Christian spirituality.

Still, as in the case of the Decalogue, the Beatitudes plays a very significant role in the field of theological ethics (and in virtue ethics in particular). Servais Pinckaers argued that the Beatitudes is relevant to our contemporary Christian moral life at both personal and social levels, for it reads like "a summary of human life crossed with questions and contradictions."[27] One writer adds that the Beatitudes makes us attentive to those human problems, invites us to find meanings in them, reminds us that our human conditions are full of God's promise, and thus affirms our deepest longing for such promise.[28] Susan Parsons further notes that in recent years many theological ethicists are interested in seeing "how [the Sermon] might come alive once more in teaching the discipline of Christian ethics."[29]

Moreover, the Beatitudes is a source for discussion of the Christian virtues demanded by Jesus Christ. It clearly extols eight corresponding virtues for the Christian moral life. Even the Pontifical Biblical Commission specifically stresses the fundamental dispositions and virtues found in the Beatitudes and states that a faithful Christian life is one that is animated by these virtues.[30]

In the area of biblical studies, Ulrich Luz claims that the Sermon provides "[a] guiding principle by which that community is to measure its own works."[31] The Beatitudes is therefore written for and spoken to the people of God in the twenty-first century as well. Indeed, Matthew 5:3–12 is important to the quest for the meaning of the kingdom of God, which is the presupposition of our entire Christian life. Besides, the contemporary and growing use of social-historical criticism within the discipline of biblical studies confirms that the Beatitudes (and the Sermon on the Mount as a whole) is concerned about not only the individual moral life but also the relevance of communities of discipleship as well as the claims of social justice.

The third and final reason for underscoring the Beatitudes is a cross-cultural one. There is a growing literature in studying and comparing the Beatitudes with counterparts found in other religions such as Hinduism, Islam, and Buddhism, especially in the area of moral virtues.[32] While a comparison between the Beatitudes and Confucianism is lacking, the whole concept of "blessed" and "happiness" in Matthew 5:3–12 is closely related to the understanding of "prosperity" within the Confucian society. Also, Confucian ethics is more and more widely accepted as a virtue-based ethics. These characteristics could be a platform for engaging such cross-cultural dialogue between Christianity and Confucianism, a point that I develop at the end of this book.

APPROACH AND STRUCTURE OF THE BOOK

By and large, the reasons above ought to convince us to take these two biblical texts as primary texts for engaging the Bible and morality. However, what are the moral teachings of these two texts, and how can we interpret their meanings for contemporary moral living?

Unfortunately, neither the major Christian figures of the past nor the Pontifical Biblical Commission nor those who are engaged in biblical ethics have offered us a satisfactory presentation of the interpretation of the texts for contemporary ethical living. Either we find an exegetical treatment of the texts (exegesis is the critical study of the original meaning of the text) or we get an ethical application or interpretation of them, but we rarely get both. Similarly, biblical theologians do not use much ethical framework, while theological ethicists do little actual exegesis. Even those recent attempts to better bridge Scripture with Christian ethics have stressed either the importance of the scriptural text or the importance of ethical hermeneutics (hermeneutics is the interpretation of the text in order to determine its meaning for today), but not both.

Insofar as methodology is concerned, however, there is an emerging consensus among contemporary scholars to bridge the gap between biblical studies and moral theology. This emerging consensus has two aspects. The first is the view that the tasks of exegesis and interpretation are almost inseparable in the area of Scripture and ethics. I find Allen Verhey's insight on Scripture being a "scripted script" very helpful in portraying and understanding this aspect.[33] On the one hand, this text has been written (what Verhey calls "scripted") in a particular time by a particular writer. As such, it needs to be exegeted. On the other hand, it is a "script" to be performed by an actor, and the performance itself becomes the interpretation of it. As such, it needs to be interpreted. Scripture as a "scripted script" thus highlights the reality that the two tasks are tightly related, and one cannot engage in one task without the other at the same time.

This view leads to a subsequent and second aspect: the growing collaboration between biblical scholars and theological ethicists in doing Scripture-based ethics, especially in terms of writing and teaching. For instance, the late ethicist William Spohn team-taught with Scripture scholar John Donahue; more recently, ethicist James Keenan has been teaching (and writing) with biblical theologian Daniel Harrington.

This consensus points to my methodological claim that one needs to take the Bible seriously by careful exegesis and to build its findings upon a sound ethical framework or hermeneutics. It is only by first acquiring a more accurate understanding of the original meaning of the text that one can obtain a more complete and consistent interpretation of the text for today. As a Christian theological ethicist, I further propose that the hermeneutics of virtue ethics is a very worthy method. Why? First, in the past few decades, virtue ethics began to resurge and become a prominent alternative to principle-based ethics. It departs from principle-based ethics in that it deals with the character of individuals and their communities, and the practices that develop those characteristics and in turn express them.[34] Second, in terms of the narratives and the overall ends of Scripture themselves, virtue ethics, above other alternatives, is the most congruent and the most able to bear the weight of interpretation. Third, as Spohn explained, it is a matter of necessity—it is simply not possible to explore Christian moral life without its being built upon some form of moral philosophy.[35]

Subsequently, in Part I, I discuss this two-step schema in bridging biblical studies and Christian ethics. Chapter 1 looks at this emerging consensus. Chapter 2 offers a contemporary understanding of the hermeneutics of virtue ethics, with special attention to the goods of virtue—namely, (1) practices and habits, (2) dispositions and character, (3) exemplars, and (4) community and communal identity. I conclude by reflecting on the relevance of virtue in reading Scripture.

In Part II, I employ this schema to treat the Decalogue. There are two versions of the Ten Commandments in the Hebrew Bible—namely, the accounts in Exodus 20:2–17 and Deuteronomy 5:6–21. Here I focus on the Exodus account, although the Deuteronomy account will be cross-referenced when necessary. The reason for choosing Exodus 20:2–17 is based on the view that, as will be discussed later, the Exodus account comes from an older source than that of the Deuteronomy edition. Moreover, the redactor of Exodus describes the Sinai event in a direct, first-person manner, while the Deuteronomy account is presented by its redactor as a recounting of the event. Readers, Christians and non-Christians alike, tend to relate to the Exodus account whenever the Ten Commandments are mentioned. It is a matter of familiarity.

For each of the commandments, I exegete them and, through a hermeneutics of virtue ethics, interpret them for contemporary Christian moral living. Subsequently, each of the chapters on the commandments contains two major parts, starting with the original meaning of the scriptural text.

Before doing so, I begin with a look at how the Decalogue as a whole was interpreted throughout history by major Christian thinkers as well as by some contemporary writers. After this review, I attend to certain critical exegetical issues of the text, like the numbering of the Ten Commandments by different traditions.

In doing hermeneutics, I do not simply propose corresponding virtue(s) for each of the commandments, but rather examine the virtuous life in light of the foundational questions of virtue ethics: Who are we? Who ought we to become? And finally, how do we get there? My answers to these three questions form the second half of each chapter. Therefore, to the first question, I reflect upon our own *self-understanding* within the larger society. The second question guides us to understand the concrete *meaning* and *content* of each proposed virtue in terms of moral formation. In other words, what does it mean to be a particular kind of virtuous person in light of each of the commandments? The last question leads us to explore the *practices* of these virtues, as well as to identify certain moral *exemplars* (predominantly) within the Christian tradition, beginning with Jesus, who is the exemplar par excellence. By practicing the virtuous acts and by imitating these models, we can partially achieve the goal of becoming a virtuous person. In sum, I develop a moral character that is in line with each and all of the Ten Commandments.

Throughout, I reflect upon the *social and communal* dimension of each virtue, for two reasons. First, the discussion of the goods of virtue indicates that there is a communal aspect in the virtuous life. By interpreting the commandments through the hermeneutics of virtue ethics, we realize that the author invites us to be a particular virtuous faith community. Second, the Decalogue itself has a social characteristic: it addresses the entire Israelite community and conveys the terms for right relationship to God and toward others. It points to the social dimension of its ethical implications.

It is important to note that I am not simply proposing certain human virtues but particularly *religious* virtues: the scriptural text is concerned in the first place with our being among the people of God.

In Part III, I treat the Beatitudes in Matthew 5:3–12 in the same manner. Here, the social characteristic of the Beatitudes is equally present: by perceiving the overall Sermon as a kingdom ethics that describes right relationship with God and with others, one may argue that the social dimension of the Beatitudes' ethical implications is implied in the broader meaning of discipleship—there is "a continuing social meaning of the inclusive call to discipleship and of merciful action."[36] Moreover, discipleship goes beyond social citizenship, for "the community is invited to enter into a deeper kind of social relationship that is based on social justice and the priority of the poor."[37]

Finally, a caveat: although I am writing as a Catholic theological ethicist and at times I turn to certain Catholic documents for insights, this book is ecumenical in orientation and is primarily written from the vantage point of theological ethics.

Moreover, I am from Hong Kong, a place deeply affected by Confucianism. Confucianism, like many major religions and traditions, goes to the texts in its search of ethical teachings—that is, its ethics is primarily the fruit of careful interpretation of its sacred texts. Throughout this book, in bridging biblical studies and Christian ethics, and in arguing for greater attentiveness on the part of the ethicists to scriptural texts, I am sure that my own Confucian background prompts me in this direction.

For this reason, at the end of the book I will discuss the possible reception of the core Christian virtues of the Ten Commandments and the Beatitudes by Confucian society. However, my discussion will be necessarily succinct: a detailed treatment will demand a separate book. Still, I am convinced that even a brief comparative exercise like this one not only demonstrates the possibility of interfaith and cross-cultural studies but also invites biblical scholars and theological ethicists to go beyond their own interdisciplinary studies. For doing interfaith or cross-cultural ethics begins not with analogous generalities but with very specific texts, and it needs to be both text-based and interpretative.

NOTES

1. In this book the term "Scripture" is used interchangeably with "Bible" and refers to those sacred writings that the Christian community considers canonical, or authoritative for belief and practice.

2. Vatican II, *Optatam Totius*, decree on priestly training issued in October 1965, http://www.vatican.va/archive/hist_councils/ii_vatican_council/documents/vat-ii_decree_19651028_optatam-totius_en.html.

3. Pope John Paul II, *Veritatis Splendor*, August 6, 1993, http://www.vatican.va/holy_father/john_paul_ii/encyclicals/documents/hf_jp-ii_enc_06081993_veritatis-splendor_en.html. See also Servais Pinckaers, "The Recovery of the New Law in Moral Theology," *Irish Theological Quarterly* 64 (1999): 14.

4. Eberhard Schockenhoff, *Natural Law and Human Dignity*, trans. Brian McNeil (Washington, DC: Catholic University of America Press, 2003).

5. The terms "Hebrew Bible" and "Old Testament" are used interchangeably throughout this book.

6. Pontifical Biblical Commission, *The Bible and Morality: Biblical Roots of Christian Conduct* (Vatican: Libreria Editrice Vaticana, 2008), 12, 132, 138.

7. The terms "Ten Commandments" and "Decalogue" are used interchangeably throughout this book.

8. John M. Grondelski, "From 'The Ten Commandments' to the 'Decalogue,'" *Journal of Religion and Film* 7, no. 1 (April 2003), www.unomaha.edu/jrf/Vol7No1/tentodecalogue.htm.

9. Phil Cavendish, "Kieślowski's Decalogue," *Sight and Sound* 59, no. 3 (Summer 1990): 162.

10. Tian Hia-hua, "Confucian Catholics' Appropriation of the Decalogue: A Cross-Textual Reading," in *Reading Christian Scriptures in China*, ed. Chloë F. Starr (London: T&T Clark, 2008), 164, 172. See also Nicolas Standaert, "The Bible in Early Seventeenth-Century China," in *The Bible in Modern China: The Literary and Intellectual Impact*, Monograph Series 43, ed. Irene Eber, Sze-kar Wan, and Knut Walf (Sankt Augustin, Germany: Monumenta Serica, 1999), 34.

11. Patrick D. Miller, "Is There a Place for the Ten Commandments?," *Theology Today* 60, no. 4 (January 2004): 473, 475. See also Robert Louis Wilken, "Keeping the Commandments," *First Things* 137 (November 2003): 33–37. The Pontifical Biblical Commission similarly claims that the Decalogue is "so important in inter-cultural dialogue." L. Melina and J. Noriega, eds., "Il rinnovamento della teologia morale: prospettive del Vaticano II e di Veritatis splen-

dor," in *Caminare nella Luce: Prospettive della Teologia Morale a partire da Veritatis Splendor* (Roma, PUL, 2004), 39–40, as quoted in Pontifical Biblical Commission, *The Bible and Morality*, 133.

12. William P. Brown, "Introduction," in *The Ten Commandments: The Reciprocity of Faithfulness* (Louisville, KY: Westminster John Knox Press, 2004), 2–4. See also Moshe Weinfeld, "The Uniqueness of the Decalogue and its Place in Jewish Tradition," in *The Ten Commandments in History and Tradition*, ed. Ben-Zion Segal (Jerusalem: Magnes Press, Hebrew University of Jerusalem, 1990), 15–19; Dale Patrick, *Old Testament Law* (Atlanta, GA: John Knox Press, 1985), 35; and Patrick D. Miller, "Ten Commandments," in *The New Interpreter's Dictionary of the Bible*, vol. 5 (Nashville, TN: Abingdon Press, 2006–2009), 517–18.

13. On the Decalogue and Judaism, see Shalom Albeck, "The Essence of Religious Faith," in *The Ten Commandments in History and Tradition*, ed. Ben-Zion Segal (Jerusalem: Magnes Press, Hebrew University of Jerusalem, 1990), 261–89; Yehoshua Amir, "The Decalogue according to Philo," in *The Ten Commandments in History and Tradition*, 121–60; Gad B. Sarfatti, "The Tables of the Law as a Symbol of Judaism," in *The Ten Commandments in History and Tradition*, 383–418; Weinfeld, "The Uniqueness of the Decalogue and its Place in Jewish Tradition," 1–44.

14. For a discussion of these reasons, see Brevard S. Childs, *The Book of Exodus* (Philadelphia, PA: Westminster Press, 1974), 435.

15. The Decalogue was one of the four major topics to be taught in the catechetical writings of the late sixteenth century. On its role in catechetical instruction, besides Childs, see David Flusser, "The Ten Commandments and the New Testament," in *The Ten Commandments in History and Tradition*, ed. Ben-Zion Segal (Jerusalem: Magnes Press, Hebrew University of Jerusalem, 1990), 219–46; Jonathan Hall, *Augustine and the Decalogue* (University of Virginia), http://people.virginia.edu/~jph8r/AugustineDec.pdf; James F. Keenan, *Commandments of Compassion* (Franklin, WI: Sheed & Ward, 1999); Patrick D. Miller, *The Ten Commandments* (Louisville, KY: Westminster John Knox Press, 2009).

16. Miller, *The Ten Commandments*, xi.

17. Stanley M. Hauerwas and William H. Willimon, *The Truth about God: The Ten Commandments in Christian Life* (Nashville, TN: Abingdon Press, 1999), 13.

18. When talking about the pericope "the Beatitudes," I use third-person singular. When I talk about the beatitudes as several blessings, I use third-person plural.

19. On the popularity and familiarity of the Beatitudes, see Hans Dieter Betz, *The Sermon on the Mount*, ed. Adela Yarbro Collins (Minneapolis: Fortress Press, 1995); Daniel J. Harrington, *The Gospel of Matthew, Sacra Pagina* (Collegeville, MN: Liturgical Press, 2007); Timothy Larsen, "Introduction," in *The Sermon on the Mount through the Ages*, ed. Jeffrey P. Greenman, Timothy Larsen, and Stephen R. Spencer (Grand Rapids, MI: Brazos Press, 2007), 13–17. For various reasons, Matthew's Sermon traditionally has drawn more attention than that of Luke's. See Jan Lambrecht, *The Sermon on the Mount: Proclamation and Exhortation* (Wilmington, DE: Michael Glazier, 1985), 20.

20. Lambrecht, *The Sermon on the Mount*, 20.

21. Lisa Sowle Cahill, "Christian Character, Biblical Community, and Human Values," in *Character and Scripture: Moral Formation, Community, and Biblical Interpretation*, ed. William P. Brown (Grand Rapids, MI: Eerdmans, 2002), 15.

22. Gregory of Nyssa, *The Lord's Prayer and The Beatitudes*, Ancient Christian Writers, trans. Hilda C. Graef (Mahwah, NJ: Paulist Press, 1954). See also Jaroslav Jan Pelikan, *Divine Rhetoric: The Sermon on the Mount as Message and as Model in Augustine, Chrysostom, and Luther* (Crestwood, NY: St. Vladimir's Seminary Press, 2000), 67, and St. John Chrysostom, *Homily 15 on Matthew*, www.newadvent.org/fathers/200115.htm.

23. Jean Daniélou, "La chronologie des sermons de Grégoire de Nysse," *RSR* 29 (1955): 372, as cited in Betz, *The Sermon*, 108.

24. Margaret M. Mitchell, "John Chrysostom," in *The Sermon on the Mount through the Ages*, ed. Jeffrey P. Greenman, Timothy Larsen, and Stephen R. Spencer (Grand Rapids, MI: Brazos Press, 2007), 22, 35.

25. Jeremy Holmes, "Aquinas' *Lectura in Matthaeum*," in *Aquinas on Scripture : An Introduction to His Biblical Commentaries* , ed. Thomas G. Weinandy, Daniel A. Keating, and John P. Yocum (New York: T&T Clark, 2005), 79–80.

26. On the Beatitudes and spirituality, see Michael H. Crosby, *Spirituality of the Beatitudes: Matthew's Vision for the Church in an Unjust World*, rev. ed. (Maryknoll, NY: Orbis, 2005); Bernard Häring, *The Beatitudes: Their Personal and Social Implications* (Slough, UK: St. Paul Publications, 1976); Max Oliva, *Beatitudes for the Workplace* (Toronto, ON: Novalis, 2009); Servais Pinckaers, *The Pursuit of Happiness—God's Way: Living the Beatitudes*, trans. Mary Thomas Noble (New York: Alba House, 1998).

27. Pinckaers, *The Pursuit of Happiness*, 37.

28. Susan Muto, "Blessed Are the Poor in Spirit and the Pure of Heart," in *New Perspectives on the Beatitudes*, ed. Francis A. Eigo (Villanova, PA: Villanova University Press, 1995), 131–32.

29. Susan F. Parsons, "Editorial," *Studies in Christian Ethics* 22, no. 1 (2009): 6.

30. Pontifical Biblical Commission, *The Bible and Morality*, 13–14, 70–71.

31. Ulrich Luz, *The Theology of the Gospel of Matthew*, trans. J. Bradford Robinson (Cambridge: Cambridge University Press, 1995), 44.

32. See Albert B. Randall, *Strangers on the Shore: The Beatitudes in World Religions* (New York: Peter Lang, 2006).

33. Allen Verhey, "Scripture as Script and as Scripted: The Beatitudes," in *Character Ethics and the New Testament: Moral Dimensions of Scripture*, ed. Robert L. Brawley (Louisville, KY: Westminster John Knox Press, 2007), 19–25.

34. Edmund D. Pellegrino and David C. Thomasma, *The Christian Virtues in Medical Practice* (Washington, DC: Georgetown University Press, 1996), 14–15.

35. William C. Spohn, *Go and Do Likewise: Jesus and Ethics* (New York: Continuum, 2000), 27–28.

36. Lisa Sowle Cahill, "The Ethical Implications of the Sermon on the Mount," *Interpretation* 41, no. 4 (April 1987): 153.

37. John Battle, "The Sermon on the Mount and Political Ethics," *Studies in Christian Ethics* 22, no. 1 (2009): 53.

Acknowledgments

I would like to express my deepest gratitude to my two Jesuit teachers and friends, Professor Daniel J. Harrington, S.J., and Professor James F. Keenan, S.J., for encouraging me to publish this work. They have been most supportive in my academic pursuit.

I am also most grateful to both Yale Divinity School and Woodstock Theological Center of Georgetown University for granting me fellowships in academic year 2010–2011 that made my research work and book writing possible. The same gratitude is extended to Ms. Sarah Stanton, the acquisitions editor; her assistant, Ms. Jin Yu; and all at Rowman & Littlefield Publishers, for their interest in my book project and for making it possible.

Moreover, I am in debt to Professor Margaret Farley, R.S.M., professor emerita of Christian ethics, and Islamic studies expert Professor Gerhard Bowering, S.J., both of Yale University, for their friendship and support. I hope they each know how much I have appreciated what they have done for me.

I also thank the members of the Overseas Ministries Study Center community at New Haven and the Jesuit communities in Fairfield University, Georgetown University, and Woodstock Theological Center, for their table fellowship and communal support during my fellowship year.

Special thanks to a few long-term Jesuit friends from abroad: Fr. James Hurley, Fr. James Gould, Fr. Caoimhín Ó Ruairc, Fr. Julio Giulietti, Fr. George Griener, Fr. Momose Fumiake, and Fr. John Clarkson. The then provincial of the Chinese province of the Society of Jesus, Very Rev. Louis Gendron, S.J., has also been very supportive of my academic training throughout his term as provincial.

Finally, I would like to express my sincere appreciation of the friendship and care of some Hong Kong Chinese Catholics from Boston. They have sacrificed their free time to help me in moving and visited me not a few times in New Haven and Washington, D.C.

May God bless all of you!

I

A Schema for Bridging Biblical Studies and Christian Ethics

In the past twenty years or so there have been positive developments within the disciplines of biblical studies and Christian ethics to bridge the two fields. Biblical scholars begin to go beyond the exegetical task to engage in interpretive hermeneutics; theological ethicists, similarly, start to pay attention to their use of Scripture in ethical reflection. We observe two contrasting realities. On the one hand, a more integrated approach has not yet been achieved, for both biblical scholars and theological ethicists have stressed either the importance of the scriptural text or the importance of ethical hermeneutics. On the part of biblical scholarship, they lack ethical frameworks as a platform for ethical analysis. For theological ethicists, Scripture is still not properly employed (and/or fully understood) but used in a way that simply perceives the Bible as a secondary support.

On the other hand, these developments point us in the right direction toward constructing a more integrated biblical ethics. Among the most recent scholars who have committed themselves to this goal, an emerging twofold consensus is noted. First, there is the view that the task of exegesis and the task of interpretation are almost inseparable in the area of Scripture-based ethics. Second, there is the growing collaboration between biblical scholars and ethicists in doing this ethics, especially in terms of writing and teaching.

From the perspective of Christian ethics, unfortunately, no consensus has been reached on what particular ethical framework should be used as the hermeneutical tool. I propose the employment of virtue ethics. As will be discussed in detail later, several important goods of virtue are helpful points of reference to the task of hermeneutics; they are particularly relevant to the task of reading Scripture as well.

Chapter One

Emerging Consensus

THE IMPORTANCE OF THE SCRIPTURAL TEXT AND THE NEED FOR INTERPRETATION

The first aspect of the emerging consensus is the fundamental view that exegesis and hermeneutics are inseparable from each other when engaging in Scripture-based ethics. Allen Verhey's insight, that Scripture is a "scripted script," is particularly helpful in portraying and understanding this inseparableness.[1] His overall argument begins with the general meanings of the two ascribed terms, "scripted" and "script." The written text as "scripted" means that it was written at a particular time by specific authors. Today it is studied as such by scriptural exegetes. The text as "script," on the other hand, can be compared to the script of a play and hence needs to be performed by the actress/actor. The performance of any script is itself an interpretation of the script. It lays out the practices and performances that should be conveyed.

Verhey further highlights the distinction between "scripted" and "script" by adopting the distinction between "object" and "instrument."[2] As "scripted," the text is "an object to us, a given, the product of the activity of others."[3] And as an object, it needs to be examined textually so as to know what sort of writing it is. As "script," the text is, however, an instrument for and an invitation to activity for the reader.

Verhey adopts these notions in the context of biblical ethics in order to understand the different tasks of biblical scholarship and Christian ethics and to highlight the relationship between them. As "scripted," the biblical texts are studied by those exegetes within the church community who "bring their knowledge of Hebrew and Greek, or their training in the tools of historical, literary, or social investigation, not just to the texts but to the community."[4] As "script," the Bible is to be performed repeatedly "in the rhetoric and

3

practices of the churches, in their theology and in their worship, in their ethics and in their politics."[5] Thus ethicists looking to the Bible for moral guidance must look to Scripture for the "prompting" toward appropriate practices, virtues, and actions. Although the task of exegesis is conventionally assigned to biblical scholars while the task of interpretation is assigned to Christian ethicists, they are related, for it is the church community that received from and formed Scripture into the canon and then interpreted and performed it.

As a whole, then, Verhey points to the need to see Scripture as *both* "scripted" and "script." The two tasks are mutually related and inseparable, and required for anyone who engages in a Scripture-based ethics. He writes, "Attention to Scripture as scripted finally *requires* attention to Scripture as a text appropriately read when it is . . . performed. And attention to Scripture as script to be performed is surely *enriched* by attention to Scripture as scripted."[6]

Verhey explains that when interpreting the text the interpreter has a responsibility "to make judgments about the sort of text it is, about the whole of which it is a part . . . about the interest appropriate to it, and about the appropriate use of this object as instrument, the performance of this text."[7] These judgments make a difference to how the text is read and used. This responsibility is, however, not purely personal: since it is the community that possesses the Bible as its canon, one's reading of the text is conditioned by (and therefore answerable to) the community to which one belongs. The community "exercises interpretative discernment by asking how each part of Scripture as scripted fits the whole."[8]

On the other hand, the performance of the script by Christian ethicists can be improved when one carefully attends to what the biblical authors did with the texts at their disposal. Different performances may emerge, and yet none of them can capture the true meaning of the text/script fully and definitely. Attending to the text can therefore function as a test for and a guide to performance.

Within the enterprise of methodological inquiry, Verhey's emphasis on Scripture as both "scripted" and "script" implies the need to pay equal attention to the scriptural text and to its interpretation. This implication points us in the right direction of engaging in Scripture-based ethics. His attempt has thus offered a worthy model, inasmuch as he both describes and, in a manner of speaking, performs his proposal.

COLLABORATION

The consensus among scholars regarding the inseparableness of the exegetical and hermeneutical tasks does not simply emerge from the theoretical level but extends to the practical level as well. This leads to the second aspect of consensus—namely, collaboration between biblical scholars and theological ethicists in terms of writing and teaching.

Signs of collaboration can be traced back to as early as the late 1970s. Some scholars have taken a step further to work hand in hand with colleagues of the other field. One of the earlier joint efforts was between biblical scholar Bruce C. Birch and Christian ethicist Larry L. Rasmussen, who coauthored *Bible and Ethics in Christian Life*. In this work they attempt to "bridge the gap between biblical studies and Christian ethics" and to "address the relationship of Scripture and ethics."[9]

Birch and Rasmussen point out that both Christian ethics and biblical scholarship "are called upon most directly to aid the faith community in traversing the distance between the primal documents of the faith—its [s]criptures—and expressions of the faith in daily life."[10] Although their pioneering work is primarily a book about the moral life with only the last two chapters dedicated to a discussion of the role of the Bible in the moral life, what is most valuable is their methodological proposal that encourages interdisciplinary work. Unfortunately, we have not seen much more published collaboration since then.[11] Rather, collaboration in the classroom setting began to emerge.

Starting in the 1980s, Spohn and Donahue engaged in team teaching when they were both faculty of the then Jesuit School of Theology at Berkeley. They taught together four times and offered a few courses on New Testament and Ethics.[12] In their "The New Testament and Christian Ethics" course in 1990, Spohn and Donahue began with a canonical description of the ethics of the New Testament, including "Jesus's Eschatological Ethics," "The Ethics of the Gospels," and "The Christological Ethics of Paul." In the second half of the course they discussed the various modes of interpretation, such as liberation, feminist, and narrative hermeneutics. However, they did not engage in demonstrating how biblical scholarship and ethical reflection interacted in concrete situations.

A more recent and developed attempt is between Harrington and Keenan, whose approach is very different from their predecessors. They have been trying to build a bridge between the two camps through their joint writings and team teaching in the past decade. Both Harrington and Keenan are interested in listening to what the other says and try to accommodate the other into their own framework and reflection. In their coauthored book, *Jesus and Virtue Ethics* (based on their team teaching of a course of the same title),

Harrington and Keenan set out a common framework that is built upon certain ethical themes—for instance, in the theme of "love as the primary virtue," Harrington first offers an exposition on the love of God and neighbor in Matthew 22:34–40; it is then followed by Keenan's reflection on the primacy of charity in moral theology proposed by Gerard Gilleman.[13] At the time of this writing, they have team-taught "Paul and Virtue Ethics" a few times, and a corresponding book of the same title has been published. Here, they continue to employ the hermeneutics of virtue ethics to interpret the selected New Testament writings—in this case, the moral teachings of Paul and the Pauline writings—and engage in interaction between the two tasks. They are convinced that "the concerns of Christian virtue ethics provide a good lens for reading Paul's letters, and that Paul and his letters provide a good lens for understanding Christian virtue ethics."[14] The specific topics covered include the following: "The shape of Paul's virtue ethics . . . faith, love, hope, virtues and vices . . . and sexual morality."[15] These teaching and writing projects illuminate their commitment to bridge the gap and better integrate Scripture and Christian ethics.

Their Jesuit colleagues in the former Weston Jesuit School of Theology in Cambridge, Massachusetts, Richard Clifford and Thomas Massaro, have also twice taught as a team in the past few years a course on social justice and the Bible that offers students "the opportunity to learn to interpret the social message of the Bible in a way that illustrates contemporary issues of social justice."[16] This seminar explores key elements of contemporary social ethics, such as the meanings of justice, power and authority, and the status of women, and it examines how the Bible illuminates them. They also introduce certain appropriate ways to use the Bible in ethical reasoning and discourse. In this way, the course predominantly focuses on the use of Scripture in a specific area of ethics. However, despite the frequent use of some official Church documents on Catholic social teaching, there is no particular ethical framework employed. The use of scriptural texts is also rather limited and scattered.

In spring 2011, Stephen Pope and David Vanderhooft, both from the theology department of Boston College, have for the first time jointly launched a course titled "God and Morality: The Ethical Legacy of the Hebrew Bible."[17] The course aims to examine several major texts—such as the Creation story, the Exodus event, the giving of the Ten Commandments, the Purity Code, and certain wisdom literature like Proverbs—from the Hebrew Bible regarding selected moral issues, including war, stealing, and lying. Vanderhooft first offers exegetical analysis of these scriptural texts, and then Pope studies their use in the subsequent history of Christian theological ethics. They also turn to some general ethical themes such as covenant and law, virtues and vices, and moral transgressions for reflection.

Finally, we see such collaboration emerge in other institutions. When I was appointed as a visiting fellow at Yale Divinity School for the academic year 2010–2011, two young professors, Carolyn Sharp and Willis Jenkins, were offering "an interdisciplinary seminar that addresses the relation of scriptural interpretation and Christian responses to poverty."[18] In particular, they

> investigate the intersections among Christian appropriations of biblical traditions (including Deuteronomy, Amos, and Ruth) and Christian interpretations of economic justice (focusing on 20th-century Catholic and Protestant social thought) in relation to contemporary confrontations with poverty and engagements with globalization.[19]

They begin with a review of the different models of Scripture and social ethics. Then they interpret those selected biblical texts related to poverty, followed by employing various social ethics models to read the texts, such as social gospel, Catholic social teaching, and liberation theology.

Although this is their first time of team teaching and they present to us different social ethics models of reading Scripture rather than employing a specific hermeneutical tool, their efforts confirm the value of collaboration between the two disciplines and signify the growing awareness of this consensus among younger scholars.

The task of exegesis and that of hermeneutics are inseparable throughout the process of doing a Scripture-based Christian ethics. This inseparableness is best described using Verhey's "scripted script." This theoretical consensus is being put into practice by some scholars through their team teaching and co-writing. I believe that the collaboration of Harrington and Keenan stands out because of their use of a coherent and sound ethical framework.

As a Christian ethicist, I take virtue ethics as a worthy hermeneutical tool for various good reasons briefly explained in the prologue.[20] Within the context of New Testament ethics, for instance, virtue ethics is "true to both the New Testament emphasis on the human response to God's gracious activity in Jesus Christ and to the ethical needs and desires of Christians."[21] It is a comprehensive approach that goes beyond character formation alone. Therefore, in the next chapter I expound the contemporary understanding of virtue ethics, focusing on the goods of virtues—namely, practices, character, exemplars, and community.

NOTES

1. On "scripted script," see Allen Verhey, "Scripture and Ethics: Practices, Performances, and Prescriptions," in *Christian Ethics: Problems and Prospects*, ed. Lisa Sowle Cahill and James Childress (Cleveland, OH: Pilgrim Press, 1996), 18–44; Allen Verhey, "Scripture as Script and as Scripted: The Beatitudes," in *Character Ethics and the New Testament: Moral Dimensions of Scripture*, ed. Robert L. Brawley (Louisville, KY: Westminster John Knox Press, 2007), 19–25.

2. Nicolas Wolterstorff, *Art in Action: Toward a Christian Aesthetic* (Grand Rapids, MI: Eerdmans, 1980), 80, as cited in Verhey, "Scripture as Script and as Scripted," 31n2.

3. Verhey, "Scripture as Script and as Scripted," 20.

4. Allen Verhey, *Remembering Jesus: Christian Community, Scripture, and the Moral Life* (Grand Rapids, MI: Eerdmans, 2002), 61.

5. Verhey, "Scripture as Script and as Scripted," 19.

6. Ibid., 20.

7. Ibid., 22.

8. Ibid., 28.

9. Bruce C. Birch and Larry L. Rasmussen, *Bible and Ethics in Christian Life*, rev. ed. (Minneapolis, MN: Augsburg, 1989), 7–8.

10. Ibid., 10.

11. In 2011, a long-awaited reference work contributed by biblical scholars and Christian ethicists was published. Cf. Joel Green, ed., *Dictionary of Scripture and Ethics* (Grand Rapids, MI: Baker Publishing Group, 2011).

12. William C. Spohn, "Teaching Scripture and Ethics," *Annual of the Society of Christian Ethics* (1990): 277. See also John R. Donahue and William C. Spohn, "The New Testament and Christian Ethics" (NTCE 4301 syllabus, Jesuit School of Theology at Berkeley, Berkeley, California, Spring 1990).

13. Daniel J. Harrington and James F. Keenan, *Jesus and Virtue Ethics: Building Bridges between New Testament Studies and Moral Theology* (Chicago: Sheed & Ward, 2002), 77ff.

14. Daniel J. Harrington and James F. Keenan, *Paul and Virtue Ethics: Building Bridges between New Testament Studies and Moral Theology* (Lanham, MD: Rowman & Littlefield, 2010), xii.

15. See Daniel J. Harrington and James F. Keenan, "Paul and Virtue Ethics" (TH 560 syllabus, School of Theology and Ministry at Boston College, Chestnut Hill, Massachusetts, Fall 2008, 2009).

16. Richard Clifford and Thomas Massaro, "Social Ethics and the Bible" (OT/MT 353 syllabus, Weston Jesuit School of Theology, Cambridge, Massachusetts, Fall 2003, 2006).

17. See Stephen Pope and David Vanderhooft, "God and Morality: The Ethical Legacy of the Hebrew Bible" (TH465 syllabus, Boston College, Chestnut Hill, Massachusetts, Spring 2011).

18. Carolyn Sharp and Willis Jenkins, "Scripture and Social Ethics" (REL 564 syllabus, Yale Divinity School, New Haven, Connecticut, Fall 2011).

19. Ibid.

20. I am not denying the possibility of employing other tools in doing scriptural ethics. Schockenhoff, for instance, in defending the relevance of natural law as the methodological approach in theological ethics, claims that the universal validity of moral precepts within a natural law framework "allows us to construct a systematic understanding of biblical ethics and of its universal claim." See Eberhard Schockenhoff, *Natural Law and Human Dignity*, trans. Brian McNeil (Washington, DC: Catholic University of America Press, 2003), x.

21. Harrington and Keenan, *Jesus and Virtue Ethics*, xiv.

Chapter Two

Reading Scripture through the Lens of Virtue

Virtue ethics is one of the oldest moral philosophies and has gone through development, decline, and revival in the past two millennia. Ancient philosophers, like Plato and Aristotle, tried to formulate an ethics of virtue, especially by developing the doctrine of the mean. During the patristic period, both Western and Eastern Church Fathers, like Augustine and Athanasius of Alexandria, offered their understandings of virtues and highlighted God as the ultimate *telos* for humanity. Aquinas then presented to us a systematic classification of virtues from which theological, cardinal, infused, and acquired virtues are defined. Unfortunately, for various reasons the discussion of virtues was slowly replaced by principle- and rule-oriented ethics in the later centuries. It was not until the second half of the twentieth century that the retrieval of virtue ethics began to emerge from philosophical, theological, and public sectors.

Within the discipline of philosophy, Alasdair MacIntyre's work has been most influential in this retrieval. Theologians, in turn, engaged in the discussion of virtue ethics, and various schools emerged based on different traditions and emphases. Among Protestant ethicists, Stanley Hauerwas is known for focusing on the notion of character and the roles of community and narrative in moral formation. The Catholic counterparts are represented by Spohn, Keenan, and Jean Porter. Keenan, in particular, is noted for engaging virtue ethics with other areas of morality and proposing a contemporary list of cardinal virtues for ordinary life. And with Spohn he also tries to bridge moral theology and other theological disciplines through virtue ethics.

Grounded in this historical development, contemporary understanding of virtue ethics has the following characteristics: It is a teleological ethics that is concerned about human good. It is interested in moral character and thus gives priority to being over doing. It also bears a kind of perfectionism that sees all aspects of life as morally relevant and urges one to moral growth. Subsequently, these characteristics pose three basic questions for the moral agent: "Who am I?" "Who ought I to become?" and "How do I get there?" I find that four important goods of virtue—practices and habits, dispositions and character, exemplars, and community and communal identity—help make virtue a fuller ethical framework.

THE GOODS OF VIRTUE ETHICS

Practices and Habits

Virtue ethics is more interested in the affairs of ordinary life than in neuralgic moral dilemmas or enormously grave actions. It is concerned about what I ought to do in daily life while moving from "who I am" to "who I ought to become." These goals can best be handled by developing practices. According to MacIntyre, "practice" denotes

> any coherent and complex form of socially established cooperative human activity through which goods internal to that form of activity are realized in the course of trying to achieve those standards of excellence which are appropriate to, and partially definitive of, that form of activity.[1]

Simply put, practice is a regular activity that forms us in such a way that certain dispositions to act in particular ways are developed. In ordinary life we are continually adopting practices that later become habits, which, as Aristotle understood, in turn become a kind of irremediable condition or a "second nature." For example, if we want to become hospitable as a person and as a community, we have to practice hospitality. At some point we so condition ourselves to this way of acting that we become hospitable. Once we acquire hospitality as a second nature, we act hospitably easily and almost naturally whenever we meet someone new. As such, we will be more disposed to the stranger than if we have not yet practiced the virtue.

In sum, practices both develop and, in turn, express the character of the moral agent. This highlights a second good of virtue—the formation of character.

Dispositions and Character

Virtue ethics at times is defined by some of its proponents as an "ethics of character." They claim that character ethics "does not altogether neglect rules, but subordinates them to the development of moral character and views them instrumentally with reference to the end."[2] It refers to "a way of thinking about and interpreting the moral life in terms of a particular vision of and a passion for life that is rooted in the nurture, formation, and socialization of a particular self-conscious community."[3]

Hauerwas retrieves virtues through his ethics of character. For him, character is inseparable from one's self-determination and is the decisive factor behind our doing and becoming. He further claims that character is "the particular direction our agency acquires by choosing to act in some ways rather than others."[4] In this way, character dominates the notion of virtue.

Others tend to incorporate character formation into a virtue ethics as an important good of virtue. For them, the question of the good life leads directly to the development of moral character, because "any adequate description of a good human life will necessarily include attributes that are not manifest in persons in the beginning of their lives, but are developmental outcomes."[5] Virtues are thus "excellences of character that are objective goods, of worth to others [and the self]," and their manifestation is the actualization of qualities that are originally potentialities within a person.[6] In addition, since the ethics of virtue is concerned about the *telos* ("end"), it calls for continual growth in our character.

Our choices and actions help form our tendencies and dispositions, which in turn help inform and direct our subsequent choices and actions. What is central to the development of moral character is the achievement of an emerging integrity—by which all the dimensions of a person, such as faculties and desires, contribute toward the eventual outcome of a virtuous person. In this fashion, virtue ethics is all about moral formation.

Since a person's character represents "the integration of [one's] life into a relatively coherent unity" and the identity of a person is formed when this integrated self is conscious, virtue ethics, as Spohn claims, inevitably considers identity. Keenan further notes that there is interplay between virtues and an anthropological vision of human identity: virtues provide practical guides to the right realization of identity, while the anthropological vision of human identity guides us in our pursuit of the virtues.[7]

Exemplars

While attending to character, virtue ethics also appreciates the role that exemplary figures play in the development of virtue and formation of character. This appreciation is built upon the fundamental presupposition that virtue is teachable. Plato, for example, made it clear that examples of moral virtues are transmitted only through storytelling, and the teaching of virtue can be achieved by the study of not just ethics but also other disciplines.[8]

Within Christianity, Athanasius once claimed that "the practice of imitating the exemplars of the faith is fundamental to the acquisition of Christian virtue . . . [and] transformation by way of the imitation of the mentor's life of virtue may result in communion, in a sharing of vision."[9] The idea of imitation and the need and role of a mentor are closely related. John Climacus of the sixth century was also convinced that a guide or a mentor who has struggled on the ladder of virtue would have the vision and critical discernment necessary to guide another.

These mentors and guides are needed in two ways. First, the virtues as skills need examples to show what they mean practically. Second, as examples they teach and encourage us to act likewise. Spohn explains that virtues "have to be displayed concretely to convey their tactical meaning."[10] In the Old Testament, Judith, for example, has been viewed as a model for liberation and the virtue of courage; Ruth and Naomi illustrate the values of loyalty and love of family.

Traditionally, as Andrew Flescher reminds us, there are two notable kinds of exemplars. The first, heroes, are "not mere moral paragons but exemplars, demonstrations of human beings living the best kind of moral life."[11] Though they distinguish themselves by excelling, heroes are ordinary persons; they represent and are (already) acting the way we should. The lives they live are "in principle accessible to anyone who becomes sufficiently virtuous."[12]

Saints, on the contrary, are extraordinary persons and differ from heroes in many ways, especially in that they "transcend their 'exemplar' status and come to embody a higher law."[13] Saints are distinctive moral agents who are extraordinarily virtuous and visionary, and who embody "an ideal of character that is not fully realizable by ordinary agents in the course of a life."[14]

The difference between heroes and saints further highlights the two different senses of "exemplar": the example of heroes "instantiates and thus clarifies general principles of morality and qualities of character that can be articulated as meaningful and understood as possible for all participants in a society."[15] The morality of saints is, in contrast, above ordinary and hence is exemplary in the sense that it "motivates us from afar, as a future ideal that impinges on us in the present."[16]

Still, we should remember that like heroes, particular saints exemplify "only certain types of sainthood, and [those] other types may be compatible with quite different human excellences."[17]

Nonetheless, these examples instruct us on how to be virtuous. We need such models in our society, who give us not just concrete guidance in the process of formation but at times "challenge us toward the *telos*, and toward fuller embodiment of the virtues."[18] In fact because of the specificity of their heroism or saintliness, they often reawaken us to appreciating a neglected virtue or a forgotten way of being.

Community and Communal Identity

Virtue ethics has often been criticized as self-centered. However, there are important arguments for a communal aspect within it. One set of arguments focuses on the roles of community in relation to virtues. First, narratives and community facilitate the practice of virtue. Second, community plays an important role in understanding virtues: the local community determines our understanding of the virtues (and so the same virtue is often expressed differently in different places). Third, the community is the proper place for virtue. In the community, people understand themselves, recognize the appropriate ends of the community, and articulate the virtues they need to develop. Fourth, virtue ethics considers identity as not just personal but also communal. Our human identity needs a story, a temporal framework that "synthesizes our diverse moments of experience into a coherent whole."[19] Personal identity "comes through a process of identification with [this] larger narrative framework—a story—and with a community that tries to live out this story."[20] Certain narratives of community define, set limits, and configure personal identity through the ideals they present to us. However, the community must be vigilant against the danger of becoming closed, for this will only lead to sectarianism.

The other group of arguments depends on the nature of virtue itself. According to MacIntyre, virtue is a social quality and is needed for "the pursuit of a good for human beings the conception of which is elaborated and possessed within an ongoing social tradition."[21] Subsequently, virtue ethicists understand the human *telos* as a flourishing in both a social and a personal way. On the other hand, many virtues depend on social connections within a community that give "point and purpose" to them. The virtue of friendship, for example, "arises within a relationship defined in terms of a common allegiance to and a common pursuit of goods."[22] Aquinas's understanding of the virtue of justice is similarly social (*ST* II.II. 58.5–6).[23]

Finally, since the time of Plato virtues have existed "not primarily for private purpose, but to form and improve our communities."[24] Insofar as our identity depends on the community, our character formation is equally communal. Within the community we do not only seek to become virtuous persons but also a particular kind of community.

These insights on community lead to three related issues. First, the emphasis of virtue ethicists on the local community raises concerns about cultural relativism.[25] We generally believe that every culture has a class of virtues to help/guide its members to answer the question of who they should become as a community. A few ethicists believe that each class of virtues is specific only to that particular culture. Many, however, believe that virtues from one culture can be analogously compared to those of another. That means that we recognize trans-cultural affinities between virtues of different cultures. Some even claim that there are universal virtues, or at least "thin" virtues in all cultures. There is a spectrum of views, ranging from those who believe in cultural contextualization to those who want to transcend the boundary of local culture. I am more inclined to follow the more progressive side here: though virtues are context sensitive, they are not ultimately confined to a limited context but remain open to revision.[26] And it is based on this view that the task of bringing a virtue-reading of Scripture into other cultural and religious systems becomes possible. However, such a task further leads to a theological question—namely, the relevance of theological ethics for contemporary cultures.

As noted earlier, Aquinas categorizes virtues into theological and cardinal virtues. Theological virtues are basically infused by God, while cardinal virtues can be acquired by Christians and nonbelievers. Furthermore, the kind of inner-worldly virtuous acts done by Christians are sometimes distinguished from those by nonbelievers by relating the former's goal with supernatural destiny, and its source with grace. Is it possible to find virtues in non-Christian communities comparable with infused theological virtues? Here we face the same issue that is found in the question of cultural contextualization: Are infused theological virtues specific only to the Christian community or can they be analogously compared? Again, I follow the progressive side in approaching this issue. Although the virtues emerging from Scripture are the result of Christian faith and have God's assistance as their source, they can still be engaged cross-culturally with non-Christian societies. A classic example is the virtue of hope.

The third issue deals with translating philosophical language into a theological one—that is, employing this moral philosophy as a hermeneutical tool for interpreting Scripture. Joseph Kotva suggests several fundamental points of reference for bridging moral philosophy and theological ethics. He notes that sanctification, like virtuous character formation itself, is a teleological process. But in the theological enterprise, the Christian *telos* is one's conformity with Christ. Its beginning, continuation, and completion radically depend on God's grace. Therefore, the concept of virtue within a theological setting is tied to the notion of grace. In addition, the *telos* as an ideal and perfection is, in both settings, a goal beyond this world.

Likewise, theological ethics sees Jesus Christ as the *telos*. He is the paradigmatic person whose humanity realizes our full human potential and offers us the content of our human *telos*. Subsequently, Jesus is the norm of humanity; a virtue framework affirms Jesus as normative humanity. Last but not least, Jesus's call to discipleship finds similarities with the good of virtue in other contexts, especially in the need and role of exemplary figures.

THE RELEVANCE OF VIRTUE IN READING SCRIPTURE

The concept of virtue can be found in Scripture, especially in the wisdom literature, such as Proverbs and the book of Sirach.[27] Some scholars are more expansive: following Athanasius's word that "the entire Holy Scripture is a teacher of virtues," they claim that the moral agenda found in Scripture is written in terms of virtue.[28]

Scholars like John Barton think otherwise. They are reluctant to claim that Scripture supports virtue ethics (or vice versa). They note that the term *virtue* is not prominent in the Bible; although the Old Testament is aware of human virtues, it does not have any specific term to express the general idea of virtue. Even in the New Testament, the term appears only a few times despite those instances that occur in the lists of vices and virtues (e.g., Galatians 5:22–23). Barton therefore argues that the Bible is not primarily about virtue.

Most scholars who entertain the question of Scripture and ethics are, however, inclined to virtue. Benjamin Farley, for example, is convinced that the Bible encourages believers to venture a biblical ethics of virtue. It contains and commends virtues and character-building motifs: in the Hebrew Bible, particular virtues among certain Hebrew figures of different historical periods are found—such as Gideon's virtue of sobriety (Judges 8:23). The wisdom literature, especially, is characterized with the provision of numerous virtues, like honesty, integrity, faithfulness, and loyalty. The New Testament similarly contains extensive lists of virtues and character-molding motifs. The Beatitudes in Matthew 5, for instance, extols eight corresponding virtues. The parables also point to a variety of virtues, like vigilance (e.g., Mark 13:32–37). For Paul, all virtues are set within the context of salvation by grace through faith. Apart from the three theological virtues of faith, hope, and charity, he also calls for various virtues based on different communal contexts, such as self-control for the Galatians (5:22) and renewal and humility for the Romans (12:2–3).

Scripture not only reveals moral virtue, value, and vision, it actually promotes them. Specifically, it "helps form and name virtues . . . and creates and renews moral vision."[29]

Scripture and Moral Character

The Bible's concrete lists and discussion of virtues provide "a touchstone and a point of reference for theological discussions of virtues and Christian character."[30] Cahill explains that Scripture orients believers (on both individual and communal levels) around certain virtues—such as forgiveness and compassion—that reflect God's self-revelation in Christ. Moreover, Scripture is the witness of Israel and the early Church both to their struggles to be

God's faithful people and to their responses to God's revelation in concrete life experiences. It shapes the community's character whenever it reflects on the community. For example, as Birch and Rasmussen note, those biblical stories that narrate Jesus's associations with the outcasts and sinners shape the followers of Christ and their faith community into an inclusive, renewing community.

Furthermore, Scripture shapes our character as distinctively Christian. It defines first the Christian virtues and thereby shapes one's character. The Judeo-Christian story provides what is needed (such as metaphors and concepts) for the shaping of Judeo-Christian character. Thus, the Bible actually occasions the formation of moral character. As a shaper of Christian identity, Scripture is the "prime source of the self-conscious identity of the community of faith."[31]

Scripture and Exemplars

During the exploration of the goods of virtue, I cited three Old Testament figures—namely, Judith, Ruth, and Naomi—as examples of role models for the virtues of courage, loyalty, and love of family, respectively. Indeed, Scripture contains many "characters" that play the role of modeling for us certain moral characters. Barton, though he does not claim that Scripture has any explicit idea of virtue ethics, similarly acknowledges that biblical stories (and their characters) have exemplary moral value in presenting humankind in its complexity. The story of David, for instance, presents to us not just a flawed life but also an examined life that "manifests a concern for how one ought to live even when this runs clearly counter to the character's own moral insight."[32] As a result, Scripture contributes to moral formation by telling the stories of those exemplary figures and of the community.

Sometimes the role of the biblical figures as exemplars for virtues is rather straightforward (e.g., James 5:11). Other times it is not. I agree with Jens Herzer that the lack of explicit references does not necessarily mean that the specific scriptural text or religious insight is irrelevant: biblical figures can play the exemplary role in an implicit manner. One particular example is the virtue of hospitality exemplified in the lives of many in the Bible.[33]

In the Old Testament one can find detailed accounts of welcome (e.g., Genesis 18) and inhospitality (e.g., Genesis 19). Certainly, in the New Testament, both the Good Samaritan in Luke 10:25–37 and the person of Jesus are vivid models for practicing hospitality. But there are others throughout. For instance, I argue that Boaz—the husband of Ruth—is also an exemplary figure in cultivating the virtue: through his unusual and exemplary words and deeds, both the land itself and the person of Ruth the Moabite are redeemed. The person of Boaz becomes a model of hospitality for individual Israelites during the postexilic period.

Scripture and Community

Since character is "a process of communal formation of individual identity," Scripture is relevant to community and communal identity. [34] Thus, I agree with William Brown that "Scripture forms community as much as community informs the reading of Scripture." [35] In addition, Patrick Miller rightly insists that the biblical texts "do not speak about a *general* understanding of community but of the formation of a *particular* community whose identity as a people is evoked by their inextricable relationship to the Lord." [36] These particular communities formed by Scripture are both historical and diverse. But Scripture forms these particular, historical, and diverse communities as moral communities. In this way, as Miller and others suggest, Scripture plays the role of generating and sustaining not just the community but its spiritual-moral formation as well. [37]

For example, the writer of the book of Ruth, in creating the character Boaz during the restoration period, aims at reforming and rebuilding the Israelite community into a hospitable community. Biblical scholars agree that the main characters of this postexilic period were "dedicated to the task of reforming Israel . . . that she might become . . . nothing less than the covenant people of God." [38] As a result, the narratives found in the books of the postexilic period are not meant merely to describe but to change the society to which the returning exiles belong. The gospels likewise do not simply portray a unique human being but also serve for training the follower to be part of the new community. *Transformation*

In short, Scripture as narrative not only describes the character (of God) but also "render[s] a community capable of ordering its existence [in a way] appropriate to such stories." [39] As Cahill rightly notes, by forming communities that are consistent with God's revelation, Scripture gains its authority in morality. The more faithful we are to the Bible, the more we recognize its authority, and hopefully vice versa.

NOTES

1. Alasdair MacIntyre, *After Virtue*, 3rd ed. (Notre Dame, IN: University of Notre Dame Press, 2007), 187.

2. David L. Norton, "Moral Minimalism and the Development of Moral Character," in *Midwest Studies in Philosophy XIII: Ethical Theory: Character and Virtue*, ed. Peter A. French, Theodore E. Uehling Jr., and Howard K. Wettstein (Notre Dame, IN: University of Notre Dame Press, 1988), 180–81.

3. Walter Brueggemann, "Foreword," in *Character Ethics and the Old Testament: Moral Dimensions of Scripture*, ed. M. Daniel Carroll R. and Jacqueline E. Lapsley (Louisville, KY: Westminster John Knox Press, 2007), vii.

4. Stanley Hauerwas, *Character and the Christian Life: A Study in Theological Ethics* (San Antonio, TX: Trinity Press, 1975), 117. See also his *A Community of Character: Toward a Constructive Christian Social Ethic* (Notre Dame, IN: University of Notre Dame Press, 1981); and Benjamin W. Farley, *In Praise of Virtue: An Exploration of the Biblical Virtues in a Christian Context* (Grand Rapids, MI: Eerdmans, 1995).

5. Norton, "Moral Minimalism and the Development of Moral Character," 181.

6. Ibid., 181–82.

7. James Keenan, "Virtue and Identity," in *Concilium 2000/2: Creating Identity*, ed. Hermann Häring, Maureen Junker-Kenny, and Dietmar Mieth (London: SCM Press, 2000), 69.

8. Gilbert C. Meilaender, *The Theory and Practice of Virtue* (Notre Dame, IN: University of Notre Dame Press, 1984), 57.

9. Joseph Woodhill, *The Fellowship of Life* (Washington, DC: Georgetown University Press, 1998), 31.

10. William C. Spohn, *Go and Do Likewise: Jesus and Ethics* (New York: Continuum, 2000), 32–33.

11. Andrew Flescher, *Heroes, Saints, and Ordinary Morality* (Washington, DC: Georgetown University Press, 2003), 172.

12. Ibid.

13. Ibid., 211.

14. Ibid., 219–20.

15. John Stratton Hawley, ed., "Introduction," in *Saints and Virtues* (Berkeley: University of California Press, 1987), xvi, as quoted in Flescher, *Heroes, Saints, and Ordinary Morality*, 177.

16. Ibid., 179.

17. Robert Adams, "Saints," in *The Virtues*, ed. Robert B. Kruschwitz and Robert C. Roberts (Belmont, CA: Wadsworth, 1987), 158. See also Susan Wolf, "Moral Saints," in *The Virtues*, ed. Kruschwitz and Roberts (Belmont, CA: Wadsworth, 1987), 137–52.

18. Joseph Kotva, *The Christian Case for Virtue Ethics* (Washington, DC: Georgetown University Press, 1996), 28, 36–37. See also William C. Spohn, *What Are They Saying about Scripture and Ethics?*, rev. ed. (Mahwah, NJ: Paulist Press, 1995).

19. Spohn, *Go and Do Likewise*, 174. Spohn refers to Mark Johnson, *Moral Imagination: Implications of Cognitive Science for Ethics* (Chicago: University of Chicago Press, 1993).

20. Spohn, *What Are They Saying?*, 81–82.

21. MacIntyre, *After Virtue*, 273.

22. Ibid., 156.

23. See Thomas Aquinas, *The Summa Theologiae of St. Thomas Aquinas,* trans. Fathers of the English Dominican Province (New York: Benziger Brothers, 1948).

24. James F. Keenan, "Virtues, Principles, and a Consistent Ethic of Life," in *The Consistent Ethic of Life: Assessing Its Reception and Relevance*, ed. Thomas Nairn (Maryknoll, NY: Orbis Books, 2008), 50. See also his "Virtue Ethics: Making a Case as It Comes of Age," *Thought* 67 (1992): 115–27; *Virtues for Ordinary Christians* (Kansas City, MO: Sheed & Ward, 1996); "Virtue Ethics," in *Christian Ethics: An Introduction*, ed. Bernard Hoose (London: Chapman, 1997), 84–94.

25. A significant example is the debate between Lisa Sowle Cahill and Jean Porter. Cahill believes that it is not enough to recognize the emergence of norms from local cultures. Rather, it is necessary to establish consensual universal norms among all cultures. Lisa Sowle Cahill, "Community and Universals: A Misplaced Debate in Christian Ethics," *Annual of the Society of Christian Ethics* 18 (1998): 3–12. See also James F. Keenan, *A History of Catholic Moral Theology in the Twentieth Century* (New York: Continuum, 2010), 214.

26. Martha C. Nussbaum, "Non-Relative Virtues: An Aristotelian Approach," in *Midwest Studies in Philosophy XIII*, ed. Peter A. French, Theodore E. Uehling Jr., and Howard K. Wettstein (Notre Dame, IN: University of Notre Dame Press, 1988), 44–45.

27. In making the claims about the relevance of virtue ethics in reading Scripture, besides Farley and Birch and Rasmussen, I also considered John Barton, *Understanding Old Testament Ethics* (Louisville, KY: Westminster John Knox, 2003); John W. Crossin, *What Are They*

Saying about Virtue? (New York: Paulist Press, 1985); Patrick D. Miller, "The Good Neighborhood: Identity and Community through the Ten Commandments," in *Character and Scripture*, ed. William P. Brown (Grand Rapids, MI: Eerdmans, 2002), 55–72.

28. Athanasius, *The Life of Anthony* and *The Letter to Marcellinus*, trans. Robert C. Gregg, *The Classics of Western Spirituality: A Library of the Great Spiritual Masters* (New York: Paulist Press, 1980), 112, as cited in Woodhill, *The Fellowship of Life* , 17.

29. Bruce C. Birch and Larry L. Rasmussen, *Bible and Ethics in Christian Life*, rev. ed. (Minneapolis, MN: Augsburg, 1989), 64.

30. Crossin, *What Are They Saying about Virtue?*, 10.

31. Birch and Rasmussen, *Bible and Ethics in Christian Life*, 181.

32. Barton, *Understanding Old Testament Ethics*, 72.

33. Jens Herzer, "Paul, Job, and the New Quest for Justice," in *Character Ethics and the New Testament: Moral Dimensions of Scripture*, ed. Robert L. Brawley (Louisville, KY: Westminster John Knox Press Press, 2007), 77–86. See also Chan Yiu-sing Luke, "A Model of Hospitality for Our Times," *Budhi: A Journal of Ideas and Culture* 10, no. 1 (2006): 1–30.

34. Lisa Sowle Cahill, "Christian Character, Biblical Community, and Human Values," in *Character and Scripture: Moral Formation, Community, and Biblical Interpretation*, ed. William P. Brown (Grand Rapids, MI: Eerdmans, 2002), 10.

35. William P. Brown, ed., *Character and Scripture: Moral Formation, Community, and Biblical Interpretation* (Grand Rapids, MI: Eerdmans, 2002), xi.

36. Miller, "The Good Neighborhood," 58.

37. See also Larry L. Rasmussen, "Sighting of Primal Visions: Community and Ecology," in *Character and Scripture: Moral Formation, Community, and Biblical Interpretation*, ed. William P. Brown (Grand Rapids, MI: Eerdmans, 2002), 389–409.

38. Raymond Foster, *The Restoration of Israel* (London: DLT, 1970), x.

39. Stanley Hauerwas, *A Community of Character: Toward a Constructive Christian Social Ethic* (Notre Dame, IN: University of Notre Dame Press, 1981), 67.

II

Exegeting and Interpreting the Ten Commandments in Exodus 20:2–17 for Ethical Living

The previous chapter reaffirms the views that Scripture exposes us to and advocates for certain virtues, shapes moral character and identity, provides exemplary models, and reforms the faith community. We are convinced that the ethics of virtue is compatible with Scripture, and the hermeneutics of virtue ethics is fitting for interpreting it. In parts II and III, this conclusion is carried over to the interpretation of the two specific scriptural texts. Still, prior to carrying out the task of hermeneutics through the lens of virtue, we need first to treat the text as "scripted"—that is, to interpret the text "textually" or "exegetically." Understanding what the text meant to the original readers in their community is a crucial and necessary step to the appropriation of the texts in contemporary society.

Chapter Three

The Decalogue in History

Philo of Alexandria was the first to make a special study of the Ten Commandments. In his treatise *De Decalogo*, he employed a kind of philosophy that focuses on the cosmic meaning of the first five commandments and the moral meaning of the remaining commandments. He perceived the commandments as hierarchically ordered.[1] His treatment also anticipated the various issues that were addressed by later interpreters, such as the question of whether the Ten Commandments were addressed to all peoples. Tertullian, for instance, answered that the Decalogue was simply the form in which the universal moral law was promulgated in a certain way.

Nevertheless, Augustine's interpretation dominated medieval writings on this topic:[2] his particular way of dividing the text and his emphasis on the two tablets has become the standard in both the Roman Catholic and Lutheran traditions. The Ten Commandments are not simply the first ten laws, but laws that stand for the entire Old Law. However, they are subordinated to the twofold commandment of love and serve as a detailed explanation of the commandment.

Augustine used the Decalogue in theological disputes, such as those with the Pelagians. Still, the most common use of the text appeared in his interpretation of scriptural numbers. Augustine perceived the understanding of scriptural numbers as an important step in exegesis and in the interpretation of the text, for "numbers are imbued with theological significance."[3] As a result, he was completely preoccupied with the number ten in his discussion of the text. Moreover, for Augustine, what is important is the basic, symbolic meaning of each commandment and not the words or even the exact order. In a manner of speaking, his exegesis belongs to a kind of symbolic interpretation in the modern sense.

Aquinas discussed the Decalogue under the section on the moral precept of the Old Law in *Summa Theologiae* (I.II. 100). However, a fuller explanation and interpretation of the Ten Commandments is found among the catechetical instructions and sermons that Aquinas gave in 1273:[4] he confirmed Augustine's view that the Decalogue and the entire law are founded in the two precepts of charity. Yet he interchanged the order of the ninth and the tenth commandments, based on the conviction that the commandment against coveting the other's goods points to a broader meaning than that of coveting the other's wife. Moreover, Aquinas correlated several commandments together according to different levels of the love of neighbor—from the person oneself to one's spouse to one's external goods. Still, what is the most influential of Aquinas's views is that he turned those negative commandments into positive ones—a view that Calvin later adopted. Thus, for example, the commandment against stealing is actually a command to protect the property of the neighbor.

Aquinas interpreted the text using scriptural texts. For instance, in explaining the term "in vain" he employed Psalms 12:3, 94:11, 4:2, and Wisdom 13:1 to signify what is false, useless, sinful, and foolish, respectively.[5] Still, the overall tone of interpretation is homiletic and catechetical rather than exegetical.

Luther similarly wrote a rather comprehensive commentary on the Ten Commandments in his catechisms, especially in the *Large Catechism* (where he spends half of the book talking just about it). In its introduction, he claimed that "anyone who knows the Ten Commandments perfectly knows the entire Scriptures" (*LC* #17).[6] However, one writer noted that Luther warned against "those who think the commandments are easy and who therefore think they have time to fulfill God's counsels."[7] For Luther, the Decalogue is based on faith rather than reason (as Aquinas held) and is "the only reliable way of knowing God's will" (*LC* #311). It is a "replication of the natural law" first written on our hearts and later on the tablets.[8]

Furthermore, Luther insisted that all commandments must be viewed in the light of the first one and that they are given in descending order of importance. What is distinctive of his reading is that the heart dominated the entire interpretation. Luther emphasized those habitual, relational behaviors, attended to the inner attitudes of the person, and called for acting from a charitable heart. For example, the commandment against adultery not only forbids adulterous acts but also all kinds of immodest and impure thoughts and hence calls for chastity and temperance in one's heart (*LC* ##202–3). Paul Grimley Kuntz rightly comments that Luther's exposition can generate a chart of virtues.

Luther's approach to the interpretation of the text is equally distinctive, innovative, and open-minded. He insisted that Christians should not read the commandments literally, for what belonged to the specific situation of the people of Israel had nothing to do with Christians directly! The two commandments against coveting, for example, were not applicable to his people and country, for they neither had slaves nor treated women as property (*LC* ##293–95). Moreover, he often expanded the interpretation to match up with the reality and experience of his audience (e.g., *LC* ##223–50)—for instance, "those who steal" also implied financial firms of his time. Last but not least, Luther argued that a more important commandment could trump the less important ones.

Luther attempted to cover almost every aspect of one's life through the commandments. He interpreted them biblically and pastorally, and he framed his interpretation socially for the sake of preaching to and instructing an ordinary audience. He did not employ literal or legalistic interpretations of the text.

Calvin also wrote on the Ten Commandments comprehensively—both in his *Institutes of the Christian Religion* and his *Sermons on the Ten Commandments*. Indeed, many would agree that no one in the Christian tradition did so with the same degree of intensity as Calvin did. For Calvin and his Reformed followers, the Decalogue is central to their theology and ethics because it sets forth divine grace—the Ten Commandments are "dynamic expressions of God's gracious will that call the church to a continuing process of conversion."[9]

Calvin perceived the Ten Commandments as a summary of the revealed moral law of God. They are so arranged as to reflect God's covenantal character. As others did before him, Calvin divided the Decalogue into two tables that reflect our duties to God and to others. He also argued that the first table is the foundation of the second. However, unlike Aquinas and Luther, he divided the commandments into groups of four and six, and separated the prohibitions against having other gods and making idols and images into two commandments.

Calvin brought the meanings of the Decalogue to a new level by perceiving each commandment as representing a broad category of behavior rather than a single solitary act (*ICR* 2.8.39). He emphasized that the Decalogue is not only about exterior behaviors but also about inner attitudes and dispositions, as Luther had done. In many ways, the interpretation looked more like what Jesus did in the Sermon on the Mount. The prohibition against killing, therefore, is also applicable to "the murder of the heart," such as hatred (*ICR* 2.8.39). Calvin further claimed that every commandment has positive injunctions and negative prohibitions. Thus, the prohibition against killing calls for holding another's life as sacred and watching over the other's preservation. Finally, Calvin understood that each commandment has a double subject—God and humankind—and interpreted the commandments realistically: the order of these commandments is based on the actual frequency of their applicability.[10]

Calvin's overall exposition of the Ten Commandments is hermeneutical and instructional rather than exegetical. He was similarly interested in the concrete ethical implications of the commandments for the community rather than the ancient meanings of the prohibitions. One Calvinist rightly comments that, for Calvin, "few people make graven images. Few are guilty of murder. But no one is free from sometimes giving his or her loyalties to the things of this world, and no one is free from sometimes hating and disregarding his or her neighbors."[11]

In sum, the interpretations of the Decalogue by Augustine, Aquinas, Luther, and Calvin are clearly homiletic, catechetical, and pastoral in nature.[12] However, the unusual ways in which Luther and Calvin interpreted the Ten Commandments invites us to focus more on the inner attitudes, thoughts, and dispositions than on external behaviors alone when reading the Decalogue. This position throws light on and supports our proposal to interpret the text through the lens of virtue.

Let us now turn to more recent attempts to interpret the Decalogue and conclude with the recent work of biblical scholars. The *Catechism of the Catholic Church* spends more than half of the entire morals section (III.2) on the Ten Commandments. Its overall structure and content is inspired by the catechisms of the past, and certain parts of its teaching are basically an affirmation of what previous councils taught (e.g., *CCC* #2068). The *Catechism* also confirms that the Ten Commandments have a special place in Scripture and in the Church's tradition—they are "a privileged expression of the natural law" and are "engraved by God in the human heart" (*CCC* ##2069–72). While it reads the Decalogue closely within the natural law tradition, it identifies certain virtues and practices that are rooted specifically in the commandments. It discusses the sociopolitical implications of these commandments, such as the right of religious freedom (*CCC* ##2104–9). It also employs many biblical texts and teachings of the early Church Fathers (e.g., *CCC* #11). The general tone of the *Catechism* is explicitly catechetical and instructional, while remaining open to other ways of interpreting the text.

In a book that marks the 450th anniversary of the publication of Luther's *Large Catechism*, the late Paul Lehmann offers his interpretation of the Ten Commandments:[13] he argues that the commandments "describe" the way God ordered the world instead of prescribing strict actions. This provides a dynamic and creative approach toward the Decalogue and invites us to read it with an attitude of discernment or what he calls "apperception." He also proposes that a relationship of "reciprocal responsibility"—which emphasizes differences among people—is intrinsic to the Ten Commandments.

In sum, his work is not an interpretation of the Decalogue per se but of its role in doing Christian ethics. James Gustafson comments that Lehmann aims at showing that Luther's interpretation of the Decalogue is congruent with certain theoretical sociological claims.[14]

Keenan anchors his treatment of the Ten Commandments in the theme of God's compassion. He claims that the right approach to interpret the text is, as Luther did, to assert "the priority of the interior disposition over the exterior action, and beg[i]n with our relationship with God and move to our relationship with one another."[15] Readers should focus on specific dispositions that help us live compassionately with God and one another, such as to be merciful and grateful, and to attend to one's deepest desire. However, Keenan's work, like many others, does not first examine the original meanings of the text but simply assumes that we already understand them.

Stanley Hauerwas and William Willimon claim that "the recovery of the commandments is crucial for our survival as a people called Christian in the face of today's challenges."[16] Yet their work is somehow different: the Decalogue is not timeless ethical principles for humanity in general; rather, it is a distinctive way through which we know of and about God and form a truthful community. True to their ethics of character and of community, they claim that our understanding of the Ten Commandments depends on the practices of a community (church). Though they insist on the need to know what the meanings of the commandments are before offering ethical advice, they greatly rely on the commentary of past Christian thinkers, rather than on contemporary exegetes.

The Pontifical Biblical Commission has also offered its brief reading of the text for contemporary moral living. It claims that the Decalogue reflects a twofold ethic: As a primitive ethic, it emphasizes exteriority, communal identity, and prohibitions. As a potentially rich ethic, it expresses universal values, is set in the framework of covenant, and is rooted in the context of liberation. The Decalogue "is not to be viewed primarily as law, but rather as gift."[17] One should understand its contents in terms of a morality of values rather than simply as precepts. The Commission thus identifies ten hierarchical, universal values, including religious homage to God and freedom. It also offers a juridical interpretation, from which it proposes a charter of rights and of freedom to the entire humanity, such as the right of families to just and protective policies. Surprisingly, the Commission employs only a few biblical texts to support its view, and its overall treatment of the Decalogue does not contain any of the exegesis that one would expect from a biblical commission.

While the Hebrew Bible scholar Walter Harrelson is concerned that Christians, for various reasons, have slowly lost their appreciation of the Decalogue,[18] it is Patrick Miller who treats the Ten Commandments substantively. Earlier, Miller proposed that the Decalogue presents itself as "a way of identifying the 'distinguishing characteristics' . . . or the marks of the good neighborhood."[19] Through the Ten Commandments, a particular community with certain characteristics is formed. Here, his approach bears a trait of an ethics of character and of community.

In his most recent exegetical exposition of the Ten Commandments, *The Ten Commandments*, Miller perceives the Decalogue as "a comprehensive framework and ground for the ethics of the Old Testament."[20] While he points out that the divine command ethics is the primary mode and starting point of the ethics of the Decalogue, still, such an ethic is a comprehensive one—it accommodates and interacts with other modes/approaches of ethical discourse as well, especially the ethics of responsibility, narrative ethics, and virtue ethics. However, Miller treats the ethics of the Ten Commandments very briefly and generally. He does not go on to offer any actual hermeneutics of individual commandments by means of those identified ethical models. Instead he provides us a fine exegetical work.

In closing, I would like to offer a few words on interpreting the Ten Commandments through the lens of virtue. In the field of Old Testament ethics, there exists a particular caricature of the Old Testament as merely a set of commandments that are "too familiarly labeled as 'legalism.'"[21] In Exodus, for example, many scholars are too quick to move from God's deliverance to God's giving of commandments and the Israelites' obedience, without attending to any relationship of Israel with God. This relationship is one of covenant that emphasizes the language of intimacy rather than of command, as demonstrated in Exodus 19:4–6. Israel's moral obligations are to be understood in the context of covenant. The Decalogue is not simply law but also covenantal obligations.[22]

Similarly, Old Testament ethics is often characterized as a kind of deontological ethics, and the Ten Commandments especially have been commonly seen as simply prohibitions or prescriptions. Yet some scholars begin to point out that the Decalogue need not be interpreted as motivated by negative reinforcement alone. Miller, for instance, insists that the Decalogue "cannot be perceived and appropriated fully without the positive formulations complementing the negative and demonstrating how expansive and total and full the response to this directive is."[23]

As far as the use of virtue ethics is concerned, reading the commandments through the lens of virtue is not a completely new enterprise. We saw from the above review that theologians and ethicists of the past and the present do not perceive the commandments as primarily about external actions. Luther and Calvin focused on the heart, internal dispositions, and habitual and relational conducts.[24] Keenan, Hauerwas, and others also, in one way or another, employ a virtue-related approach in reading the text. Nowadays, more and more scholars would agree that the Ten Commandments are related to one's interior life, especially one's attitudes and dispositions. Brevard Childs acknowledges that such internalization "does not ever seem to have been completely absent within Israel" and hence "the process of internalization cannot be fully dismissed and stands on the edge of the commandments."[25] Keeping the commandments can become both a commitment and a habit. In this way, the Decalogue is useful in the formation of Christian character.

Moreover, the Decalogue is not only concerned with the individual's dispositions, habitual conducts, and character, but also with the Israelite community itself. Because the addressee is not simply individual Israelites, "[t]he focus is on protecting *the health of the community*, to which end the individual plays such an important role."[26] The norms emerging from the Decalogue "are much more akin to statements about the character of life in community than they are to cases of violation of the law of the community and what punishment is to be dealt out."[27] Even if one continues to perceive the Decalogue as a kind of "natural law," that law can be discovered only through "transformed witnesses who embody the whole law."[28] As a result, the Decalogue is not self-interpreting but depends on the practices of a community formed by God.

Now I turn to some exegetical issues regarding the text, but with this caution: I spend more pages in exploring the exegetical issues and the original meaning of the Ten Commandments than that of the Beatitudes. This is partly because of the problems that scholars of Old Testament ethics face: "First, ordinary readers, not inured to these [OT] stories by constant attention as biblical scholars are, notice . . . that they are often far from morally edifying. . . . Second . . . it is often not easy to decide what is being commended [or] deplored."[29]

NOTES

1. For example, Philo perceived adultery as more serious than killing and hence put the commandment against adultery before that of killing (table 1). See Paul Grimley Kuntz, *The Ten Commandments in History: Mosaic Paradigms for a Well-ordered Society*, ed. Thomas D'Evelyn (Grand Rapids, MI: Eerdmans, 2004). See also Robert Louis Wilken, "Keeping the Commandments," *First Things* 137 (November 2003): 34–35.

2. See Jonathan Hall, *Augustine and the Decalogue* (University of Virginia), http://people.virginia.edu/~jph8r/AugustineDec.pdf. See also Augustine, "Quaest de Exodo," in *Sancti Aureli Augustini: Quæstionum in Heptateuchum Libri VII* (Vindobonae: F. Tempsky, 1895); *The First Catechetical Instruction*, Ancient Christian Writers series, vol. 2, trans. Joseph P. Christopher (Mahwah, NJ: Paulist Press, 1978).

3. Hall, *Augustine and the Decalogue.*

4. Thomas Aquinas, "Explanation of the Ten Commandments," in *The Catechetical Instructions of St. Thomas Aquinas*, trans. Joseph B. Collins (New York: Joseph Wagner, 1939), http://dhspriory.org/thomas/TenCommandments.htm. For the original Latin text *Collationes in decem praeceptis*, see also www.corpusthomisticum.org/cac.html.

5. The Hebrew numbering of the Psalms is used throughout this work.

6. Martin Luther, "The Large Catechism," in *Triglot Concordia: The Symbolical Books of the Evangelical Lutheran Church: German-Latin-English* (St. Louis: Concordia, 1921), www.bookofconcord.org/lc-3-tencommandments.php.

7. Timothy J. Wengert, "Martin Luther and the Ten Commandments in the Large Cate-chism," *Currents in Theology and Mission* 31, no. 2 (April 2004): 113–14. See also *LC* #316.

8. Philip Turner, "The Ten Commandments in the Church in a Postmodern World," in *I Am the Lord Your God: Christian Reflections on the Ten Commandments*, ed. Carl E. Braaten and Christopher R. Seitz (Grand Rapids, MI: Eerdmans, 2005), 11.

9. John Burgess, "Reformed Explications of the Ten Commandments," in *The Ten Com-mandments: The Reciprocity of Faithfulness*, ed. William P. Brown (Louisville, KY: Westmin-ster John Knox Press, 2004), 80. See also John Calvin, *Institutes of the Christian Religion*, trans. Henry Beveridge (Grand Rapids, MI: Eerdmans, 1989), www.spurgeon.org/~phil/calvin; *John Calvin's Sermons on the Ten Commandments*, ed. and trans. Benjamin W. Farley (Grand Rapids, MI: Baker Books, 1993).

10. For example, false witness, which happens more frequently than stealing, is listed after stealing.

11. Burgess, "Reformed Explications of the Ten Commandments," 84.

12. See also Joseph A. Slatterly, "The Catechetical Use of the Decalogue from the End of the Catechumenate through the Late Medieval Period" (PhD diss., Catholic University of America, 1979).

13. Paul L. Lehmann, *The Decalogue and a Human Future: The Meaning of the Command-ments for Making and Keeping Human Life Human* (Grand Rapids, MI: Eerdmans, 1995).

14. James M. Gustafson, "Commandments for Staying Human," *Christian Century* 112, no. 37 (December 20–27, 1995): 1247–49.

15. Keenan, *Commandments of Compassion*, vii–viii, xiii.

16. Stanley M. Hauerwas and William H. Willimon, *The Truth about God: The Ten Com-mandments in Christian Life* (Nashville, TN: Abingdon Press, 1999), 13.

17. Livio Melina and Jose Noriega, eds., "Il rinnovamento della teologia morale: prospettive del Vaticano II e di Veritatis splendor," in *Caminare nella luce: Prospettive della teologia morale a partire da Veritatis splendor* (Roma: PUL, 2004), 39–40, as cited in Pontifical Biblical Commission, *The Bible and Morality: Biblical Roots of Christian Conduct* (Vatican: Libreria Editrice Vaticana, 2008), 133.

18. Walter J. Harrelson, *The Ten Commandments and Human Rights* (Macon, GA: Mercer University Press, 1997).

19. Patrick D. Miller, "The Good Neighborhood: Identity and Community through the Ten Commandments," in *Character and Scripture*, ed. William P. Brown (Grand Rapids, MI: Eerdmans, 2002), 56.

20. Patrick D. Miller, *The Ten Commandments* (Louisville, KY: Westminster John Knox Press, 2009), xi.

21. Walter Brueggemann, "Foreword," in *Character Ethics and the Old Testament: Moral Dimensions of Scripture*, ed. M. Daniel Carroll R. and Jacqueline E. Lapsley (Louisville, KY: Westminster John Knox Press, 2007), vii.

22. Thomas W. Ogletree, *The Use of the Bible in Christian Ethics: A Constructive Essay* (Philadelphia, PA: Fortress Press, 1983), 49–53. For a more juridical approach, however, see Bruce C. Birch, "Divine Character and the Formation of Moral Community in the Book of Exodus," in *The Bible in Ethics: The Second Sheffield Colloquium*, ed. John W. Rogerson, Margaret Davies, and M. Daniel Carroll R. (Sheffield: Sheffield Academic Press, 1995), 119–35.

23. Miller, *The Ten Commandments*, 21.

24. Therefore, I attend closely to the insights of Luther and Calvin in my interpretation of the Ten Commandments.

25. Childs, *The Book of Exodus*, 396.

26. Terence E. Fretheim, *Exodus* (Louisville: John Knox Press, 1991), 221.

27. Harrelson, *Ten Commandments*, 10.

28. Hauerwas and Willimon, *The Truth about God*, 18–19.

29. John Barton, *Understanding Old Testament Ethics* (Louisville, KY: Westminster John Knox Press, 2003), 2–3.

Chapter Four

Some Preliminary Questions

The Decalogue is often seen as part of the larger story of the revelation of YHWH in the wilderness as recorded in the book of Exodus. However, neither the Decalogue nor the book of Exodus is intended to stand by itself. Therefore, in order to offer an exposition of the text that is faithful to the Pentateuch, we need to look at both the book of Exodus and the Pentateuch as a whole and attend to certain preliminary questions.

WHAT IS THE PLACE OF THE DECALOGUE IN THE PENTATEUCH AND THE BOOK OF EXODUS?

The Pentateuch

The first five books of the Hebrew Bible are collectively known as the Pentateuch and are traditionally called "the book of Moses" or "the Torah," although such designations are problematic: there is no reliable evidence to support the claim that Moses was the author.[1] It presents not just laws and regulations but also narratives. In addition, the term "Torah" actually refers to historical teaching rather than law. The Pentateuch thus is better understood as "[a] story of the prehistory of Israel, from creation to the death of Moses on the threshold of the promised land."[2]

According to the dominant "Documentary hypothesis" (or "Four sources theory") of Julius Wellhausen, the Pentateuch is basically comprised of four different documents, each of which comes from a distinct source: the Priestly source (P), the Deuteronomist source (D), the Elohist source (E), and the Yahwist source (J). The first two sources are rather easy to identify, as reflected in the main body of Leviticus and Deuteronomy, respectively.

However, the E and J sources, which represent a good deal of narratives in the Pentateuch, are more difficult to distinguish.[3] This is partly because a narrative may come from more than one document (e.g., the flood story in Genesis contains both J and P sources), hence making the identification difficult.

On the other hand, one common view is that the subsequent order of dating of these four sources is J, E, D, and P, and the overall completion of the Pentateuch should be no earlier than the postexilic period (around the sixth century BCE). The Yahwistic source probably comes from the southern country (Judah), while the Elohist source is associated with the northern kingdom of Israel.

The Book of Exodus

Grounded on the "Four sources theory," the majority of the content in Exodus comes from the Priestly document. The rest is from either the J or the E document; some are even composite in nature. Nevertheless, the book has gone through a number of redactions before the present, final edition was completed.[4]

The content of Exodus reveals not only its sources but also its connectedness with the rest of the Pentateuch. First, the book continues the legacy of Genesis by telling a more extended and continuous story of the birth of a people.[5] The connectedness between Exodus and the next two books is much smoother—the theme of instructions and how the regulations are carried out continues through Leviticus into Numbers. In Deuteronomy, we further note that the major events found in Exodus are presented again, though in different styles.

Taken together, Exodus is well connected with other parts of the Pentateuch and deals with some of its central events. Martin Noth and others remark that Exodus is the heart of the entire Hebrew Bible and is pivotal for the faith of the Israel community. Still, these scholars also agree that the book is a distinctive, integrated unit itself: structurally it contains both a prologue (1:1–7) and an epilogue (40:34–38). Theologically, its beginning introduces the people as slaves of Egypt, while its conclusion reveals that they now commit freely in covenant with YHWH.

In this light, Exodus basically tells the story of the birth and origins of the people of Israel whose survival relies on YHWH as manifested especially in the pivotal event of exodus.[6] Yet some scholars, like John Collins, claim that it has a cultic rather than historical purpose—to remind the people of their obligation to worship God.

In any event, the book can be divided into parts, although the way biblical scholars divide the book differs.[7] Some suggest that the overall structure of the book attests to a thoughtful design, based on the observation of structural symmetry, numerical presentations, repetition of key words in the text, and so on.[8]

Nevertheless, Exodus contains a broad variety of literary types, including sagas and tales (e.g., 2:1–10; 4:24–26), poetic writings and hymns (e.g., 15:1–21), and corpus of laws (e.g., 21:1–23:19).[9] And many of the narratives, as Collins suspects, like the rescue of infant Moses, could be primarily legendary and folkloristic in nature, for similar motifs are found in the literature of neighboring peoples. On the other hand, those statutes and regulations found are generally in line with the legal tradition of the ancient Near East. Dale Patrick thus claims that "no area of biblical studies has benefited more from the recovery of ancient Near Eastern literature than law."[10]

The diverse literary forms of the book logically point to different themes:[11] the revelation of YHWH and the liberation from slavery, for example, are two important themes in the book of Exodus. These themes further bear certain theological significance for the Israel community. First and foremost is the assertion of God's immanence, transcendence, and mercy toward the people. Another important theological contribution is the idea of covenant itself. One scholar rightly claims that "covenant consciousness suffuses all subsequent developments in Israel's history."[12] The laws, therefore, are taken up into this covenantal relationship between Israel and YHWH. All these help the Israelites become a redeemed, covenantal people of God.

WHAT DOES THE TERM "DECALOGUE" MEAN? IS THERE ONLY ONE DECALOGUE IN THE BIBLE?

The English term "Decalogue" is derived from two Greek words *deka* and *logoi*, which in turn are translated from their Hebrew parallels *'eshr mylym*, which literally mean "ten" and "words," respectively. "Decalogue" was first used by Clement of Alexandria in the second century CE, and its designation can be traced first to Exodus 34:28, and later in Deuteronomy 4:13 and 10:4. The term is sometimes referred to as "covenant" or "treaty" (e.g., Exodus 31:18) and "law" (e.g., Exodus 24:12). Still, the term "commandment" is commonly used.

The Two Decalogues

Most Jews and Christians know that there are two versions of the Decalogue found in the Pentateuch, one in Exodus 20:2–17 and the other in Deuteronomy 5:6–21. They are different in contexts, contents, and date of composition:

The Exodus version, as the text reveals, is claimed to be the direct words of YHWH to all the Israelites at Mount Sinai after being delivered by YHWH from slavery in Egypt. The Deuteronomy account, in contrast, is said to be told by Moses on the plains of Moab before entering the land of Canaan. The commandments in this account are thus perceived as "part of Moses' recollection and recapitulation of the journey." [13]

Their differences in content are mostly nominal except for the commandment on observing the Sabbath—specifically, the Exodus version's rationale for observing the Sabbath lies in the creation story. The rationale of the Deuteronomy version, in contrast, lies in the liberating act of the exodus story. Other identified differences include the insertion of a reference in Deuteronomy 5:16 (in honoring parents) and differing sequences in Exodus 20:17 and Deuteronomy 5:21. These changes, as Umberto Cassuto points out, are related to a customary literary practice of that time—that when someone's speech is cited and later is being referred to by someone else, that speech will not be repeated word for word. [14]

On the other hand, the Exodus version seems to be older than that of Deuteronomy, although some would counterargue that the Deuteronomy version is more original. [15] Still, as will be discussed later, some scholars attempt to restore the "original" form of the Ten Commandments and propose their own reconstruction of the Decalogue.

Other "Decalogues" in the Bible

Apart from the Deuteronomy version, we also come across a number of texts in the Pentateuch that are sometimes termed by scholars as "decalogue," such as Ezekiel 18:5–9. [16] They are thought to contain or can be modified to lists of ten even though their settings and contents are quite different from that of the Ten Commandments. Among these "decalogues" Exodus 34:11–26 shows clear resemblance in form (but not content) to the Decalogue and thus is often called the "ritual Decalogue." Another text that demonstrates a certain degree of parallels is the so-called curse ritual in Deuteronomy 27:15–26.

Nevertheless, we are mindful that these texts do not constitute another version of the Decalogue but "only that some of its provisions exhibit a parallel style, scope, and subject matter." [17] The Exodus 20 and Deuteronomy 5 accounts alone are explicitly called "Decalogue." They seem to serve as a paradigm for other "decalogues" and create a certain disposition among ancient Israelites to collect such lists.

The Closeness of the Decalogue and the Hebrew Bible

The identification of those "decalogues" gives support to the claim that the Decalogue is related to the entire Hebrew Bible. Research by scholars on the linguistic style and specific contents of the Decalogue, as well as the interaction between law and narrative, further affirm the close relationship between the Ten Commandments and the Hebrew Bible. First, several key Hebrew terms in the Decalogue, such as the particle "not" and noun "vanity/falsehood," are found in the Pentateuch in particular ways.[18] Second, the specific prescriptions and prohibitions of the Decalogue can be identified and found throughout the Hebrew Bible, though some are more explicit than others.[19] Third, the linkage between the Decalogue and the narratives of the Hebrew Bible can be understood in light of the interaction between law and narrative. One writer says, "The laws must also be seen as the narrator's way of painting the merciful but just character of YHWH for the reader. . . . Attention to the narratives provides explanations for why . . . the Decalogue . . . begin[s] with cultic regulations."[20]

In brief, the above exploration confirms that the Ten Commandments are not a stand-alone text but are integral to the Hebrew Bible. In fact, the Decalogue finds its place in the New Testament writings as well. A classic example is the narrative of the rich young man in Mark 10:17–22, which contains a rather complete listing of the Decalogue, and its two originally independent units (vv18–20 and 21–22) seem to represent the two tablets of the Decalogue.[21]

WHAT ARE THE CHARACTERISTICS OF THE DECALOGUE?

The Genre and Nature of the Decalogue

Since the Hebrew term for Decalogue originally meant "ten words" instead of "ten commandments" of God, many scholars argue that the literary form of the Decalogue is not law like the rest of the legal instruction in the Pentateuch. Some further suggest that since the negative Hebrew word *lo'* ("not") in the commandment is followed by an indicative rather than an imperative, it is better to understand the Decalogue as a covenant.[22] Still, Childs rightly comments that one has to acknowledge that the Ten Commandments, though distinguished from it, are closely associated with the Old Testament law.

According to Thomas Dozeman, the notion of "law" in the Hebrew Bible has a wide variety of meanings, ranging from teaching, statutes, commandments, and testimony to covenant. Law, in this context, has a dynamic character and is derived from the word or voice of God. In contrast to our modern understanding of law, as one scholar points out, the law in the Hebrew Bible is a kind of "wisdom-law" in that it is not restricted to written forms but focuses on the shared experience and is open to further consideration.[23]

Nevertheless, the legal materials in the Pentateuch can be classified in different ways. One way is to group the laws into "series" and "codes": Patrick explains that the former contains a relatively small number of similarly formulated rules, while the latter consists of a large number of rules covering a broad spectrum of topics.

Another way is to organize them according to their types—namely, apodictic and casuistic laws. The first, apodictic type points to a kind of absolute, unconditional categorical declaration of right and wrong. It pronounces absolute prohibitions without qualification. Apodictic laws are often presented in series, either as summaries or treatment of a specific topic. They seem to be related to proclamation in a cultic setting, such as during the assembly of the Israelites in their renewal of covenant with YHWH (e.g., Deuteronomy 31:9–13). The second, casuistic type of laws, on the contrary, points to what is conditional—it contains "qualifying phrases and clauses defining the facts of the case and the duties of the party held responsible."[24] One typical example is the rule and penalty on injuring another person. These laws are based on juridical reasoning and are logically ordered. They also demand actual practice of the law. They are indicative in nature and are juridical laws.

In light of this understanding, the specific literary form of the Decalogue can be understood in two ways. First, the Ten Commandments are some sort of legal series rather than codes. Second, they belong to the apodictic form of law. Albrecht Alt, the German biblical scholar who was the first to propose the distinction between apodictic and casuistic laws, thus claims that the Decalogue is "Israel's covenant law, the community's absolute requirement from the God of the Covenant."[25]

Later archaeological findings offer us yet another helpful insight: scholars like Miller and Collins observe that there are some parallels between the Decalogue and the ancient Hittite treaties of the fourteenth century BCE. Ancient Near Eastern treaties normally occur not between equals but between a feudal lord (or a suzerain) and the vassal(s). The vassals swear an oath to the lord and make provisions that often contain apodictic prohibitions or commandments in written form. In this way, the Ten Commandments resemble the stipulations of those treaties. Moreover, such a parallel provides additional evidence to the above-suggested association between the Decalogue and the covenant.

Finally, the terse nature of the Decalogue has resulted in diverse interpretations. Philo referred to the commandments as summaries of particular Mosaic laws, while Aquinas perceived them to be moral precepts. Some modern interpreters have suggested that they are categorical imperatives. Others perceive the Ten Commandments as a list of prohibitions in the form of a declaration. One scholar even claims that they are a kind of ancient Israel "criminal law."[26] However, many would reject this extreme proposal and insist that the Decalogue does not constitute concrete legislation at all. Rather, they claim that the Ten Commandments are a summarized list of moral principles for the Israelites. From a theological perspective, the Ten Commandments can further be understood as "statements of what the believer who has experienced God's grace *will* do, not commands of what he *must* do to deserve or earn God's love."[27]

The Source and Function of the Decalogue (in Exodus 20)

If one adopts the Documentary hypothesis, then Exodus 20:2–17 comes from the Elohist document and was written around the eighth century BCE.[28] However, there is no consensus among scholars regarding the precise origin and dating of the Ten Commandments. As said earlier, some attempt to trace the original form of the Decalogue. They turn specifically to the above-mentioned Deuteronomy 27:15–26 to point out that there is resemblance between the Decalogue and the curses. They conclude that the curse ritual in Deuteronomy "may have well provided some impetus to the creation of the Ten Commandments," even though it is unlikely that the Ten Commandments simply emerged from it.[29] No matter whether one agrees or not, what is certain is that the final form of the Decalogue reveals a history of composition and redaction, and certain commandments have undergone expansion or contraction for various reasons (e.g., verse 8).[30]

Apart from undergoing redaction, some suspect that the Decalogue in Exodus 20 was skillfully inserted between two verses (19:25 and 20:18) that were originally connected—19:25 contains a reference to Moses's delivery of YHWH's directives to the people, while 20:18–20 says that the Israel community was waiting for Moses to speak to them what YHWH had spoken to him.

Regarding its function, the Decalogue has long been serving as a foundation of law for the Israel community, especially since the time when King Josiah enacted it as God's law.[31] Ancient Israelites also employed it in teaching and in the worship of the community.

HOW ARE THE TEN COMMANDMENTS (IN EXODUS 20) NUMBERED AND DIVIDED?

The number "ten" seems to be a deliberate choice for the sake of easy memorization rather than for some theological reason. Yet contemporary scholars continue to ask, "Which of the commandments in fact make up the list of ten?"[32]

Different Christian (and Jewish) traditions enumerated the Decalogue differently (see table 1 at the end of this book).[33] During the time of writing the Septuagint version of Exodus (around the third century BCE), verse 3 and verses 4–6 were counted as two separate commandments. Philo maintained this view, which has been generally shared by Reformed and Orthodox Christians. However, the later Jewish Talmud (oral instructions) understood 20:2 as the first commandment and combined verse 3 with verses 4–6 to form the second commandment. Such an arrangement, as one Jewish scholar defends, seems "better to acknowledge the form of covenant common in the ancient world" in which the superior's deed done will be acknowledged at the beginning of the covenant.[34]

Augustine followed the Talmudic tradition in putting verses 3–6 together but counted it as the first commandment. He then divided verse 17 into two so as to retain ten commandments. Both the Roman Catholic and Lutheran traditions basically took up this Augustinian position.[35] Still, the two traditions differ from one another: Roman Catholic tradition follows Augustine in arranging the order of the last two commandments according to the word order of Deuteronomy 5:21. Luther, on the contrary, continues to use the word order of Exodus 20:17. In addition, by subsuming the prohibition against images into the first commandment, some suspect that Augustine (and therefore Lutherans and Catholics) would not interpret the prohibition against images literally. In this way, iconography (except that depicting God) and the like could be preserved.

In sum, there are three major variations: (1) Some traditions count Exodus 20:2 as the first commandment while others do not. (2) Exodus 20:3–6 is treated as either one single commandment or two separate ones. (3) Some split Exodus 20:17 into two commandments and others count it as just a single one. I agree with Miller that each way of numbering the Decalogue has its own justification and offers a particular angle of understanding the emphases and unity of the commandments. For instance, including 20:2 as part of the first commandment may provide a context of divine mercy to the Decalogue. Or, as Hauerwas and Willimon note, in not dividing verses 3–6 into two commandments, one might avoid the danger of Deism.

With regard to the division of the commandments, it seems natural to divide them into two groups grounded on the observations that Moses received two tables from YHWH (Exodus 34:1) and that the Decalogue consists of both prohibitions and positive commandments. Still, how they are divided is debatable. For the Jews and some Reformed Christians, the commandments are divided into two equal halves based on the assumption that symmetry and balance are distinctive of holy objects. A more common view is that the first tablet contains obligations to YHWH while the second tablet describes obligations to one's neighbor. However, even such a common view does not bring complete agreement: Should the commandment on honoring parents be placed in the first tablet or the second, since it can also be analogously understood as honoring God? Subsequently, some divide the commandments into groups of four and six, or three and seven. Harrelson, while wondering if the two tablets represent two identical copies of the entire Decalogue rather than a division of the commandments, creatively suggests that the commandments be divided into four parts based on the contents of the commandments themselves.[36]

While different schemes on dividing the Ten Commandments continue to emerge and the discussion goes on, other less controversial issues concerning the internal structure of the Decalogue are also raised, such as the lack of consistency in terms of the length of each commandment, and the variations in style. The Decalogue simply does not have a coherent structure comparable to, as we shall see, that of the Beatitudes.

Finally, scholars disagree on where the emphasis of the Decalogue should lie. They also wonder who the addressees are. One view is that the use of second-person singular and masculine verbal forms in the formulation implies that "the addressees were free male heads of household and property owners in the community."[37] As we shall see, the verb used in the commandment against adultery does not require any object and hence can refer to both men and women. Miller thus asks if the redaction could open up the scope of the text to include women.

MY OWN APPROACH

Many of these issues do not have a definite view, and debates continue among scholars. Instead of getting further into these debates, I state some theses that express my own approach in this work. They serve as exegetical guidelines in the exegesis that follows.

First and foremost, despite some contemporary criticisms of the Documentary hypothesis, I basically adopt this dominant view, for other hypotheses do not really resolve all the textual problems. Subsequently, the Ten Commandments in Exodus seem to be associated with the Elohist source that came from the Northern Kingdom of Israel around the eighth century BCE, and the final form of the text was done shortly after the Babylonian exile (which was ended in approximately 539–537 BCE). The Exodus Decalogue is an older version than its Deuteronomy counterpart, and for this reason I focus on Exodus 20 in this book.

Second, while the Decalogue and Exodus can be treated as independent, self-integrated units, they are closely connected with the Pentateuch and the entire Hebrew Bible both in terms of literary forms and contents. This interconnectedness is essential to our understanding of the commandments.

Therefore, while each commandment is treated individually for clarity's sake, I will highlight how the commandments are related to each other and to those related texts from the Old Testament throughout the exegesis of each commandment. And I will not divide the commandments into groups, as such division risks segregation and undermines their interconnectedness.

Third, some scholars have attempted to argue that the enumeration of the Decalogue of certain Reformed traditions is more faithful to the original intention. I continue to adopt the tradition from which I come—namely, the Roman Catholic tradition. However, I will turn to Exodus 20:17 (instead of Deuteronomy 5:21) for the discussion of the ninth and the tenth commandments in order to preserve exegetical coherence. Moreover, inasmuch as I take into account the view that Exodus 20:2 can be treated on its own, I still count it as part of the first commandment. And the common issue of the last two commandments in verse 17 (i.e., coveting) will first be discussed before they are treated separately according to the word order.

Fourth, no matter whether we treat the Decalogue as treaty or apodictic law or summary of prohibitions, we have to acknowledge that it is closely associated with other legal ordinances and statutes of ancient Israel and Near Eastern countries. And it continues to play a very important role for the moral life of the Israelites and has a great ethical value to Israelite society.

NOTES

1. One commonly observed counterevidence is that it is just not possible that Moses wrote about his own death at the very end of the Pentateuch (Deuteronomy 34:5–8). See John J. Collins, *Introduction to the Hebrew Bible* (Minneapolis: Augsburg Fortress, 2004), 47–50.

2. Collins, *Introduction*, 47.

3. Some contemporary scholars, like Thomas Dozeman, simply abandon these two sources totally and counterpropose that the Pentateuch was composed by various editors in two stages—namely, D composition and the final P edition. See Thomas B. Dozeman, *Commentary on Exodus* (Grand Rapids, MI: Eerdmans, 2009), 35–43.

4. On the historical formation of the book, see Martin Noth, *Exodus* (Philadelphia: Westminster Press, 1962).

5. See Nahum M. Sarna, "Book of Exodus," in *Anchor Bible Dictionary*, vol. 2, ed. David Noel Freedman (New York: Doubleday, 1992). However, some scholars like John Van Seters stress the literary separation between the two books. See John Van Seters, "Confessional Reformulation in the Exilic Period," *VT* 22 (1972): 448–59, as cited in Dozeman, *Commentary on Exodus*, 19.

6. This pivotal event is indicated in the title of the book itself: the Hebrew term *tse'th* ("going out, release from slavery") is translated into Greek as *exodos* ("exodus"). See William Johnstone, "Book of Exodus," in *The New Interpreter's Dictionary of the Bible*, vol. 2 (Nashville, TN: Abingdon Press, 2006–2009), 371.

7. Collins's proposal is noteworthy. See his *Introduction*, 107. See also Waldemar Janzen, *Exodus* (Scottdale, PA: Herald Press, 2000), 18–19.

8. For additional evidence of thoughtful design and examples, see Sarna, "Book of Exodus," 695–96.

9. See G. W. Coats, *Exodus 1–18* FOTL IIA (Grand Rapids, MI: Eerdmans, 1999), 155–74.

10. Dale Patrick, *Old Testament Law* (Atlanta, GA: John Knox Press, 1985), 28.

11. Some of the themes are related while others are originally independent, such as the deliverance from Egypt and the rescue at the sea.

12. Sarna, "Book of Exodus," 699.

13. Patrick Miller, "Ten Commandments," in *The New Interpreter's Dictionary of the Bible*, vol. 5 (Nashville, TN: Abingdon Press, 2006–2009), 517.

14. Umberto Cassuto, *A Commentary on the Book of Exodus*, trans. Israel Abrahams (Jerusalem: Magnes Press, Hebrew University, 1967), 250.

15. See Bernhard Lang, "The Number Ten and the Iniquity of the Fathers: A New Interpretation of the Decalogue," *Zeitschrift für die alttestamentliche Wissenschaft* 118, no. 2 (2006): 218–38.

16. Cornelis Houtman, *Exodus*, vol. 3, trans. Johan Rebel and Sierd Woudstra (Kampen, Netherlands: Kok, 1993–2000), 9.

17. Patrick, *Old Testament Law*, 38.

18. See Wilfried Warning, "Terminological Patterns and the Decalogue," *Zeitschrift für die alttestamentliche Wissenschaft* 118, no. 4 (2006): 513–22.

19. For a complete list of the scriptural passages in sequential order, see Walter C. Kaiser Jr., *Toward Old Testament Ethics* (Grand Rapids, MI: Zondervan, 1991), 82.

20. Joe M. Sprinkle, "Law and Narrative in Exodus 19–24," *Journal of the Evangelical Theological Society* 47, no. 2 (June 2004): 251–52. For a discussion of the interaction between law and narrative, apart from Fretheim, see also J. P. Fokkelman, "Exodus," in *The Literary Guide to the Bible*, ed. R. Alter and F. Kermode (Cambridge, MA: Harvard University Press, 1987), 62, as cited in Dozeman, *Commentary on Exodus*, 461–62; Nanette Stahl, *Law and Liminality in the Bible*, JSOT Sup 202 (Sheffield: Sheffield Academic Press, 1995), 11–26, 51–73.

21. For additional examples, see Brevard S. Childs, *The Book of Exodus* (Philadelphia, PA: Westminster Press, 1974), 428. However, Harrelson argues that Jesus only selectively mentions certain commandments. See Walter J. Harrelson, *The Ten Commandments and Human Rights* (Macon, GA: Mercer University Press, 1997), 133–46.

22. Paul L. Maier, "Enumerating the Decalogue: Do We Number the Ten Commandments Correctly?," *Concordia Journal* 16, no. 1 (January 1990), 19.

23. Bernard S. Jackson, *Studies in the Semiotics of Biblical Law*, JSOT Sup 314 (Sheffield: Sheffield Academic Press, 2000), 70–92, as cited in Dozeman, *Commentary on Exodus*, 458.

24. Patrick, *Old Testament Law*, 22.

25. Albrecht Alt, "The Origins of Israelite Law," in *Essays on Old Testament History and Religion* (Garden City, NY: Doubleday, 1966), 79–132, as cited in Harrelson, *Ten Commandments*, 19. Alt's view did not go unchallenged, however. See Childs, *The Book of Exodus*, 390.

26. Anthony Phillips, *Ancient Israel's Criminal Law* (Oxford: Blackwell, 1970), 10.

27. Horace D. Hummel, *The Word Becoming Flesh* (St. Louis: Concordia, 1979), 74, as cited in Maier, "Enumerating the Decalogue," 19.

28. Some scholars, like Patrick and Miller, however, note that such identification is problematic. For example, the text contains certain expressions that are distinctive to either the D document or P document. Moreover, if one takes the view that the Deuteronomy version is an older and more original text than the Exodus one, the Decalogue in the latter would be attributed to a much later date.

29. Harrelson, *Ten Commandments*, 27.

30. For a discussion of reasons, see Childs, *The Book of Exodus*, 400.

31. Rupert E. Davies, *Making Sense of the Commandments* (London: Epworth Press, 1990), 6–18.

32. Harrelson, *Ten Commandments*, 38.

33. We have to bear in mind that in the Hebrew Bible, the Decalogue is not numbered.

34. Frank E. Eakin Jr., *The First Tablet of the Commandments: A Jewish and Christian Problem* (Scranton, PA: University of Scranton Press, 2004), 15. Houtman, however, notes that there is no single view among the Jewish traditions either.

35. Since the Council of Trent, the Roman Catholic tradition has included verse 2 as part of the first commandment.

36. For a glance of the outline, see his *Ten Commandments*, 39.

37. Miller, "Ten Commandments," 519.

Chapter Five

The First Commandment in Exodus 20:2–6

20:2—I am the Lord your God, who brought you out of the land of Egypt, out of the house of slavery. [1]

20:3–6—You shall have no other gods before me. You shall not make for yourself an idol, whether in the form of anything that is in heaven above, or that is on the earth beneath, or that is in the water under the earth. You shall not bow down to them or worship them; for I the Lord your God am a jealous God, punishing children for the iniquity of parents, to the third and the fourth generation of those who reject me, but showing steadfast love to the thousandth generation of those who love me and keep my commandments. [2]

WHAT DID THE TEXT COMMAND?

Exodus 20:2 is one of the key occasions for disagreement on enumerating the Ten Commandments. Some scholars argue that it is a prologue, partly because it does not contain any command but is simply a declaration like those found in the ancient Near Eastern countries—where the kings were accustomed to make solemn proclamations by first recalling their deeds. However, I agree with others that this view, though convincing, does not exclude the possibility that the verse can be part of the long, first commandment. It is partly because verse 2 also contains the first-person singular as verses 3–6 do, and together they can form a distinctive unit of the "I-THOU" relationship.

This proposed "I-THOU" relationship leads us to consider that the commandment is not just the first but also the most fundamental one and is constitutive for the relationship between YHWH and Israel. The claim that the Hebrew Bible is simply an application of, a commentary on, or a narrative elaboration of it, is therefore plausible.[3] Nevertheless, the first commandment without doubt is a lengthy and multifaceted formulation.

First, it contains an introduction. Literally, Exodus 20:2 can be understood as a kind of self-introduction[4]—YHWH introduces God-self as the God of Israel and claims God's ownership that is grounded in the deliverance of the Israelites from the bondage of slavery. Here, YHWH does not only give God's name but also God's identity. And the revelation of name not only conveys a presence but it establishes a covenantal relationship and forms the context in which the first commandment (and the remaining ones) is lived out. 20:2 thus helps lay the ground for the ethical life of Israel.

Exodus 20:3 is a short verse that contains only a prohibition. Its grammar, structure, and content are distinctive but at times puzzling. First, the verse in Hebrew does not have an imperative verb. One wonders if it is simply an introduction to verses 4-6. Second, the use of the singular form for "There shall not be to you" (*lo'-yihyeh le-kha*) seems to emphasize that one should not even associate with one god. Similarly, the employment of *elohim acheirim* ("other gods") in the plural tends to clarify that such prohibition is applicable to all the deities. Third, the uncertainties regarding the proper translation of the phrase *'al-panai* ("before my face") lead to various interpretations. Here, I take the view that "before me" may be a more useful literal translation—it implies that no other gods can appear in the sanctuary where YHWH is worshipped and hence foretells the prohibition of the making or worshipping of idols. Fourth, the overall message seems to contrast with other claims found in the Hebrew Bible regarding the exclusive existence of YHWH (e.g., Isaiah 45:21).[5]

Finally, the explicit differences between verse 3 and verses 4–6 have further led some traditions to view them as two separate commandments. However, there are good reasons to argue that they form a single unit. For instance, since images played an important role in the worship of deities, verses 4–6 flow logically from verse 3 and become a complement, an explication, and an elaboration of the verse.

Still, a glimpse of verses 4–6 gives the impression that they form a subunit of their own. In verse 4, the people are told not to make any image, idol, or carved object (made of wood, stone, or metal). These images and objects are generally cultic images that represent the divine; hence, some claim that the prohibition does not apply to the use of visual arts, such as those pictures of cherubim placed in YHWH's tent (e.g., Exodus 26:1). Both the term "form" and the subsequent specification seem to be a later addition that aims at broadening the scope to all kinds of earthly representation and pointing out that this prohibition is absolute.

The purpose of such a deliberate prohibition, from a sociohistorical dimension, could be to counteract the common practice of making (and worshipping) idols and other representations among the heathen peoples, or to oppose what the Egyptians (who are called the iron-smelters) did. Still, it could also be to prevent any comparison between God and the object made, or to reject the idea of the incarnation of the deity that was commonly believed in the ancient world.

Nonetheless, the real puzzle is whether verse 4 includes the images of YHWH or not. Those who perceive verses 4–6 as a separate commandment would probably interpret the text as a prohibition of images of YHWH, stressing that the term "for yourself" refers to Israel's own worship. They also argue that it is YHWH's own mandate and that God reveals himself in a voice (i.e., his word) but not in any visible form. Moreover, idols and images are unable to establish any relationship between the deity and the people (e.g., Jeremiah 10:4–5). To worship them is to deny the basic nature of God, which is his relatedness with the world. It would also place YHWH on the same level with other deities and thus erode his uniqueness for the Israelites.

Those who see verses 3–6 as a single unit, in contrast, tend to claim that the flow of the text implies that it is basically directed against pagan deities. Consequently, the concern of 20:3–6 is the worship of YHWH. In other words, the central issue is the nature of true worship and not God's revelation that is already dealt with by verse 2.

We find an additional prohibition, a motivation clause, and a sanction in the next two verses. We also note that in verse 5 the preceding verse's singular object (i.e., idol) is changed to the plural suffix "them." For me, it makes sense to propose that the verse originally comes right after 20:3 and actually refers to those deities. It forbids one to bow down and serve these other gods. In this way, 20:5 smoothly incorporates itself to the first prohibition in verse 3.[6]

The identification of YHWH as a jealous God is a recurring motif in the Pentateuch (e.g., Deuteronomy 6:15). Most scholars agree that jealousy points to a mutually exclusive relationship between two parties that is best depicted in the metaphor of a monogamous marriage. The use of "reject" and "love" further suggests that verses 5 and 6 are to be understood within the imagery of marriage. Here, YHWH insists on an exclusive, covenantal relationship with the people of Israel and will not tolerate competing gods. The rationale behind this claim is that Israel as a nation owes its existence to YHWH alone (as indicated in verse 2). Therefore, breaking this exclusive, covenantal relationship would mean committing an unfaithful act and thus deserve severe punishment by YHWH.

The subsequent sanction seems to raise tough questions on the matter of suffering the consequences of one's ancestors and on God's righteousness itself. A communal reading, however, would perceive this threat as a warning addressed to the entire nation rather than to individuals. Moreover, Cornelis Houtman convincingly suggests that should the punishment be understood literally, it does not pose serious problems either, for the duration rightly reflects the number of generations to suffer the consequences in the course of the nation's life, or the number of descendants the family head could have in a normal life span.[7] Furthermore, the later addition of the phrase "of those who reject me" implies that only those descendants who actually follow the evil deeds of their family head will experience retribution. Lastly, such transgenerational punishment is usually employed in story (e.g., 2 Samuel 12:10) and creedal-type (e.g., Numbers 14:18) formulation rather than in legal settings. The declaration that God's mercy and steadfast love will infinitely be extended to all those who are loyal to the covenant and keep the commandments further gives the Israelites hope and comfort.

Summarizing, I too argue that verses 3–6 form a single unit, and that the overall meaning and function of 20:2–6 is all about true worship of YHWH. It first informs the Israelites who their true object of worship is. He is identified by name and by his salvific act. Second, the community is to worship YHWH alone, especially for what the covenantal relationship demands. Although the commandment does not reject the existence of other deities but only denies their efficacy, it helps "protect YHWH's sovereignty as well as his religious prerogatives in Israel."[8] It also reflects and reminds the Israelite community of the need to break away from its surrounding world radically. Third, the first commandment points to the issue of idolatry—for the making of images of deities (especially from precious materials) and the worshipping of these deities rather than worshipping YHWH alone has been a growing concern, especially for the prophets. These collective practices of the community defile the covenantal relationship between YHWH and Israel. Being the bride of YHWH, Israel's idolatry is an adulterous act against YHWH.

Both the concern about true worship and the issue of idolatry point to not just a theological but also a moral issue for the Israelites. In the economic and political life of the entire community, while the commandment does not deny the presence of other powers, it reminds the Israelites about the temptation of turning to these other powers or realities and choosing them as the ultimate center of their lives. This is reflected, for example, in the words of Job: "If I have made gold my trust, or called fine gold my confidence . . . I should have been false to God above" (31:24–28). It thus, as Miller points out, challenges the seeking of wealth (as commonly expressed in terms of precious metals and gems) and possessions rather than YHWH; it also undercuts the validation of divine kinship by refusing to identity political figures with divine authority.

Finally, by claiming that 20:2–6 is about true worship of YHWH, the first commandment reveals a positive mandate for Israelites, too: they have to worship and love the Lord with all their hearts, all their souls, and all their might, and to follow, fear, obey, serve, and trust YHWH (Deuteronomy 6:4–9; 13:4). This lays the ground for the virtue that the Israelites need to cultivate.

UPHOLDING TRUE WORSHIP

Keenan and John Holbert suggest that the moral value of the first commandment is about God's mercy and *hesed*; others highlight the awareness of the presence of God in a time of secularism.[9] Our study shows that it is primarily about worshipping the one true God who has a covenantal relationship with God's people. Therefore, while acknowledging that one of our contemporary religious challenges is that of secularism and atheism, and so on, our moral reflection is, as Miller and a few others point out, grounded in what one should do with the one true God who is in front of us.[10] Still, who is this God that stands before us?

"Gods" in Our World

Christians nowadays would hardly think of themselves as violating the first commandment. However, in reality there are many things among and within us, Christians and non-Christians alike, that could replace God as the object of our worship. Luther rightly said that when we set our hearts and put our trust upon one thing, that one thing would become our god (*LC* #3). Indeed, philosophers likewise tell us that when we make that which is originally a means into an end, we simultaneously turn them into gods.[11] In spiritual terms, we elevate them to a status that is as important as God. They become false gods and a substitute for God. They come before our relationship with God and hinder God's gifts of freedom from slavery and freedom for God. We are no longer able or free to worship the one true God.[12]

I share Miller's concern that the major and powerful god that contemporary secular society worships is wealth and power, and those economic and sociopolitical systems that it creates.[13] Yet another influential and ever-growing god in the past few decades is science and technology itself. For example, we observe the emergence of those thinkers who believe that science and technology alone can solve all our human problems.

Unfortunately, false gods are found within our Christian faith as well. When we focus solely on external manifestations of God, such as miracles and sacred objects, we likewise encounter a false god. William Barclay rightly points out that even "a system of Church government can and does become an end in itself, so that people end by being more concerned with the way in which the Church is governed than with the Church itself."[14] Barton and Corwin Stoppel are similarly aware that we could turn our Christian traditions and religions into gods as well![15]

The Meaning of Upholding True Worship

Now that the true object of our Christian worship is identified, we can proceed to pursue the meaning of true worship. I identify three distinctive features. First, we choose God above all that could become false gods and avoid clinging to them. However, as Miller rightly says, we need not deny or reject their basic values. Second, we have to commit ourselves wholeheartedly to this God without reservation—an attitude clearly spelled out in the *Shema* (Deuteronomy 6:4–9). In other words, we worship God with all that we are and have. Luther similarly insisted that the commandment demands the totality of our heart and confidence in God (*LC* #13).

Third, as Calvin's exposition shows, true worship includes several important aspects, each one of which brings out a unique character of God (*ICR* 2.8.16): (1) adoration with submission of one's conscience that recognizes God's majesty, (2) trust in God's power and goodness, (3) invocation that reflects our need of God and confirms that God is the source of our aid, and (4) thanksgiving that expresses our gratitude for the blessings we receive from God. Miller similarly proposes trust, submission of conscience, reverence, and praise as the crucial elements of true worship for today.

Upholding True Worship as a Virtue

The *Catechism of the Catholic Church* reaffirms the teaching of past catechisms that the commandment embraces the three theological virtues of faith, hope, and charity (##2086–94). It also perceives the virtue of worship as a specific facet of the virtue of religion, for the latter virtue disposes us to the proper attitude of worship (##2095–2103). Obviously, the *Catechism* adopts the view of Aquinas, who perceives the virtue of religion as a part of justice—pay due worship to God (*ST* II.II. 81.5).

Still, Calvin also identifies certain relevant virtues that are rooted in those aspects of true worship. First, true worship calls for the virtues of reverence and humility. When we humbly come in front of God to give God homage, we acknowledge God's majesty. Second, our acknowledgment of God's majesty is also based on faith (and trust) in God and God's power and goodness, and so on. Third, and subsequently, the virtue of true worship demands obedience toward God. Fourth, since trust and faith anticipate that God will answer our prayers, true worship thus implies the virtue of gratitude on our part. Lastly, the virtue of detachment is needed so as not to cling to whatever may come between God and us.

In sum, the virtue of upholding true worship is a complex one that contains a cluster of relevant virtues—as we shall see later, the virtues extracted from these terse verses tend to be multifaceted in nature. Upholding true worship in our Christian life requires the living out of other virtues as well as engaging in different practices.

The Practice of True Worship

Aquinas taught us that both interior and exterior acts are to be practiced in the virtue of religion. Therefore, the practice of true worship likewise contains both interior and exterior actions (*ST* II.II. 81–91). Interiorly, we recall God's mighty acts in our lives on the one hand, and our unworthiness in front of God on the other. This interior act is the primary and most important act of worship. Exteriorly, worship finds expressions within and outside the liturgy, in our verbal expressions, physical gestures and movements, and the use of created things. They may be used for different reasons—for instance, when presenting things to God we offer sacrifices and make vows, and when calling upon God's name we sing praise to God. Miller adds that thanksgiving is one of the most fundamental practices of keeping the commandment.

On the other hand, while not confining our worship of God to a particular place or time or gesture, scheduled and well-structured worship can help nurture a habit within us, make our worship more focused, and invite others to participate more easily. This in turn points to the practice of communal worship. Many would agree that true worship is never a private virtue but is communal in nature.

The Exemplars

The earthly Jesus is not just a man of prayer but also a teacher of worship. When tempted by the devil in the wilderness, he refuses to cling to those created things that could become idols and false gods (Matthew 4:1–11). Jesus also clarifies that one cannot serve two masters at the same time, and so we need to choose and worship God without reservation (Matthew 6:24). Furthermore, he points out that true worship is not achieved by external manifestations but inner obedience to do the will of God (Matthew 7:21).

Throughout the history of Christianity, many saintly people have lived a life of true worship to God. Some of them further helped others do so by promoting certain worships and devotions. Within the Catholic tradition, for example, Visitandine Sister Margaret Mary Alacoque and Jesuit Father Claude de la Colombière helped give new life to the devotion to the Sacred Heart of Jesus among the faithful.[16]

In our contemporary world, the founder and promoter of the Taizé community, Brother Roger, comes to mind. The distinctive worship style of Taizé has provided a unique sacred space for many young people to live out a community life of worship and reconciliation. However, while their style of worship is famous for making tremendous use of music, songs of different languages, silence, and icons, what is exemplary is the Taizé community's awareness that these are not an end in themselves:

> For the community, the music has never been an end in itself. It is a means to facilitate the worship of God. That is why the brothers, although they respect and strive for technical competence, place the accent not on performance but on participation. [17]

The Social, Communal Aspect of the Virtue of True Worship

As noted above, the virtue of true worship has a strong communal nature. Yet its importance is not limited to formal, communal worship within the Christian community itself. It also has an impact on the wider society. Capitalism, nationalism, science and technology, and other forms of economic and sociopolitical systems have become ever-growing gods and idols. The virtue of true worship challenges and helps us be more aware of their insidiousness—Stoppel rightly notes that they employ similar forms of worship found in Christian (and other religious) traditions, such as the use of symbols/icons, the creation of "holy" places, the demand of loyalty, and so on. Upholding true worship also helps us reject the temptation to place any economic and sociopolitical system or ideology, and human invention—no matter how helpful they are in the advancement of the society—higher than God or to replace God ultimately.

Moreover, the virtue of true worship throws light on the question of and debate on religious pluralism and tolerance in society. Briefly speaking, since true worship of God understood in the light of the first commandment does not focus on an exclusive claim of God, cultivating the virtue of true worship allows and supports the right of individuals and communities to their own "religious rapport with God." [18]

As a whole, to live out the first commandment faithfully is both a religious and moral matter. It is not so much about insisting on the one true God or avoiding making visible expressions of God as it is about worshipping God truthfully in our personal and communal life, and respecting others' freedom to uphold their true worship in the same manner.

NOTES

1. All the scriptural texts quoted in this work are taken from the New Revised Standard Version (NRSV). In some translations the term YHWH is used instead of "Lord." Also, "I am the Lord your God" is sometimes translated as "I, the Lord, am your God."

2. Although the *Catechism of the Catholic Church* does not count verse 6 as part of the first commandment, I take the liberty to include it here for it forms a single unit with verse 5. On the meaning of the text, see also Dale Patrick, "The First Commandment in the Structure of the Pentateuch," *Vetus Testamentum* 45, no. 1 (January 1995): 107–18.

3. See Patrick D. Miller, "Preaching the First Commandment in a Pluralistic World," *Journal for Preachers* 27, no. 4 (Pentecost 2004): 8.

4. It was a well-known view in ancient Near Eastern traditions that deities introduce themselves by name so as not to be confused with other deities. Also, verse 2 shows parallels in terms of form and function with texts like Exodus 34:5–7—namely, introducing YHWH to the people.

5. The disharmony is partly because verse 3 focuses on the relationship of YHWH with Israel rather than on the question of monotheism. In real life the ancient Israelites did worship other deities (especially the Canaanites' god Baal) alongside YHWH (e.g., 2 Kings 21:1–7). See John J. Collins, *Introduction to the Hebrew Bible* (Minneapolis: Augsburg Fortress, 2004), 127–28.

6. Walther Zimmerli, "Das zweite Gebot," *Gottes Offenbarung* (1963), 237ff, as cited in Brevard S. Childs, *The Book of Exodus* (Philadelphia, PA: Westminster Press, 1974), 405.

7. Cornelis Houtman, *Exodus*, vol. 3, trans. Johan Rebel and Sierd Woudstra (Kampen, Netherlands: Kok, 1993–2000), 27–28.

8. Dale Patrick, *Old Testament Law* (Atlanta, GA: John Knox Press, 1985), 43.

9. See John C. Holbert, *The Ten Commandments* (Nashville, TN: Abingdon Press, 2002); David Klinghoffer, *Shattered Tablets* (New York: Doubleday, 2007).

10. See also David Bentley Hart, "God or Nothingness," in *I Am the Lord Your God: Christian Reflections on the Ten Commandments*, ed. Carl E. Braaten and Christopher R. Seitz (Grand Rapids, MI: Eerdmans, 2005), 55–76.

11. See Ernest J. Lewis, *Light for the Journey: Living the Ten Commandments* (Waco, TX: Word Books, 1986), 30–31.

12. See Paul E. Capetz, "The First Commandment as a Theological and Ethical Principle," in *The Ten Commandments: The Reciprocity of Faithfulness*, ed. William P. Brown (Louisville, KY: Westminster John Knox Press, 2004), 174–92.

13. See Patrick D. Miller, *The God You Have: Politics and the First Commandment* (Minneapolis: Fortress Press, 1994), 24.

14. William Barclay, *The Ten Commandments* (Louisville, KY: Westminster John Knox Press, 1998), 11.

15. See John Barton, "'The Work of Human Hands' (Psalm 115:4): Idolatry in the Old Testament," in *The Ten Commandments: The Reciprocity of Faithfulness*, ed. William P. Brown (Louisville, KY: Westminster John Knox Press, 2004), 194–203; G. Corwin Stoppel, *Living Words: The Ten Commandments for the Twenty-first Century* (Cambridge, MA: Cowley, 2005), 34.

16. See also Jeanne Weber, "Devotion to the Sacred Heart: History, Theology, and Liturgical Celebration," *Worship* 72 (1998): 236–54.

17. GIA Publications, Inc., "Taizé Community," www.giamusic.com/bios/taize.cfm.

18. Pontifical Biblical Commission, *The Bible and Morality: Biblical Roots of Christian Conduct* (Vatican: Libreria Editrice Vaticana, 2008), 46.

Chapter Six

The Second Commandment in Exodus 20:7

You shall not make wrongful use of the name of the Lord your God, for the Lord will not acquit anyone who misuses his name.

WHAT DID THE TEXT COMMAND?

Exodus 20:7 is the second commandment according to the Catholic and Lutheran traditions. It is about the use of the divine name for certain purposes, and it contains both a motivation clause and a sanction. Its distinctiveness, as Miller claims, lies not just in the fact that 20:7 is one of the only two commandments that contain a sanction (the other is the first commandment) but also because its sanction is rather direct and specific—God's retribution.

According to ancient Near Eastern beliefs, a divine name carries an inherent power that gives access to the deity, for one's name penetrates one's own deepest identity.[1] Knowing a name also allows one to have power over the other, as in the story of Jacob's encounter with the divine messenger (Genesis 32:22–32).

In the Hebrew Bible, Deuteronomy 14 is often seen as an explication of the commandment on using the divine name.[2] Still, we find links between the profanation of YHWH's name and statutes on religious and daily practices, like the Holiness Code (Leviticus 18–22). There are also numerous occasions and accounts in which YHWH's name is mentioned and used, such as invoking God's name (e.g., Genesis 4:26) and swearing by the name of the Lord (e.g., Jeremiah 4:2). These show that calling upon God's name is a common practice among the Israelites.

Within the Decalogue, Miller demonstrates that the second commandment flows rather smoothly from the first: it reinforces the preceding verses
by focusing on a specific aspect of God's reality and identity—the name of
YHWH. This connectedness is reflected in Deuteronomy 6:13 in which what
is said in 20:2–7 is positively expressed in the key words "fear," "serve," and
"name." In other words, using the divine name properly is crucial to how the
Israelites fear and serve God. More specifically, the commandment is inti-
mately connected to the preceding one in these significant ways: (1) they are
the only two commandments that include a sanction; (2) the name of God
was primarily spoken and heard in, and originated from, the sanctuary and
worship; (3) invoking God's name in worship is the avenue for the presence
and blessing of God.

Nevertheless, the commandment is also related to the subsequent commandments in terms of form, content, or language: the next two commandments also use the third person in reference to YHWH (see below) and
employ the phrase "the Lord your God." They all include the motivation
clause as the second commandment does. The commandment on observing
the Sabbath likewise deals with the "use" of something (i.e., name and time).
Moreover, 20:7 uses the same Hebrew term *shawe'* ("in vain") found in the
Deuteronomy version of the commandment against false witnessing. Thus,
both the second and the eighth commandments can be set in the context of
swearing.

However, as noted, 20:7 uses the third person in reference to YHWH. It
therefore grammatically departs from the first commandment, which uses the
first person in reference to YHWH. This rhetorical shift of voice, as one
writer comments, "creates distance between YHWH and the Israelites, which
aids in conveying the meaning of the command . . . that holiness is not
casual."[3] Nevertheless, the interrelatedness between the second commandment and the first, third, fourth, and eighth commandments hints that its
corresponding moral value is connected to those of these commandments.

With regard to its content, at first glance, the second commandment is
rather straightforward and seems to be self-evident. Still, Dale Patrick, Patrick D. Miller, and others note that there are a couple of issues that need
attention, especially the use of certain Hebrew terms/phrases in the verse.
The understanding of these phrases is important in determining the ethical
meaning of the commandment.

The first is the Hebrew phrase *tissa et shem adonai*, which literally means
"carry/lift up the name of Adonai." It is a rather unusual expression, for in
the Hebrew Bible lifting up the hand(s) is the normal gesture that signifies
swearing (e.g., Daniel 12:7).[4] Thus, the phrase seems to echo the language of
prayers during which the name is raised to Heaven or being heard publicly
(e.g., Psalm 16:4b). However, it was a common practice in ancient Israel to
take oaths in God's name (e.g., 1 Samuel 20:42). Therefore, the phrase can,

as well, be understood as a synonym for taking an oath by invoking God's name. Still, it is equally arguable that the phrase refers to "the use of a name" in general.

The second issue is the exact meaning of the above-mentioned Hebrew term *shawe'*. Here, there are dichotomous views. Some interpret the term narrowly to mean "falsehood." They argue that the same Hebrew term is used in Exodus 23:1 to speak of making false report in a court. The Deuteronomy version of the commandment against false witness also uses this term to mean falsehood. Those allusions to the second commandment likewise seem to interpret the term as "swearing falsely" (e.g., Hosea 4:2).

Those who hold an opposite view find such narrow usage rather problematic. They point out that the term has a substantive meaning and could mean, among other things, "using something lightly or without clear purpose."[5] In particular, it appears in a number of occasions in the Hebrew Bible, such as Psalm 31:6, to mean "vanity" and "emptiness." The term thus should not solely be equated with "falsely."

The discussion and debate on these two issues lead to the fundamental question of whether the commandment refers to a more general prohibition of using God's name for any empty purpose, or a narrower and more specific prohibition of "swearing falsely."[6] Here I take the view that the overall commandment embraces a broader prohibition, partly because a more inclusive usage will not exclude the prohibition of employing God's name in swearing. Another reason is that although the people of Israel, for the sake of protecting the divine name, were not allowed to use YHWH's name in certain specific circumstances—such as cursing (e.g., 2 Kings 2:24) and defilement (e.g., Ezekiel 43:8)—in reality it has been a common and important religious practice to use the name of YHWH to call upon God (e.g., Genesis 4:26), to prophesy (e.g., Jeremiah 11:21), to praise (e.g., Psalm 69:30), and so on.

Moreover, Childs tells us that for various reasons the second commandment was formulated into the present canonical form so as to broaden its application.[7] It became a general command that is concerned about the use of God's name in all kinds of practices, and the scope of prohibition was likewise diverse and expandable.

The motivation clause of the commandment seems to cause some confusion as well. It does not offer concrete reasons for the wrongful use of the divine name. Rather, its content seems redundant. One possible explanation is that it serves as a reminder to the community that using God's name in vain is a very serious matter, and one has to take full responsibility for its outcome. In this way, it gives weight to the seriousness of the commandment and justifies the sanction attached to the commandment. Surprisingly, as Houtman notes, the sanction does not clarify how the retribution is to be carried out even though it would be imminent, as told in 1 Kings 8:31–32.[8]

No matter whether one takes a narrower or broader interpretation, the overall rationale behind the prohibition remains the same and is rather self-explanatory. It points to the holiness of God's names, such as Elohim, Adonai, and YHWH. Although some scholars, like Miller, believe that the prohibition aims at protecting the name "YHWH" in particular—for it is the name "YHWH" that is revealed by God and called upon by the Israelites (e.g., Exodus 6:2–8)—the immediate function of the commandment is to protect and respect the divine name in all its manifestations.

In so doing, the commandment first forbids the Israelites to invoke God's name lightly and in vain. In the case of swearing, although God's name may be called upon in oath (either to act as a witness to the promise and a judge of performance, and an enforcer of the provisions of the oath, or to act as a witness to the authenticity of one's testimony and a punisher of lies), the commandment basically is concerned with the practice of making promises/testimony and other forms of oath-taking.

As pointed out earlier, a name is closely tied to certain inherent power and identity. Simply put, God's identity is God's holiness. A broad and inclusive view of the commandment implies that calling upon God's divine name for whatever purposes and in whatever circumstances would involve God's holiness and the use of God's power, which should only occur according to God's divine will. Therefore, the commandment has a deeper meaning: it aims to respect God's holiness and warns the Israelite community against any attempt to coerce or manipulate God for its own purpose or fulfillment, as described in the story of Balaam in Numbers 22–24. It is a very serious matter. Moreover, Houtman and Harrelson rightly remind us that the misuse of God's name not only disrespects God but also could harm one's fellow, as the false prophets did in proclaiming false peace to the Israelites. Therefore, the prohibition indirectly protects the well-being of our neighbor. Still, the commandment could have a more explicit positive value: Israelites have to respect God's holiness by invoking God's holy name in a constructive way, such as lifting it up in prayers, in worship, and in praise, as the psalmist urges the people to do (e.g., Psalm 7:17). These practices in turn reinforce the relationship between the virtue of upholding true worship and the virtue that corresponds to the second commandment, which I treat now.

RESPECTING GOD'S HOLINESS

Some ethicists focus on the question of invoking another person's name, while others highlight the issue of taking an oath in the name/presence of God. There are also those who believe that it is all about the integrity of our profession of faith and acting out this faith.[9] Our exegetical exposition of the text indicates that the second commandment is, as one writer puts it, fundamentally theocentric: it focuses on God's holiness, which is God's identity and is signified by God's name.[10] It also upholds a broad usage rather than pertaining narrowly to oath-taking. The explicit key word here is "respect."

Claiming Everything in God's Name

When I lived in a Western country for the first time, I was struck by how often people unconsciously uttered "For God's/Christ's sake!" or "Goddamn it!" in their conversations. Although these phrases are more than simply tolerated, one wonders if there is a need to invoke God's name purposelessly.

Within Christianity, the scenario is quite different. We often invoke God's name in our actions with a purpose. For instance, in the sacrament of baptism, parents and godparents invoke God's name and publicly promise God and the community the responsibility of teaching the children in the practice of the faith. Unfortunately, throughout Christian history, there have been times when Christians invoked God in a questionable way, particularly by claiming (either verbally or symbolically) that wars and persecutions against other groups were waged in the name of God, such as the Crusades in the eleventh century or the Inquisitions held during the Counter-Reformation period.[11]

In our contemporary world, writers like David Klinghoffer and Joan Chittister offer helpful reflections:[12] a subtle way of invoking God for our self-serving intention is the cherry-picking of scriptural texts and employing the Bible as proof-texting in our arguments. The justification of our own actions and agenda by claiming to be God's will, or to speak on God's behalf, is somehow a manipulation or abuse of God, too. Indeed, Christians, past and present, have co-opted God's name in many different ways, especially when using it to prove ourselves and our piety or righteousness, to judge others, or to avoid what is required of us.

From a slightly different perspective, Hauerwas and others suggest that we not only manipulate God but also marginalize and even silence God by our loose talk about God. By marginalizing and silencing God, we could rid God of divine holiness and ultimately see God as a "non-entity."[13] In sum, invoking God's name is such a common scenario that it can do good or cause harm to our relationships with God and others.

The Meaning of Respecting God's Holiness

We have first to understand that we are not forbidden to invoke God, for God has willingly disclosed himself and his name to us. What is needed is to use it in a rightful and truthful way. Both Luther and Calvin have provided important insights. Luther said,

> We are . . . commanded to employ [God's name] for truth and for all good. . . .
> So also when there is right teaching, and when the name is invoked in trouble
> or praised and thanked in prosperity, etc. . . . For all this is bringing it into the
> service of truth, and using it in a blessed way. (*LC* #64)

Therefore, we are called to act in an active manner. Calvin called this active
respect "religious veneration." He elaborated the meaning of this aspect as
follows:

> First, [we] must bespeak his excellence, and correspond to the sublimity of his
> sacred name; in short, must be fitted to extol its greatness. Secondly, we
> must . . . always maintain [his sacred word and adorable mysteries] in due
> honor and esteem. Lastly, we . . . must laud every action which we attribute to
> him as wise, and just, and good. This is to sanctify the name of God. (*ICR*
> 2.8.22)

Calvin's insights, in contemporary language, point to honor God with a
sense of reverence and awe, and with praise. Yet, as Keenan hints, since
giving due respect is the first step to charity, we need to invoke God's name
lovingly as well. These active actions and attitudes give content to the virtue
that corresponds to the commandment—namely, respecting God's holiness.

Respecting God's Holiness as a Virtue

A virtue as such points in the first place to purity of heart. Our invocation of
God should always have God's holiness as its end rather than as a means for
our own, often self-serving agenda. Subsequently, we need first to cultivate
the virtue of integrity in the sense that our external acts and speech correspond to our internal thoughts.[14] The virtue of integrity in turn points to the
virtues of truthfulness and honesty (which is not restricted to oath-taking
alone).

Next, we have the virtues of charity and justice in sight. As stated above,
respecting one's name is the first step of charity. The virtue of respect for
God's holiness thus becomes the first step to loving God. Justice, on the
other hand, provides us with the needed standard: to respect means not to
deprive others of what belongs to them.[15] Then the theological virtue of faith
is also called upon since invoking God's name with respect is a verbal
manifestation of our faith.

Last but not least, the virtue of respect for God's holiness is essentially
part of the virtue of religion that particularly "governs our use of speech in
sacred matters" (*CCC* #2142). Thus, this virtue shares some of those virtues
attached to the virtue of upholding true worship and is likewise multifaceted.

The Practice of Respecting God's Holiness

Now that the virtue of respect for God's holiness is particularly related to the use of speech, its practice for Christians naturally leads to the issue of prayer. For some Christians, prayer is the most religious way of invoking God's name. Among the various Christian traditions, the Catholic tradition is known for developing various kinds of formal and communal prayers.

Another religious practice in which the invocation of God (and God's name) is involved is the habit of giving praise to God. The prayer that Jesus himself teaches us begins with giving praise to the name of our Heavenly Father—Hallowed be thy name! As the above quotation from Calvin points out, whenever we praise God, God's name may be glorified. Nevertheless, in the Bible the psalmists often give praise to the Lord and invite the community to join them in doing so (e.g., Psalm 100). Psalm 145 even tells us why we praise God: God's greatness, goodness, compassion, and all that God has done. Therefore, praying with the Psalms is a good way to express our praise to God.

However, when we pray to and praise God by means of formal prayers, we need to do so in a manner that corresponds to the values signified in the formula rather than simply uttering the words.

On the other hand, Calvin insightfully suggested the practice of simplicity of speech and making oaths only under the most extreme conditions.[16] The latter injunction in turn promotes the practice of discernment and self-examination. In simple terms, as Barclay writes, we need to ask ourselves if we invoke God's name carefully, truthfully, and necessarily.[17]

The Exemplars

The psalmists illustrate with diverse examples how and when we can and should invoke God in our prayers and praise. Still, Jesus shows us the virtue of respect for God's holiness in its fullest. Jesus teaches us how to pray and praise God in the first place (Matthew 6:9). He insists that doing God's will rather than simply calling upon God's name is the true expression of respecting God's holiness (Matthew 7:21). Jesus also advises us not to make any oath to God, whether God's name is mentioned or not (Matthew 5:33–37). Last but not least, during his last moments in the world, Jesus demonstrates to us in concrete terms how to invoke God in the most human and honest way: "My God, my God, why have you forsaken me?" (Matthew 27:46). In contemporary spiritual terms, prayer is a conversation that signifies one's personal relationship with God.

In the early period of Christianity, Saint Cecilia was known not just for her martyrdom (or being the patroness of Church music and musicians) but also for her readiness to invoke God and give praise to God both verbally and nonverbally, even at the moment of death.[18]

Today, especially within the Catholic tradition, the international Apostleship of Prayer, begun in the nineteenth century, has been encouraging the faithful around the world to habitually offer themselves and invoke God's name by praying with the universal Church as a community for the needs of the Church and the world.[19]

The Social, Communal Aspect of the Virtue of Respecting God's Holiness

Although invoking God's name in prayer, praise, and oath-taking is normally a personal act, the example of the international Apostleship of Prayer (as well as Christian liturgy) shows that it can be an active, communal act as well. Still, the virtue has vivid social implications. I name three of them. First, respecting God's holiness can be helpful in the issue of interreligious dialogue and Christian ecumenism. Like the virtue of upholding true worship, it points to the right of individuals and faith communities in the society to have their beliefs and religious practices/symbols (which reflect the holiness of their God) respected by others (as the Pontifical Biblical Commission upholds). In light of this virtue, no other religion or faith community can simply claim the support of God to criticize, much less attack, another religion or religious tradition.

Second, within the Christian community it challenges abusive use of the Bible and other biblical teachings to justify dominance or bigotry. A concrete example was apartheid in South Africa. The apartheid state was criticized for "[using] Romans 13:1–7 to give an absolute and 'divine' authority to the State" and to justify its status quo of racism, capitalism, and totalitarianism. The local Church there was also criticized for the abuse of the Gospel teaching of reconciliation in resolving the struggle between justice and injustice.[20]

Third, the virtue raises the concern about the invocation of God by Christian politicians and organizations as they pursue secular political power. In this way, we need to reconsider how church and state should be related to one another.

In conclusion, the second commandment is all about respecting our Creator, starting with God's name. It has introduced us to the important moral quality of "respect" (or "valuing"), which, as we shall see, becomes the background virtue for our interpretation of the subsequent commandments. In this way, respecting God's holiness and God's name is the first step to respecting God's creatures.

NOTES

1. See Thomas B. Dozeman, *Commentary on Exodus* (Grand Rapids, MI: Eerdmans, 2009), 486–87.

2. For reasons that support this claim, see Patrick D. Miller, *The Ten Commandments* (Louisville, KY: Westminster John Knox Press, 2009), 85–86.

3. Dozeman, *Commentary on Exodus*, 487.

4. Herbert B. Huffmon, "The Fundamental Code Illustrated: The Third Commandment," in *The Ten Commandments: The Reciprocity of Faithfulness*, ed. William P. Brown (Louisville, KY: Westminster John Knox Press, 2004), 207–8.

5. See Brevard S. Childs, *The Book of Exodus* (Philadelphia, PA: Westminster Press, 1974), 411; Walter C. Kaiser Jr., *Toward Old Testament Ethics* (Grand Rapids, MI: Zondervan, 1991), 88; Miller, *The Ten Commandments*, 70–71.

6. Harrelson, however, has a different opinion. See Walter J. Harrelson, *The Ten Commandments and Human Rights* (Macon, GA: Mercer University Press, 1997), 63.

7. For a discussion of the reasons of broadening its implication, see Childs, *The Book of Exodus*, 412.

8. Cornelis Houtman, *Exodus*, vol. 3, trans. Johan Rebel and Sierd Woudstra (Kampen, Netherlands: Kok, 1993–2000), 36–38.

9. Ernest J. Lewis, *Light for the Journey: Living the Ten Commandments* (Waco, TX: Word Books, 1986), 52.

10. John C. Holbert, *The Ten Commandments* (Nashville, TN: Abingdon Press, 2002), 40.

11. An example of symbolic proclamation is the fact that during the Second World War, German soldiers would bear the badge "Gott mit uns" on their uniforms. See Stanley M. Hauerwas and William H. Willimon, *The Truth about God: The Ten Commandments in Christian Life* (Nashville, TN: Abingdon Press, 1999), 48. See also Gerd Krumreich and H. Lehmann, eds., *"Gott mit uns": Nation, Religion und Gewalt im 19. und frühen 20. Jahrhundert* (Göttingen: Vandenhoeck & Ruprecht, 2000).

12. See David Klinghoffer, *Shattered Tablets* (New York: Doubleday, 2007), 72; Joan Chittister, *The Ten Commandments: Laws of the Heart* (Maryknoll, NY: Orbis Books, 2006), 30. See also G. Corwin Stoppel, *Living Words: The Ten Commandments for the Twenty-first Century* (Cambridge, MA: Cowley, 2005), 48.

13. Holbert, *The Ten Commandments*, 38. See also Ephraim Radner, "Taking the Lord's Name in Vain," in *I Am the Lord Your God: Christian Reflections on the Ten Commandments*, ed. Carl E. Braaten and Christopher R. Seitz (Grand Rapids, MI: Eerdmans, 2005), 87.

14. The virtue of integrity will be discussed in more detail in chapter 22.

15. The virtue of justice will be discussed in more detail in chapter 11.

16. See Calvin, *John Calvin's Sermons on the Ten Commandments*, ed. and trans. Benjamin W. Farley (Grand Rapids, MI: Baker Books, 1993), 87–88.

17. William Barclay, *The Ten Commandments* (Louisville, KY: Westminster John Knox Press, 1998), 15.

18. See Paul Burns, ed., *Butler's Lives of the Saints* (Collegeville, MN: Liturgical Press, 2003).

19. Apostleship of Prayer, "Mission," http://apostleshipofprayer.org/mission.html.

20. "Kairos Document," http://medbib.com/Kairos_Document.

Chapter Seven

The Third Commandment in Exodus 20:8–11

Remember the Sabbath day, and keep it holy. For six days you shall labor and do all your work. But the seventh day is a Sabbath to the Lord your God; you shall not do any work—you, your son or your daughter, your male or female slave, your livestock, or the alien resident in your towns. For in six days the Lord made heaven and earth, the sea, and all that is in them, but rested the seventh day; therefore the Lord blessed the Sabbath day and consecrated it.

WHAT DID THE TEXT COMMAND?

The commandment on observing the Sabbath is, after the first commandment, the longest in the Decalogue. Both its unusual length and other features, as Childs notes, partially explain scholars' great interest in this commandment. They observe that its formulation differs remarkably from that of the Deuteronomy version. The commandment also seems to have rich extrabiblical materials that help explain its historical origins.

However, by the same token, these scholars also raise many questions that lead to debates. For instance, there is no consensus on whether the Hebrew term *shabbat* ("Sabbath") is primarily derived from a verbal form (which means to rest or cease from work) or a nominal form.

Still, one of the main concerns among Old Testament scholars has been the origin of the Sabbath.[1] Despite the common view that the term and its practice were derived from similar practices of the neighboring peoples, other contrasting hypotheses continue to emerge. Harrelson, for example, is convinced that Israel's prohibition of work on the Sabbath is a unique custom in the ancient Near Eastern world. Others suggest that its distinctiveness lies in the fact that the Sabbath became a sacred day of worship for the Israelites.

Nevertheless, few doubt that observing the Sabbath had been a long, familiar institutional social practice among the Israelites, for the exhortation to "remember" already gives a hint that the commandment had been given to and observed by the Israelites in the past (Exodus 16:22–30). As will be seen in the later discussion on coveting, others further suggest that the third commandment is related to the commandments against coveting in terms of content and function.

Within the broader context of the Hebrew Bible, we find similar formulations of Sabbath observance (e.g., Exodus 31:12–17). Many of them are rather short in length, such as Leviticus 23:3. However, these formulations have different emphases and contents. For example, in Exodus 31:12–17 the Sabbath is understood as a sign of the covenant between YHWH and the people. It contains a sanction that is not found in Exodus 20:8–11.

Even the Deuteronomy version, as noted in the earlier chapter, is strikingly different. The differences lie not just with the insertion of the phrase "as the Lord your God commanded you" but more importantly with the replacement of the "creation" tradition with the "exodus" tradition, which implies a change of focus. The Exodus version, as we shall see, focuses on why the Sabbath is holy and is cosmological in perspective; the Deuteronomy version, in contrast, emphasizes why it must be observed and is soteriological in purpose. Exodus 20:8–11 is theological, while Deuteronomy 5:12–15 is more historical (or humanitarian).[2]

As a whole, we can claim that 20:8–11 is unique in its own regard and holds an important place in both the Ten Commandments and the social life of Israel. Still, the various emphases, contents, and rationales found in these different formulations lead some to believe that there may be an original, shorter form of the commandment, and that the present form has gone through certain developments.[3]

Apart from being one of the longest commandments, 20:8–11 is also the only one that contains both a positive command (keep the Sabbath holy) and a negative prohibition (do not work on the seventh day). I thus agree with Miller that one may perceive the commandment as containing two commands that are woven together through the notion of "Sabbath." Yet Childs reminds us that it is a carefully constructed unit as well: it begins with a positive command (v8), followed by guidelines for its fulfillment (vv9–10), and ends with a rationale for observing the command (v11). Within this unit is also a parallel between what the Israelites should do and what YHWH has already done.

With this well-thought-out framework in mind, we now examine the meaning of the commandment. Verse 8 is a command to remember the Sabbath and to keep it holy. Childs rightly notes that the use of the infinitive absolute for the two verbs ("remember" and "keep") could imply that the mandate to remember points to an *active* observance (Exodus 2:24).[4] Moreover, we learn from Cassuto that since holiness connotes a certain separateness and sublimity, the phrase "keep it holy" points to setting the Sabbath apart from the rest of the week and dedicating it to the Lord. As a result, we can join others to consider that worship is implicitly called for on this holy day. Indeed, the two acts (keeping it holy and worshipping) are almost inseparable (e.g., 2 Kings 4:22ff).

The following two verses (vv9–10) form a unit in which the prohibition is found. This unit describes the manner in which the Sabbath is kept holy—first in terms of permission to work during the first six days, then a prohibition to work on the seventh day.[5]

The Hebrew word for "work," *melachah*, basically means "a creative act, not necessarily a physically taxing or tiring one."[6] However, there is no detail regarding what constitutes work or what one should do (apart from *not* to work) in setting aside the seventh day. This ambiguity thus leads to diverse interpretations of the prohibition (especially within the Jewish tradition), ranging from preparation of meals to traveling (e.g., Exodus 16:29).

In contrast to the lack of details regarding work/labor, verse 10 provides a rather substantive list of the constituency involved. However, this provision still leads to various interpretations:[7] some claim that the list seems to highlight the number "seven" on which the Sabbath is based; others attend to the categories themselves and conclude that no exception is allowed. Still, if one focuses on the last category, then the commandment anticipates the circumstances of the near future—the people of Israel will dwell in its towns and cities. Nonetheless, these different views, as I see them, reveal that Sabbath observance is universal and timeless, and its focus is one's inner attitude rather than one's external deeds.

Verse 11 is comprised of two independent sentences. The first sentence offers a rationale for observing the command that is in accord with the manner described in verse 10. The recall of the creation story here implies that the Sabbath itself is a recollection of the creation of the world by God. Thus, I agree that, for Israelites, the command to cease from work and to rest grows out of the faith experience and not out of humanitarian grounds, as some commentators would suggest. The next sentence points out that the Sabbath is holy because God not only blesses it but also sanctifies it. In this way, verse 11 grounds the sanctity of the Sabbath in the light of God's own act of creation. It is both cosmological and theocentric in perspective. The overall emphasis is on why the Sabbath is holy.

Regarding the role of the commandment in the life of the Israelite community, Houtman and Harrelson rightly claim that the first and immediate function is to provide a rationale for the existing practice and an opportunity for every member to rest. The above consideration regarding the connection between "keeping it holy" and "worship" supports Miller's view that the Sabbath requirement can become a paradigm and basis for the celebration of (and worship in) many religious festivals for the Israelites, such as the feast of unleavened bread. In this way, the Sabbath brings joy and happiness to the people (e.g., Isaiah 56:2–8). Moreover, it seems possible that observing the Sabbath could serve as a means for the Israelites to observe rhythms as nature does. Taken together, Sabbath observance has an explicit, practical significance.

Still, the commandment is also significant to the Israelites existentially:[8] Sabbath observance becomes an institutional practice that defines Jewish identity. It is actually a gift instead of a command per se because the focus is the well-being of the Israelites.[9] It brings joy to and demands certain responsibilities from them.

Consequently, the Israelites must take the third commandment seriously. Although the commandment does not contain any sanction, several scriptural texts make it clear that the profanation of the Sabbath deserves the death penalty, and whosoever works on the Sabbath will be cut off from the community. The observance is an absolute requirement for all to attain happiness and prosperity, and, when transgressed, brings misfortune (e.g., Isaiah 56:4–7; Jeremiah 17:24–27). Unfortunately, elsewhere the prophets complained that the Sabbath had been largely commercialized by the people of Israel (e.g., Nehemiah 13:15–17).

Finally, as hinted in the above findings and those of many scholars, the commandment is not just crucial to the identity and happiness of the Israelite community but is also important for the moral life of the people. Here, then, we recognize, first, that rest becomes as important and sacred as work itself. The commandment relativizes the importance of work and hence frees the Israelites from the danger of slavery to work. YHWH remains the master of time. Second, positively it calls not only for physical rest but also for communal celebration as a way to treasure the sacred time given to them as a gift. Third, the gift aspect of the commandment, the experience of joy, and the consecration of the Sabbath by God in turn invite the Israelites to bring happiness to others. Fourth, and subsequently, the Israelites actually imitate God and bear witness to what God did. Lastly, since the rationale of the commandment lies in the creation tradition, it attends to the universal creation experience of all humankind more than the particular liberating experience of the Israelites.

In sum, the commandment delivers a multifold moral message. Observing the third commandment is thus not as simple and passive as one would imagine but calls us to treasure this sacred time actively and communally. How can these practical and moral significances be lived out nowadays?

TREASURING THE SACRED TEMPORAL SPACE

Some writers attend to the meaning of holiness, while others are concerned about the relationship between the Jewish Sabbath and Christian Sunday observance.[10] Our examination hints that the key ethical issue seems to focus on treasuring the sacred time itself.

However, a caveat is needed here: Since the time of St. Paul, the Sabbath was not an obligation for Christians (Colossians 2:16). Rather, they gathered on Sunday, the Lord's Day (Acts 20:7). Historically, Christians continued to work on Sundays and yet kept the Lord's Day holy by celebrating together through the Eucharist the Lord's death, resurrection, and return. In this way, the Sunday observance and the third commandment were not really matched, though the Lord's Day gradually took the place of the Sabbath. It was not until the third century that Sunday rest was explicitly mentioned, and Eucharistic celebration and resting on Sunday were together later decreed by both ecclesial and civil authorities. Christians were commanded to keep the Lord's Day holy just as the Jews kept the Sabbath holy. Then, in the sixth century, servile work was officially prohibited by the Church, and the masters of the serfs were obliged to let the serfs rest and celebrate the Eucharist together.[11]

For Jews, therefore, the Sabbath observance first emphasizes imitating God, who rested, and then calls for communal worship. For Christians, Sunday observance is for the sake of celebrating the Lord's death and resurrection, and in so doing, they stop performing "servile" work and rest. What is in common to both is the need to worship and rest.

Here, then, I adopt the view of Luther: that what is needed is to regularly set apart a special temporal space in which we rest and focus our thoughts on God. For Christians, however, this sacred temporal space is the Lord's Day on which the Lord rose.

Sunday Is Just Another Workday

When I was the acting director for our vocational school for the handicapped in Cambodia over a decade ago, one of my duties was to assist our sewing class graduates (mostly young women), like Sovanny, to get a job in garment factories in the city. She "luckily" got a job and worked six days a week from 8 a.m. to 5 p.m. with a monthly salary of US$30. There was even a reward of

US$5 if she did not absent herself from work for a full month. However, she was also expected to work on Sundays and accept overtime work during the week in order to be qualified for the reward program.

Many writers would note that similar working conditions are found among workers in the United States, especially the undocumented immigrant workers and those whose jobs do not provide medical insurance for themselves and their families. Even those who have secured a stable job often work in an environment that emphasizes speed and efficiency. Sunday becomes a time to catch up on those unfinished tasks. The changing nature of work in our society further forces us to take up home-based jobs that make Sunday no different from the rest of the week. [12]

As we consider the reception of the third commandment, we might do well to realize that until we work for greater fairness for all, some, because of inequity, might not have the freedom to rest on the Lord's Day and celebrate the Eucharist. It was after all, this inequity that prompted the Church's concern about "servile" work.

The Meaning of Treasuring the Sacred Temporal Space

The foundation of the third commandment is the imitation of what God did. Both our exegetical findings above and Abraham Heschel's view suggest that treasuring the sacred time denotes imitating God's rest, joy, and sanctification of this temporal space. [13]

First, we imitate God who rests after work (Genesis 2:2). However, Christians hold a distinctive understanding and practice of rest: it is not for the sake of regaining strength for labor; rather, labor is a means, and rest signifies the end of God's creation work. Moreover, as Calvin highlighted, rest has both physical and spiritual dimensions that permit God to work in us (*ICR* 2.8.28). Hauerwas and Willimon thus comment that this spiritual dimension points to the recognition of our own limitations, trust in God's governance of the world, and the enjoyment of this sacred time as God-given.

Second, we imitate God, who enjoys God's work and rest (Genesis 1:31). For Christians, the sacred time is a venue that "enables, encourages, and is marked by genuine rejoicing in the Lord." [14] We rejoice in the Lord specifically by coming together on the Lord's Day to celebrate the Paschal Mystery. Aquinas, in his *Explanations of the Ten Commandments*, claimed that this celebration consisted of offering sacrifice, hearing God's Word, and contemplating divine things. Luther and Calvin added that we come together to praise, sing, and pray to God, and emphasized that hearing and serving the Word of God is crucial and fundamental, for it makes the time holy and distinguishes our celebration from that of non-Christians (*LC* ##84, 93–95; *ICR* 2.8.28, 34).

Third, we imitate God who continues to sanctify us. Treasuring the sacred time does not mean "doing nothing"; rather, it recalls what God has been actively doing—the carrying out of works of mercy. Aquinas rightly claimed that while Christians should avoid servile work on the Lord's Day, they are allowed to do so provided that their work is done out of necessity, of the service for the Church, of the good of the neighbor, and of obedience to our superiors. Here, we find the insights of the past continue to enrich our present-day understanding.

Treasuring the Sacred Temporal Space as a Virtue

The threefold meaning of treasuring the sacred time implies a threefold characteristic of its virtue. Imitating God, who rests, points to the virtue of gratitude for the rest that we have and the time that God created as a gift for us. By letting God work in us and in the world when we take rest, we learn, as Calvin rightly said, to be "dead to our own affections and works" (*ICR* 2.8.28). Here, then, we need to recognize what we have been given. For many, this requires the virtue of patience as we wait for the next week to begin. I believe that the fact that God continues to sustain the weekly order calls in play the virtues of humility, trust, and hope in God as well. [15]

Imitating God, who rejoices, and celebrating the Lord's resurrection point to the virtue of joy, which is rooted in our gratitude. We need to cultivate the sense of rejoicing that the early Church had and which was commanded by Paul: "Rejoice in the Lord always!" (Philippians 4:4–7).

Finally, as we celebrate the Lord's resurrection, we celebrate God's continued work of sanctification in us, and this prompts us to appreciate the virtue of religion, which is also required in the previous two commandments. Therefore, the virtues of true worship and respect for God's holiness need to be emphasized in our Sunday liturgy. Still, as we shall see, the virtue of mercy is also called in to regulate the implied works of mercy.

The Practice of Treasuring the Sacred Temporal Space

Three types of practices are needed for the cultivation of the threefold virtue of treasuring the sacred time. First, we thank God whenever we are able to rest, be it our daily or weekly rest. Holbert rightly reminds us that when we rest, we need to create moments of silence so as to acquire spiritual rest as well. The contemplation of the divine things, as suggested by Aquinas, is a good exercise for acquiring spiritual rest and discerning what brings true happiness to our hearts. Slowly, we are able to detach ourselves from what seems more important in the eyes of the world.

Second, the best way to rejoice and celebrate, as far as much of the Christian tradition is concerned, is the communal celebration of the Sunday Eucharist. [16] Barclay and others are right to claim that praying as a group, studying God's words or discussing the meaning of faith together, or sharing a meal with one another are also valuable ways of treasuring what is sacred in today's busy lifestyle.

Third, we have to carry out works of mercy that provide necessary means for everyone to rest, rejoice, and worship God, especially for the less advantaged. For instance, while we need to work for the rights of those who are not free on the Lord's Day, employers need to guarantee reasonable wages and grant sufficient holidays to employees even to the point of sacrificing a certain portion of their own profit, so that employees do not have to give up their entitled rest for the sake of earning adequate income. It is a matter of both justice and mercy.

The Exemplars

Jesus observes the Sabbath as other Jews of his time do (e.g., Luke 4:16). However, Jesus demonstrates to us that the real meaning of the observance is that the Sabbath is made for humankind and not vice versa (Mark 2:27). Specifically, to sanctify the Sabbath means to do God's will and to liberate the people from the bondage of sin. Thus, on a number of Sabbaths Jesus continues God's merciful work by doing good (e.g., John 5:1–18).

Within the Catholic tradition, the late Pope John Paul II is known for recalling the Lord's Day and recovering the doctrinal foundations of this practice. In his apostolic letter *Dies Domini* the pope expresses the deep concern that "changes in socioeconomic conditions have often led to profound modifications of social behavior and hence of the character of Sunday" (#4).[17] Specifically, he offers a Trinitarian view of the Lord's Day that is similar to the threefold understanding I have presented above, and emphasizes the need for solidarity through works of mercy and justice (##55–73).

The Social, Communal Aspect of the Virtue of Treasuring the Sacred Temporal Space

Both the threefold meaning of the virtue itself and the apostolic letter reveal that treasuring the sacred time is never an individual and private practice. In practical terms, we cannot celebrate or rejoice on our own. An appointed and agreed-upon time allows the community to come together for this purpose. Indeed, true rest "comes when we know ourselves as members of a community held in God's hand."[18] An individualistic view of celebrating the Lord's Day, on the contrary, risks the danger of serving and idolizing the self.

Moreover, many would agree that the virtue, which emerged from Exodus 20:8–11, has a socioeconomic implication, though less stressed than in its Deuteronomy counterpart. It is because the call to rest is a radical protest to what the capitalist world preaches. For instance, in 1999 the Catholic and

Lutheran Churches of Germany issued a joint declaration supporting the maintenance of a work-free Sunday, *Menschen Brauchen den Sonntag*, rejecting calls by industry leaders for operating factories 24/7.[19]

The commandment and its virtues also criticize the unjust reality that only the rich can have the luxury to rest while the poor (and even ordinary people) have to sacrifice their entitled free time in order to earn a living. In this way, it challenges the wealthy and the powerful not to exploit those who labor for them. Both the poor and the rich should be able to treasure what is sacred equally and communally. The commandment and its virtue thus confirm the twofold right of all humankind—freedom of restful/qualitative time and of worship, as the Pontifical Biblical Commission advocates.

On the other hand, by taking rest and coming together for joyful celebration on the Lord's Day, family and community members are able to grow and strengthen their bonds, echoing Klinghoffer's conviction that the commandment helps counteract social isolation. Last but not least, Christian works of mercy performed on the Lord's Day promote the good of the neighbor and contribute to the good of the society. All in all, the third commandment presents to us the most communal-centered Christian virtue.

NOTES

1. For a discussion of different views, see Cornelis Houtman, *Exodus*, vol. 3, trans. Johan Rebel and Sierd Woudstra (Kampen, Netherlands: Kok, 1993–2000), 40–42. See also Walter C. Kaiser Jr., *Toward Old Testament Ethics* (Grand Rapids, MI: Zondervan, 1991), 89; John J. Collins, *Introduction to the Hebrew Bible* (Minneapolis: Augsburg Fortress, 2004), 129.

2. David Novak, "The Sabbath Day," in *The Ten Commandments for Jews, Christians, and Others*, ed. Roger E. Van Harn (Grand Rapids, MI: Eerdmans, 2007), 78. See also Terence E. Fretheim, *Exodus* (Louisville, KY: Westminster John Knox Press, 1991), 230.

3. Scholars disagree about what this original form might be. Childs, for instance, claims that the original form simply commands one to observe or not to desecrate the Sabbath.

4. See Fretheim, *Exodus*, 229. Miller further claims that "remember" and "observe" (used in the Deuteronomy version) are supplementary to each other.

5. The phrase "the seventh day," for Hebrews, lasts from sunset of Friday until sunset of Saturday.

6. David Klinghoffer, *Shattered Tablets* (New York: Doubleday, 2007), 85.

7. See Umberto Cassuto, *A Commentary on the Book of Exodus*, trans. Israel Abrahams (Jerusalem: Magnes Press, Hebrew University, 1967), 245; Patrick D. Miller, *The Ten Commandments* (Louisville, KY: Westminster John Knox Press, 2009), 122; Thomas B. Dozeman, *Commentary on Exodus* (Grand Rapids, MI: Eerdmans, 2009), 492.

8. See also K. Grünwaldt, *Exil und Identität: Beschneidung, Passa und Sabbat in der Priesterschrift* (Frankfurt am Main: Anton Hain, 1992), as referenced in Houtman, *Exodus*, 44.

9. Miller notes that the gift aspect is present especially in the story of manna in Exodus 16. The Deuteronomy version, in contrast, highlights the command aspect of the observance.

10. See Kathryn Greene-McCreight, "Restless until We Rest in God: The Fourth Commandment as Test Case in Christian 'Plain Sense' Interpretation," *Ex auditu* 11 (1995): 29–41.

11. See James F. Keenan, *Commandments of Compassion* (Franklin, WI: Sheed & Ward, 1999), 16–17; *Catholic Encyclopedia*, s.v. "Sabbath," www.newadvent.org/cathen/13287b.htm; "Sunday," www.newadvent.org/cathen/14335a.htm.

12. Without doubt, there are also workaholics who keep themselves busy so as to have a sense of purpose and security.

13. Abraham J. Heschel, "A Palace in Time," in *The Ten Commandments: The Reciprocity of Faithfulness*, ed. William P. Brown (Louisville, KY: Westminster John Knox Press, 2004), 216. As we shall see, this threefold view indirectly echoes Pope John Paul II's Trinitarian interpretation.

14. Joan Chittister, *The Ten Commandments: Laws of the Heart* (Maryknoll, NY: Orbis Books, 2006), 47.

15. Marguerite Shuster, "Response to 'The Sabbath Day,'" in *The Ten Commandments for Jews, Christians, and Others*, ed. Roger E. Van Harn (Grand Rapids, MI: Eerdmans, 2007), 83.

16. The "Official Church Responses" to the WCC Lima Statement on *Baptism, Eucharist, and Ministry* stressed the importance of regular Sunday celebration of the Eucharist. Cf. www.liturgybytlw.com/Lectures/BEMEuch.html.

17. Pope John Paul II, *Dies Domini*, apostolic letter on keeping the Lord's Day holy, May 31, 1998, www.vatican.va/holy_father/john_paul_ii/apost_letters/documents/hf_jp-ii_apl_05071998_dies-domini_en.html.

18. Shuster, "Response to 'The Sabbath Day,'" 85.

19. The Evangelical Church in Germany and the German Bishops' Conference, *Menschen Brauchen den Sonntag*, www.ekd.de/sonntagsruhe/archiv/texte/menschen_brauchen_den_sonntag.html.

Chapter Eight

The Fourth Commandment in Exodus 20:12

Honor your father and your mother, so that your days may be long in the land that the Lord your God is giving you.

WHAT DID THE TEXT COMMAND?

The fourth commandment is the second in the Decalogue that contains a positive command. It also has a motivation clause as the previous ones do. However, the motivation clause seems to be much more specific and is modified in the Deuteronomy version—the Deuteronomy writer added the phrase "as the Lord your God commanded you" just as he did with the third commandment.

As mentioned in chapter 4, the commandment has been subject matter for debate among scholars—whether it should be placed in the first tablet or the second. Miller notes that, for Christians, one of the contributing factors to the issue is the ambiguous words of Jesus in Matthew 19:18–19 ("Honor your father and mother; also, [y]ou shall love your neighbor as yourself"): by placing this commandment at the end of his citation of the first table and next to the "love your neighbor" commandment, it is unclear if Jesus perceives honoring parents as a summary of the first table or as a synonym for the commandment on love of neighbor.

Scholars like Dozeman attempt to resolve this issue by claiming that the commandment contains a number of "bridging" features that can link the commandments directed toward God and those toward one's neighbor. For example, the fourth commandment is the last commandment that refers to

God. There exists also a close relationship between God and parents. While agreeing with that, Miller notes that these and other arguments tend to highlight more the commandment's connection with those commandments directed toward God than those toward one's neighbor.[1]

Another debate raised by this commandment is whether it has a positive or negative origin. Childs notes that those parallel texts that appear in the Torah are predominantly formulated negatively (e.g., Leviticus 20:9). It is thus argued that the commandment has a negative origin, prohibiting anyone to *dishonor* one's parents. Still, references found in the wisdom literature are generally presented in a positive style (e.g., Proverbs 1:8).

In brief, while these two debates sound more theoretical than practical, they highlight the unique status of our parents in our relationships with God and with others. They also reveal the basic attitude of the commandment, which is to "do good" rather than "avoid evil."

Although a positive formulation of Exodus 20:12 tends to enjoy a comprehensive and expansive nature that its negative counterparts in the fifth through tenth commandments lack, there are several issues that deserve our attention. The first and major issue is the meaning of the Hebrew verb *kabbed* ("honor"). According to Miller, the verb literally means "to make heavy" and is applied to treating someone who is of great weight. In the context of familial relationships, it is often interpreted as obeying parents. However, the verb not only refers to obedience narrowly but also has a wide spectrum of meanings in the Hebrew Bible, ranging from "prize highly" to "show respect" and "revere" (e.g., Proverbs 4:8; Leviticus 19:3), and indirectly means "care for" and "show affection" (e.g., Psalm 91:15). When having YHWH as the object of honor, the term further implies "worship," "fear," and "give reverence to" (e.g., Psalm 86:9).

Among the different possible meanings, Houtman and Dozeman note that the notions of "reverence" and "respect" have been brought up elsewhere, especially in the wisdom literature. Still, scholars observe that the notion of "caring for" is commonly found, particularly in those stories of caring for the aged parents, such as the account of Ruth toward her mother-in-law (Ruth 1:16–17). Actually, its practices were extended to the deceased parents through burial rites and ancestral worship (e.g., Genesis 50:1–14). Nevertheless, according to wisdom literature, caring for the aged parents points first to the provision for their physical needs, such as food and clothing (e.g., Proverbs 3:9). Proper attitudes toward them include the following: do not despise, forsake, or be angry with them, but be patient and kind to them, especially when their minds fail (e.g., Sirach 3:1–16).

As a whole, some authors are convinced that caring for aged parents is the heart of honoring. Others, in contrast, insist that the commandment goes beyond caring for the aged parents, for they give us life from the beginning. This latter view reintroduces the notion of "obedience" as an important way of understanding the term "honor." I am convinced that both attitudes are necessary throughout our lives: "obeying" and "caring for" the aged parents are not mutually exclusive but are required at different stages. As we shall discuss below, the emphasis varies according to the status of the addressee.

In saying so, we need to qualify the notion of obedience. Patrick and Miller remark that it normally refers to the relationship between nonadult children and their parents. Thus, the duty of obedience ceases when the children have grown up. Moreover, although obedience implies not only "listening" but also "heeding," the examples found in the Hebrew Bible point out that we listen to specific words and heed only what is good and helpful. If the parents turn against God, their authority ceases and the child is no longer obliged to obey their commands (e.g., 1 Kings 15:13–14).

The second issue is concerned with the object and addressee of the commandment. At first glance, it is rather self-evident that the object is our earthly parents. Still, as Childs and Houtman point out, we can find additional information from the Hebrew Bible. Normally, parents are portrayed as aged, their minds are failing, and they are no longer able to take care of themselves (e.g., Sirach 3:13). The signs of aging, such as physical infirmities, make them vulnerable, embittered, and seen as a burden to and less valuable in society (e.g., Ruth 1). Yet being elderly is not a totally negative reality in ancient Israel—it is also a sign of wisdom and uprightness (e.g., Job 12:12). Moreover, it is assumed that parents are worthy of honor by their children. In sum, this additional information gives weight to the claim that caring for aged parents is a core meaning of the commandment.

Regarding the addressee, both the previous conclusion and the use of singular second-person masculine verbs and pronouns support the claim that the commandment addresses the free male adult members of the Israelite community rather than children. As a result, the fourth commandment seems to emphasize the need to care for one's aged parents. Still, I find Miller's proposal practical: the audience of the fourth commandment is not restricted to a certain age or gender, but adult children are an important starting point of the commandment and its ethical reflection.

A third issue concerns the rationale for honoring parents. Again, scholars like Houtman and Miller note that the Hebrew Bible provides various reasons: parents are the visible representatives of God through which divine authority is exercised. They are also the first and closest people we should care for in our relation with others. Moreover, father and mother are the begetter and bearer of the child, respectively (e.g., Proverbs 23:22). Thus, one should return a certain degree of the care and nourishment provided by them. In this way, the obligation is primarily driven by our response or *responsibility* toward them. However, the motivation clause in the commandment also states clearly that those who honor their parents will receive long life. That means that it is for one's own sake that the Israelite honor his parents. It suggests what Miller calls the logic of "reciprocality": having a long life implies that one will be cared for and honored by one's children when they become old themselves. Either way, we have to acknowledge that the rationale is not based on love or quality of relationship.

On the other hand, some link the promised "land" with the land of Canaan and perceive that the failure to observe the commandment will lead to the fall of the nation and the loss of the land. Others counterpropose that "the land" is not confined to any specific piece of land but wherever God's promise continues. The mention of the land aims to merge the obligation with the broader scheme of salvation history. While this debate sounds unimportant, what is relevant to our interpretation is the fact that most scholars would agree that the beneficiary of this land is the entire Israelite community: the notion of "long life" and the phrase "that your days may be long" envision not only an extension of one's chronological life but also the blessing of the community in which one lives.

Unfortunately, the Hebrew Bible reveals that acts of dishonoring parents are found within the community, such as lack of respect, chasing them away, or wishing them annihilation (e.g., 2 Kings 2:23). Some of these acts, such as verbal insults (like "curse") and physical violence (like "striking"), deserve severe punishment—including death (e.g., Exodus 21:15, 17).

Finally, most scholars agree that the fourth commandment not only points to a reward/promise[2] but also reflects significant religious and cultural insights for the Israelite community; it touches on the relationship between YHWH and his earthly representative in terms of their authority and order. It also treats mothers and fathers as equals (within the setting of family). Furthermore, the commandment highlights the importance of a family—it is upon the bedrock of the family that the continuation of the community and its identity as the people of YHWH are built.

Still, these scholars also point out that the commandment is significant for the ethical life of the community. First, as Cassuto suggests, the formulation seems to assume a kind of "measure for measure" ethical principle similar to what Miller suggested above—if you honor your source of life on earth, you will be rewarded with long life on earth as well. Second, to honor one's parents is a moral obligation required of all Israelites regardless of the situation of their elderly parents. It is a high social ideal for all. On the contrary, dishonoring parents is a serious threat and a sign of lawlessness and collapse of the social order (e.g., Micah 7:6). Thus, it is often condemned by the prophets along with unjust social practices, such as ill treatment of the resident aliens and widows (e.g., Ezekiel 22:6–7). Third, by concentrating on Deuteronomy 16:18–18:22, some believe that the commandment calls to Israel's attention the question of obeying religious/civil authority. However, I follow Miller's view that such an extension is only implicit and inferential. It is partly because the possibility of extending the commandment to authority outside the family setting relies on whether these community offices reflect the teaching of God as parents do.

By far, we have seen that the scope of the meaning of honor and the status of the addressee determine the emphasis of the commandment. Each Israelite has a responsibility to act out this commandment, and it is for the good of both one's family and the entire community. Yet, being a positive command, verse 20:12 is more interested in the cultivation of positive emotions and attitudes than the prohibition of certain acts.

THE VIRTUE OF HONORING PARENTS

Hauerwas and Willimon claim that the commandment aims at reminding adult parents that they are responsible for the nurture of their children just as their parents were. Others, on the contrary, concentrate on how young children should obey their parents. There are also those who focus on other family values beyond the relationship of parents and children, such as harmony. Our finding points to the need to focus more on the moral attitude of adult children toward their aged parents.

Being Parents in the Twenty-first Century

In the past century, the growing divorce rate and other sociological changes have led to changes in the understanding of parenthood. The relationship between parents and children likewise has been changing. Specifically, respect for parents by young people has been deteriorating. In the United States, some suggest that the success of reality shows like *Nanny 911* (from which desperate parents seek help) only verifies this problem.[3]

Sadly, the lack of respect and honor is found in adult children as well, just as in the time of ancient Israel. Statistics indicate, for example, that over one-third of elderly Americans who have reported maltreatment by their supposed caretakers are abused by their own adult children.[4] Apart from such physical and mental abuse, aged parents are at times simply abandoned by their children. Some writers suspect the growing individualistic (and self-centered) ethos as well as the consumer culture, which sees old commodity as valueless, have indirectly contributed to the growth of this disturbing reality.[5]

Of course, some grown-up children have to leave their aged parents behind for other reasons, like working in a distant place. They also find "trying to balance the responsibilities of their own families and working lives and the desire to care for parents . . . highly stressful."[6] As many writers observe, these children reluctantly either let their aged parents live on their own or transfer them to nursing homes.[7] A sense of guilt could emerge, especially when hard decisions like these are to be made. Christian adults further feel that the fourth commandment adds extra weight to their guilt feelings.

The Meaning of Honoring Parents

Why should Christians honor their parents in the first place? Aquinas adopted the views of Augustine and Aristotle and explained that we do so out of love and on account of the benefits they granted us, respectively. Specifically, we are indebted to our parents for the gifts of life, nourishment, and instruction. Here the unique gift of life makes the status of parents higher than that of any other earthly authorities. The gift of faith that they helped us receive is another reason for honoring them (*CCC* #2220). Thus, for Christians, honoring aged parents is never merely a matter of mutual responsibility or duties to be fulfilled.[8]

Luther offered a comprehensive understanding: "[that the parents] be held in distinction and esteem above all things . . . that also in our words we observe modesty toward them . . . that we show them such honor also by works . . . that we serve them, help them, and provide for them . . . not only gladly, but with humility and reverence, as doing it before God" (*LC* ##109–11). For Luther, honor is most pleasing to God and is the highest work that we can do next to worshipping God (*LC* ##125–27). Finally, Luther explained that since parents are given to us by God, they are not deprived of our honor in any circumstances—no matter whether they are abusive, violent parent(s) or not (*LC* #108). Here, Luther showed us that honor is not conditional the way obedience is.

Calvin upheld Luther's view in his own writing but pointed out that honor contains three parts—namely, reverence, gratitude, and obedience (*ICR* 2.8.36–37).

Contemporary writer Barclay similarly summarizes honor in three points: (1) There is a sense of gratitude—we owe our parents a twofold debt of life through birth and nourishment. (2) There is also a unique sense of obedience—obedience out of a balance between control and respect for our freedom. (3) There is a necessity of support, especially to the aged parents—we have to see to it that they are not left in need while not causing an unbearable burden to ourselves. Here, Barclay's understanding anticipates the necessity of discernment.

Honoring Parents as a Virtue

The diverse and expansive meaning of "honor" as ascribed in the commandment and Christian traditions shows that honoring parents requires the cultivation of certain attitudes. However, honoring parents is itself an attitude of unselfishness.[9] In fact, honoring parents has been treasured by the ancient

Greek philosophers (such as Plato) as an important virtue next to honoring the gods. [10] In our contemporary world, the virtue of honoring parents is all the more necessary than in the past, partly because our parents now live much longer than before.

As a virtue many would agree that it is first related to the virtue of gratitude, because the gift of life (and faith) comes from God via our parents. The virtue of honor also demands the cultivation of the virtues of modesty, humility, and reverence toward our parents, for they are representatives of God. Since the object of honoring is primarily our aged parents, the virtues of patience and understanding are also required. Moreover, we need to respect their freedom and wishes and at the same time discern our own capacities. Therefore, the virtue of prudence is in play. Still, the late Pope John Paul II rightly reminds us that honoring aged parents is necessarily connected with the virtues of charity and justice, for it is both out of love (of God and of neighbor) and the debt we owe our parents that we honor them. As a whole, honoring aged parents is never a simple virtue in real life.

The Practice of Honoring Parents

Several corresponding practices can be proposed here. In the first place, we express gratitude with gladness and by words and deeds. Second, we avoid the use of words or behaviors that may hurt them physically and/or mentally (especially their dignity). Luther rightly said, "Do not accost them roughly, haughtily, and defiantly, but yield to them and be silent, even though they go too far" (*LC* #109). Third, Keenan suggests that we attentively listen to their needs, life experiences, and even complaints. Patient listening lays the ground for discernment and proper caring for them. Fourth, we care for them "with our body and possessions . . . and provide for them when they are old, sick, infirm, or poor" (*LC* ##109–11). One young writer rightly adds that it also includes the care of their mental and spiritual well-being—honoring their decisions, and affirming their dignity, wisdom, and experiences. [11]

For Christians, this young writer further claims that the practices of reconciliation and forgiveness are prerequisite steps to honoring parents who might have hurt us in the past. Within the Catholic tradition, many begin to realize that the sacrament of anointing of the sick—through which the aged, sick, or dying parents receive God's special grace—is a distinctive practice of honoring them. Christian liturgies, like funerals and prayers for the dead, further extend our honor toward them as the ancient Israelites did.

The Exemplars

Jesus is well aware of the tricks played by the people of his time who do not want to care for their elderly parents (Mark 7:10–13). However, based on the narrative of the childhood Jesus (Luke 2:41–51), some wonder if Jesus could be a model for us. The seeming disobedience of Jesus, as some ethicists infer, is to point out that "parents are to be honored as they honor God."[12] I agree with those who believe that Jesus does keep the commandment faithfully. Specifically, they rightly suggest that the speculation that Joseph died young implies that Jesus would have been Mary's sole caretaker. In addition, two narratives from the gospel of John depict Jesus's honor of Mary (2:1–11; 19:26–27). Last but not least, Jesus honors his Heavenly Father by respecting his name and doing his will (Matthew 6:9; John 4:34).

Throughout human history and in almost every culture, we come across stories of how ancient figures exemplify the virtue by carrying out humbling and self-sacrificing deeds. For instance, in my own Chinese culture, one ancient folk story tells of a poor man named Xiang, who loosened his clothes and lay on the ice to melt it, in search of fish to feed his stepmother.[13] And within Christianity, the following moving words of Augustine also disclose his respect and gratitude for his mother Monica:

> [M]y God, our maker, what comparison can there be between the respect with which I deferred to her and the service she rendered to me? Now that I had lost the immense support she gave, my soul was wounded and my life, as it were, torn to pieces, since my life and hers had become a single thing. (IX.12.30)[14]

While these examples of the past coincidently portray the honoring of our loving mothers, I am convinced that in our contemporary society there are many adult children (sons and daughters) who daily honor their parents (fathers and mothers) in ordinary but equally exemplary ways.

The Social, Communal Aspect of the Virtue of Honoring Parents

Honoring parents helps build up the family. Since the family is the sociopolitical basis of our society, many would agree that honoring parents becomes a means and the first step to building society. Moreover, the reality described above shows that the lack of honor by adults (and of obedience by children) to their parents can lead not only to familial problems but also to social ones. Mass media, for instance, subtly portrays parents as incompetent adults. The growing acceptance that "parents are friends of their children" further blurs the necessary boundary between parents and their children. Society's tolerance (and even promotion) of unhealthy individualistic and consumer cultures, as well as certain political systems, also contributes to the belief among young adults that "no authority need be acknowledged unless it personally suits us."[15] All these undermine the need to honor our parents. Conversely, society ought to promote the fourth commandment.

Therefore, by honoring our aged parents, we challenge these values, views, and cultural norms of our modern society. In practice, as some rightly insist, honor would also urge the government to both provide preventive and constructive measures that attend to the problem of elder abuse (e.g., through education) and to assist adult citizens who care for their aged parents (e.g., by means of health care policy and subsidies). In this way, the virtue associated with the Fourth Commandment parallels the Confucian view that if we are able to manage our family through the cultivation of virtues, we will be able to manage the society and the world as well.

NOTES

1. For a discussion of these arguments, see Patrick D. Miller, *The Ten Commandments* (Louisville, KY: Westminster John Knox Press, 2009), 170–74.
2. Fretheim argues that causal relationship does not exist in the formulation and hence rejects the idea of "promise" or "reward."
3. David Klinghoffer, *Shattered Tablets* (New York: Doubleday, 2007), 102–3; Anathea E. Portier-Young, "Response," in *The Ten Commandments for Jews, Christians, and Others*, ed. Roger E. Van Harn (Grand Rapids, MI: Eerdmans, 2007), 100.
4. See Klinghoffer, *Shattered Tablets*, 107–8.
5. See Ernest J. Lewis, *Light for the Journey: Living the Ten Commandments* (Waco, TX: Word Books, 1986); Portier-Young, "Response," 105.
6. G. Corwin Stoppel, *Living Words: The Ten Commandments for the Twenty-first Century* (Cambridge, MA: Cowley, 2005), 75.
7. I find noteworthy Harrelson's question on whether keeping the aged parents at home is necessarily a good thing to do or not. See his "No Contempt for the Family," in *The Ten Commandments: The Reciprocity of Faithfulness*, ed. William P. Brown (Louisville, KY: Westminster John Knox Press, 2004), 242–43.
8. "Duty" is highlighted by the *Catechism of the Catholic Church* (##2199, 2217–18).
9. See Pope John Paul II, *Letter to Families*, February 2, 1994, www.vatican.va/holy_father/john_paul_ii/letters/documents/hf_jp-ii_let_02021994_families_en.html.
10. See Plato, *Laws*, Bk. IV, trans. Benjamin Jowett, http://philosophy.eserver.org/plato/laws.txt; Aristotle, *Nicomachean Ethics*, trans. J. A. K. Thomson (London: Penguin Books, 1976), 9.2.8.
11. Portier-Young, "Response," 106.
12. Stanley M. Hauerwas and William H. Willimon, *The Truth about God: The Ten Commandments in Christian Life* (Nashville, TN: Abingdon Press, 1999), 71.
13. Guo Ju-jing, *The Twenty-Four Filial Exemplars*, trans. David K. Jordon, http://weber.ucsd.edu/~dkjordan/scriptorium/shiaw/TwentyfourEnglish.pdf.
14. Augustine, *Confessions*, trans. H. Chadwick (Oxford: Oxford University Press, 1991), 174.
15. Hauerwas and Willimon, *The Truth about God*, 75.

Chapter Nine

The Fifth Commandment in Exodus 20:13

You shall not murder [kill].

WHAT DID THE TEXT COMMAND?

The fifth commandment is the first that deals with relationships among equals in society. It is among the three shortest formulations (the others are the sixth and the seventh) in the Decalogue. Each of them is formed by two Hebrew words and contains no motivation clause or sanction. Their brevity has sometimes led scholars to comment that these three commandments offer no new insight for ancient Israel (and our contemporary civil societies as well) because even the ancient Near Eastern world would similarly prohibit these acts.

Still, for the Israelites these prohibitions are unusual in that they are incorporated into the Decalogue: [1] the fifth commandment relies on previous commandments for its claim—life is given by God through our parents and hence belongs to God and God alone. On the other hand, the protection of human life is the starting point in moving out into the realm of life with others. The protection of other aspects of life, like marriage, reputation, and property, flows naturally from this fundamental protection. In this way, Exodus 20:13 and the remaining commandments share the same general objective of protecting another Israelite's life. They all embody not only ethical but also clear religious values.

In contrast to this version, all the identified parallel texts within the Hebrew Bible have much longer formulations by adding particularity; for instance, in Deuteronomy 27:24 the law prohibits taking another's life by killing in secret. In other cases, the manner, object, or penalty of taking life is clarified (e.g., Exodus 21:14). Moreover, there are many legal texts that deal with other issues of life-taking and protecting life (e.g., Deuteronomy 19:1–22:8). As we shall see, Numbers 35 specifically contains a detailed, extended discussion of killing that throws light on our understanding of the fifth commandment.

Apart from these legal texts, the Hebrew Bible also contains a good number of narratives that involve intentional killing or murder, such as the well-known stories of Cain's murder and the plot to kill Joseph (Genesis 4:1–16; 37:1–20). As Miller notes, though they do not explicitly use the word "murder" in the texts, many of these narratives, such as David's plot to let Bathsheba's husband be killed in a war (2 Samuel 11–12), are intentional killings done by the powerful in society. As a whole, these parallel texts show that life-taking can be a legal matter as well as a moral issue.

Although the prohibition of the commandment looks self-evident, there exists a dichotomy regarding its translation:[2] the older English Bible translates the commandment as "You shall not kill," while more recent translations adopt the phrase "You shall not murder." The root cause of this dichotomy seems to lie in the exact meaning of the Hebrew word *ratsach*—does it refer to the specific unauthorized, intentional killing of another, or taking a human life in general?

Those who opt for a narrower meaning note that other words are used throughout the Hebrew Bible to illustrate killing, and these words appear far more frequently than *ratsach* does.[3] They claim that *ratsach* points particularly to "illegal killing inimical to the community" or "illegal impermissible violence."[4] Some of them, while not focusing on the legal aspect, believe that it refers to blood vengeance or all kinds of willful killing.[5]

Among those who argue in the opposite direction, one scholar maintains that the verb has diverse (and at times ambiguous) meanings and uses, ranging from accidental killing to killing out of hatred.[6] Others, however, suggest that the original meaning of the verb has gone through noticeable development from a broader to a more specific one.

There are also those who, like Miller, claim that the commandment clearly forbids some other forms of killing. Even taking another's life unintentionally (or without hatred) "does not mean that the act of killing is removed from the frame of reference of the commandment."[7]

Taken together, it seems more appropriate to uphold the more inclusive translation, "You shall not kill." It points to taking seriously the other's life and, as we shall see, even unintentional killing deserves some form of penalty. Also, it challenges those killings done in the name of the society. And the emphasis is more on intentionality and the inner movement of the will than on the legality of the outward act alone. Hence, the commandment would also prohibit any violent acts against another person out of hatred (or other inner movements) that might result in taking another's life.

We now turn to some issues that are not pronounced in the commandment. The first deals with the subject and object of the verb. The general view is that the lives of individual Israelites (men and women) are the presupposed objects of protection. Yet some biblical texts inform us that the lives of the slave and even of the thief (but not the fetus in the womb) seem to be protected, too (Exodus 21:20–25; 22:1–2). In line with the more inclusive view that I hold regarding killing, I too claim that all human beings are objects of protection.

Regarding those who are responsible for the act itself—in the case of intentional killing—apart from the one who literally performs the killing, a wide range of people are understood as "murderers" by the community. They include those who approve the act, assist in the act, abuse their authority against the weaker members, and (under certain circumstances) avenge murder (e.g., 2 Samuel 12:9; Numbers 35:27). They deserve the death penalty (e.g., Numbers 35:16). Those who take the life of another unintentionally are not called murderers, even though they are still responsible for the death of the victim. They are allowed to take refuge in certain designated cities for a fixed period of time (e.g., Joshua 20:1–6).

A second issue concerns the rationale behind the prohibition itself. Childs notes that the ancient understanding of God's lordship of life, manifested in Genesis 9:6, is in view: we are created in the image of God. Our lives belong to God, who alone has the authority to claim them. We are God's agents and bearers of life only. Taking a person's life violates God's dominion and our vocation. Moreover, for Israelites, taking a life pollutes creation and despoils God's created order (Leviticus 17:11). As a whole, Miller rightly comments that the commandment is directly grounded in what we call nowadays "the theological anthropology" of the Hebrew Bible.

The violation of God's lordship of life is thus a very serious matter in ancient Israelite society. As mentioned earlier, the one who kills intentionally deserves the death penalty. No atonement or ransom is allowed to substitute for the death penalty (Numbers 35:31). The death penalty is the only solution because murder means killing God in effigy. The murderer's life is thus now owed to nobody but God alone.[8] Yet the fifth commandment does not include that sanction. It thus gives the impression that certain kinds of killing are permissible.

One related issue emerging from the discussion of the death penalty is the institution of capital punishment in ancient Israel. It is one of the only two legitimate procedures for taking a life.[9] In the Hebrew Bible the matter is treated on several occasions, such as Deuteronomy 21:22–23 (which gives instruction on how it is to be conducted) and Leviticus 24:10–23 (which is concerned with matters regarding the community and fairness toward all people). Generally speaking, the legitimacy of capital punishment is grounded in the view that the community acts on behalf of God to take the life of the one who kills against God's will.

The other legitimate procedure is the institution of war. Throughout the history of Israel, there had been wars that were permitted or even ordered by YHWH (e.g., 1 Samuel 15:2–3). Some thus boldly interpret the commandment as not referring at all to killings in war. However, the Deuteronomic Code (20:1–20) allows exemptions from military service, lays out guidelines for the conduct of war, insists on first seeking peaceful measures, and forbids indiscriminate destruction.[10] Miller rightly comments that these exemptions aim at preventing wrongful killing in war. Thus, one can hardly hold that the fifth commandment exempts matters of war from its ambit.

As a whole, the object of the commandment points to the protection of the life of the neighbor. However, its significance is not limited to individuals but to the entire society of Israel as well. I take Harrelson's view that the commandment is not so much concerned with what would happen in the case of its specific violation as with what kinds of action would destroy human life in a community. It shapes the Israelites' understanding of those violent acts against other human beings within society. Specifically, deliberately taking the life of another person undermines society and its order. Subsequently, the commandment restricts blood vengeance to the community alone. In this way, the function of the commandment is, as Collins rightly summarizes, to regulate life-taking under the control of the community rather than either allowing for personal vendettas or preventing all killing.[11]

Moreover, as Miller, Houtman, and others point out, the commandment offers specific ethical insights to the Israelites. It first clarifies that life is sacred but not absolute—that is, it does not mean that under no circumstances can life be taken by legitimate authority in society. We have to take life seriously, and our protection of life is out of respect for God's dominion. Second, in light of the fifth commandment, the oft-discussed *lex talionis* (i.e., those "life for a life" sayings) in Exodus 21:18–27 and elsewhere cannot be governed by the principle of justice alone. Miller explains that *lex talionis* does not serve as a general ethical principle but highlights the appropriateness of punishment and the danger of inappropriate punishment. In other words, other moral values are taken into account. Third, many of the above-cited narratives bring out the social aspect of the ethics of this commandment—it challenges the violence done by the powerful in Israelite society. Fourth, the commandment also contains a positive ethics for the Israelites: the advance of the well-being of our neighbors. For example, we find in the Hebrew Bible the positive statute for building a parapet on the roof to prevent the accidental fall of anyone that may cause death (Deuteronomy 22:8).

Moreover, since the driving force behind violent and murderous acts is often hatred, jealousy, or greed, the Israelites are called to attend both to their inner emotions and feelings that evoke killing, as well as the positive cultivation of affection for others.

In conclusion, a short commandment as such needs even more attention in order to understand more fully its meaning. And a broader interpretation allows us to retrieve those unspoken concerns of the text, especially those positive moral and religious values that promote and respect God's gift of life.

THE VIRTUE OF RESPECT FOR LIFE

One contemporary writer rightly notes that the fifth commandment often provokes a mixed reaction from people:[12] On the one hand, many Christians may find the prohibition irrelevant, since we would not think to kill another person. On the other hand, we would agree that it is the most important commandment, for what is at stake is life itself.

Nevertheless, many Christians (especially Catholics) quote this commandment when arguing against controversial practices, like abortion and euthanasia. I agree with Holbert that these issues, while important and timely, are not the most basic concerns of the commandment. Indeed, as our exposition shows, the positive attitude of respect for life is a more foundational issue. We need to get the foundational issue out there, as well as our opposition to these life-taking practices. As Keenan notes, Christians oppose many of these life-taking practices because we first respect life.

Is Life Cheap?

As shared in an earlier chapter, I worked in Cambodia over a decade ago. During my two years of living with land-mine victims in our boarding school, I visited on a few occasions the infamous "S-21 Prison" in Phnom Penh and the "Killing Fields" museum just outside the capital. The prison was converted from a high school and was used to interrogate and torture people. The museum, on the other hand, was the place where over fifteen thousand civilians were executed and their bodies dumped. Each time I looked at those lined-up skulls through the glass windows, or when I passed by those fenced spots outside our school where unmarked land mines are found, or when I listened to the stories of our handicapped students after school about how they lost their family members during the Khmer Rouge regime, I could not stop asking myself, "Is life so cheap? Is it not worth more than those five-dollar mines? When do we learn to respect life?"

The Meaning of Respect for Life

The fact that "our lives are a gift from God and hence belong to God" alone offers a sound argument for respecting life. Today the Catholic Church uses the term "sanctity of life" in this regard. By employing the term "sanctity," it emphasizes that human life is more than a gift but is derived from and possessed by the divine. Therefore, whatever is sanctified is absolutely inviolable and demands reverence. Consequently, sanctity of life refers to the inviolability of life and to the reverencing of life. Keenan adds, "When sanctity of life is used in the restrictive sense, it underlines the dominion of God. When it is used in the more universal and general sense, it emphasizes our stewardship."[13]

The sacredness of life is built upon the fact that human beings are created in the image of God. The *Catechism of the Catholic Church*, while in continuity with the traditional view of *imago dei,* further claims that the sacredness of life is derived from the involvement of "the creative action of God and the permanent, special relationship with the Creator" (#2259). Taken together, respect for life means respect for what is sacred and respect for God who is the Creator and source of this sacred life. God alone has the absolute right to give life and bring an end to life. This "respect for God" reminds us of the second commandment we studied earlier.

In line with Jesus's interpretation of the commandment as narrated in the gospels, respect for life draws our attention to the inner movement of the heart. Both Aquinas and Luther thus specifically addressed the issue of handling our anger as a preliminary and important aspect of respecting life. Aquinas, in *Explanations of the Ten Commandments,* reminded us to have self-control and be aware of our words and expressions of anger, even though anger can be justified. He even proposed five practical ways of avoiding anger. Luther, on the other hand, suggested that we should "learn to calm our wrath, and to have a patient, gentle heart" (*LC* #187).

Based on the parable of the last judgment in Matthew 25, Luther further highlighted another important aspect of respect for life—the protection of the life of our neighbor. Consequent positive attitudes toward others include meekness, generosity, patience, calmness, and peace.[14] In a similar fashion, Calvin claimed that respect for life means defending the life of our neighbor; being vigilant in warding off harm, and promoting whatever tends to the other's tranquility. In doing so, we need to acquire a sincere desire for these practices. However, Calvin made it clear that we should defend our neighbor according to our capacity (*ICR* 2.8.39–40). He also highlighted the protection of the soul of our neighbor and was concerned about the "murder of the heart," as Aquinas was.[15]

The respect for the spiritual aspect of life is also shared and expounded by contemporary writers like Chittister: our words and deeds can either promote or destroy another's future and hope. Within the Catholic tradition, respect for human life is extended to include respect for human dignity, which itself embraces respect for the soul, the bodily health, and the integrity of the other person until the moment of death (*CCC* ##2284–2301). By far, we see that respect for life has a strong religious element and covers a lot of aspects, from external acts to inner attitudes that help define its corresponding virtue.

Respect for Life as a Virtue

Subsequently, respect for life as a virtue has two aspects. First, it points to those virtues that liberate us from the temptation to anger and revenge, such as the virtues of calmness, patience, and gentleness at which Luther hinted. Moreover, we need to acquire the virtue of temperance so as to better control our anger. Of course, anger can be virtuous—"when one is angry because it is justly fitting to be angry and within proper limits."[16] Yet our angry words are often an expression of pride (to create the feeling that we have power and importance); as a result, humility is needed to help us recognize our dependence on one another and to treasure nonviolence.

Second, the virtue of respect for life points to those virtues that assist us in protecting the life of our neighbor. Again, the insights of Luther and Calvin are helpful here. Respect for life calls, in the first place, for the cultivation of the Christian virtues of charity and justice, as discussed in chapter 6. Charity is the fundamental attitude from which respect is formed, especially toward those who hurt us. In the light of this view, the virtues of peacemaking with our enemy and of sincerity are involved.[17] Justice, on the other hand, provides us with the needed standard: to respect means not to deprive others of what belongs to them—in this case, life. Finally, vigilance and prudence are important in understanding the needs of others and in discerning how much we can do to protect the lives of others and promote their well-being. Here, the virtue of respect for life shares certain common virtues found in the second and the fourth commandments, and it anticipates the following ones, which are also grounded in respect.

The Practice of Respect for Life

In order to promote the well-being of our neighbor (and ourselves), we first must acquire the habit of carrying out charitable works that will benefit our neighbor's life at different stages, from its beginning until its end. Within the Catholic tradition, for example, the sacrament of the anointing of the sick is an exemplary practice that expresses our respect for the life of the dying (*CCC* ##2299–2300).

To those who hurt us and lead us to anger or even to hatred and revenge, the practice of forgiveness and reconciliation is likewise beneficial (Matthew 5:23–25). Habitual discernment further helps us make prudent judgments regarding how we should promote the life of the other in different situations.

Regarding the handling of our anger, I find Aquinas's Scripture-based practical advice very helpful:[18] not to be provoked to anger quickly (James 1:19); to be aware of its duration and intensity and growth into hatred (Ephesians 4:26; 1 John 3:15); and to be aware of our words and expressions that could lead us to pride (Matthew 5:22). In short, we need both internal and external practices.

The Exemplars

Christians often quote the teaching of Jesus in the Sermon on the Mount as an exemplary way of interpreting the ethical meaning of the fifth commandment (Matthew 5:22). Still, Jesus protects life in the concrete, for example, by ordering Peter to put away his sword during Jesus's arrest in Gethsemane (Matthew 26:52). Most of his miracles are acts of healing (both spiritual and physical) and concrete examples of respecting and promoting life (e.g., Mark 3:1–5).

Jesus is also a model on the matter of anger. Even when Jesus shows anger in his confrontation with the Pharisees, it is solely out of the virtue of righteous anger rather than hatred.

Throughout the history of Christianity, various Christian groups promoting pacifism have emerged, such as the Mennonites, the Amish, and the Quakers. They insist on total rejection of violence based on the above-mentioned teaching of Jesus. While their position on pacifism may not be widely accepted, their nonviolent lifestyle and commitment have demonstrated what a society that respects life could be. In the Catholic Church, for instance, the U.S. Conference of Catholic Bishops pointed to Dorothy Day and Martin Luther King as contemporary models of nonviolence.[19]

The late Pope John Paul II has also been seen as a promoter and exemplar of respect for life through his writings, particularly *Celebrate Life* (1979), *Donum Vitae* (1987), and *Evangelium Vitae* (1995).

In *Evangelium Vitae*, the pope expresses his deep concern about the emerging "culture of death" in our world:

> A life which would require greater acceptance, love and care is considered useless, or held to be an intolerable burden, and is therefore rejected in one way or another. . . . In this way a kind of "conspiracy against life" is unleashed. This conspiracy involves not only individuals . . . but goes far beyond, to the point of damaging and distorting, at the international level, relations between peoples and States.[20]

Here, the virtue of respect for life can help challenge this culture of death.

The Social, Communal Aspect of the Virtue of Respect for Life

The above quotation highlights that respect for life is not simply an individual virtue but one that has a strong social character as well. On the one hand, the virtue helps strengthen the order of the society on all levels. For instance, it points us to the need for promoting peace and reconciliation on the national and international levels. By adopting the language of "right," the Pontifical Biblical Commission claims that respect for life further promotes the right to life, which includes the right to be born, to be educated and live, and to die a natural death.

Chittister adds that the virtue of respect for life could also address social policies such as health care, housing, education, and working conditions. The *Catechism of the Catholic Church* correctly explains that these practices are not simply social programs but fundamental living conditions that allow its citizens to grow and develop (#2288). They are "the very essence of what it means to sustain life for others."[21] We thus have to ask ourselves whether our current social policies concerning these essential means promote life or not.[22]

NOTES

1. See Umberto Cassuto, *A Commentary on the Book of Exodus*, trans. Israel Abrahams (Jerusalem: Magnes Press, Hebrew University, 1967), 246–47; Walter J. Harrelson, *The Ten Commandments and Human Rights* (Macon, GA: Mercer University Press, 1997), 95; and Patrick D. Miller, *The Ten Commandments* (Louisville, KY: Westminster John Knox Press, 2009), 222.

2. Wilma Ann Bailey, "'You Shall Not Kill': The Meaning of RSH (rtsh) in Exodus 20:13," *Encounter* 65, no. 1 (Winter 2004): 39.

3. Ibid., 41. The verb and its noun/participle form predominantly appear in legal codes, narratives, and the prophetic/wisdom literature.

4. Johann Jakob Stamm, "Sprachliche Erwägungen zum Gebot 'Du Sollst nicht toten,'" *TZ* 1 (1945): 81–90, as cited in Brevard S. Childs, *The Book of Exodus* (Philadelphia, PA: Westminster Press, 1974), 420.

5. H. Graf Reventlow, *Gebot und Predigt im Dekalog* (Gütersloh: Mohn, 1962), as cited in Childs, *The Book of Exodus*, 420.

6. For a detailed discussion of these diverse meanings and applications, see Bailey, "'You Shall Not Kill,'" 41–53. However, Miller and others comment that Bailey's arguments are not without problem. See Childs, *The Book of Exodus*, 421; Miller, *The Ten Commandments*, 224–62.

7. Miller, *The Ten Commandments*, 226.

8. Certain atonement can be permitted in other serious crimes that also deserve the death penalty—such as striking/cursing parents and adultery. See Walter C. Kaiser Jr., *Toward Old Testament Ethics* (Grand Rapids, MI: Zondervan, 1991), 91–92.

9. Stephen Kaufman, "The Structure of Deuteronomic Law," *Maarav* 1, no. 2 (1978–1979): 135, as cited in Miller, *The Ten Commandments*, 234.

10. The seemingly contradictory statute of total annihilation in verses 15–17, as Miller tries to resolve it, is a conditional one—verse 18 indicates that the statute has the first commandment in view.

11. John J. Collins, *Introduction to the Hebrew Bible* (Minneapolis: Augsburg Fortress, 2004), 129.

12. Bernd Wannenwetsch, "You Shall Not Kill—What Does It Take? Why We Need the Other Commandments If We Are to Abstain from Killing," in *I Am the Lord Your God: Christian Reflections on the Ten Commandments*, ed. Carl E. Braaten and Christopher R. Seitz (Grand Rapids, MI: Eerdmans, 2005), 149–50.

13. See James F. Keenan, "The Concept of Sanctity of Life and Its Use in Contemporary Bioethical Discussion," in *Sanctity of Life and Human Dignity*, ed. Kurt Bayertz (Dordrecht: Kluwer Academics, 1996), 2.

14. See J. Georg Walch, ed., *Luthers Sämtliche Schriften*, 2nd ed. (St. Louis, MO: Concordia, 1880–1910), 3:1262, as cited in Wannenwetsch, "You Shall Not Kill—What Does It Take?," 156. See also *LC* ##189–94.

15. That is, killing the soul by "inducing it to commit mortal sin." See Aquinas, "Explanation," http://dhspriory.org/thomas/TenCommandments.htm.

16. Ibid.

17. The virtue of peacemaking will be discussed in chapter 23.

18. Aquinas, "Explanation."

19. See U.S. Conference of Catholic Bishops, *The Challenge of Peace*, www.usccb.org/sdwp/international/TheChallengeofPeace.pdf.

20. Pope John Paul II, *Evangelium Vitae*, Encyclical Letter from March 25, 1995, http://www.vatican.va/holy_father/john_paul_ii/encyclicals/documents/hf_jp-ii_enc_25031995_evangelium-vitae_en.html.

21. Joan Chittister, *The Ten Commandments: Laws of the Heart* (Maryknoll, NY: Orbis Books, 2006), 72.

22. One concrete social practice is capital punishment. I will briefly touch on this issue in chapter 12.

Chapter Ten

The Sixth Commandment in Exodus 20:14

You shall not commit adultery.

WHAT DID THE TEXT COMMAND?

Like the fifth commandment, Exodus 20:14 is among the shortest formulations in the Decalogue. Generally, it is concerned with certain sexual behaviors that are unacceptable in the community. Some scholars, like Dozeman and Harrelson, try to explain the Israelites' concern about these matters from a social perspective: ancient Israel was "a patrilineal society in which paternity is essential for inheritance law."[1] This and other reasons partly contribute to the explicit rejection in the Torah of certain sexual activities, such as those listed in Deuteronomy 27:20–23.

Although not all of these scriptural texts consider the act of adultery itself, we find a good number of parallel texts on prohibiting it (e.g., Deuteronomy 22:22–24). The prohibition also appears—in tandem with murder, stealing, and false witness—in those "lists" of the prophets (e.g., Jeremiah 7:9) and in other "decalogues." Furthermore, wisdom literature writers are known for prominently warning against adultery and identifying its danger and social consequences (e.g., Proverbs 7).

In brief, these references, in one way or another, affirm the gravity of adultery and the great concerns of the writers. Still, the rather large number of scriptural prohibitions against adultery further leads some to conclude that adulterous acts were all too common within the Israelite community. Indeed, the attempt to commit adultery had been a prominent feature of the stories of the patriarchs; among them the affair between King David and Bathsheba is the most famous and significant example (2 Samuel 11–12).

On the other hand, the sixth commandment is connected to other commandments in various ways. At first glance, it seems to share the same object with that of the ninth. Moreover, if one perceives the purpose of the commandment as safeguarding marriage, then 20:14 joins the commandment on honoring parents in protecting the institution of the family. In addition, the sixth commandment is indirectly connected to the first because, as noted in chapter 5, adultery has been a metaphor used by the prophets for idolatry. Therefore, we can confidently suggest that adultery is not simply a private affair between two people but touches other issues.

Regarding the meaning of the commandment, we first turn to the Hebrew verb *na'af* ("commit adultery") for insights. Houtman observes that it is not a commonly used verb in the Hebrew Bible. Widely used instead is the term "to lie with," which simply expresses sexual intercourse (e.g., Genesis 19:32–34). Similar terms employed include "take/go into" (e.g., Genesis 38:2) and "come in to" (e.g., Genesis 38:15–16). They all take a feminine object. In other words, the "object" of the verb is specified. The verb *na'af*, by contrast, as Miller points out, is a stand-alone general term without any object attached. Thus, the object of adultery can be a man or a woman. Still, this verb has an "internal" qualification: it refers to having a sexual relationship outside marriage. Some ancient Israelite idioms further hint at a unique understanding of adultery: "[A] man can only commit adultery against a marriage other than his own, the woman only against her own."[2] What is decisive is the marital status of the woman involved. Men (married or not) commit adultery *only* with married or betrothed women.

Second, Childs informs us that adultery has been treated very differently from fornication in the Hebrew Bible. For instance, as will be seen later, adulterers are sentenced to death while fornicators are not. Even offenses like seduction and rape only demand indissoluble marriage with the victim and/or monetary compensation (e.g., Deuteronomy 22:28–29). This in turn gives the impression that fornication and other premarital sexual relations are not grave matters.

Third, subsequently, one may further deduce that having sexual intercourse with a woman who is not married/betrothed may be permissible for men. This deduction points to the issue of laxity regarding polygamy and prostitution. In the case of polygamy, beginning with Lamech (Genesis 4:19) a good number of patriarchs (especially Solomon) have more than one wife. The Hebrew Bible hints that it is generally permitted, although one has to follow certain limitations in favoring one wife over the other (Exodus 21:10). Still, monogamy remains the norm in view and is especially praised (e.g., Proverbs 31:10–31) because polygamy often brings complications that threaten the entire Israelite community. Ancient Israel seems to tolerate prostitution, too. However, since by definition prostitution refers to casual sexual intercourse between two persons who are unrelated, it is at least morally condemned.

In sum, we may comment that there exists an apparent double standard (and inequality) among the Israelites in treating married men and women who are involved in extramarital sexual relations.[3] A married woman is perceived as the sole determining factor for adultery and is alone to be blamed for causing damage to her marriage and family. Married men, in contrast, are never criticized for hurting *their own* wives or marriages, though—as we shall see—if they commit adultery, they are put to death for violating the other man's marriage. Moreover, the specific nature of the Hebrew verb for adultery and the comparisons between adultery and other sexual behaviors further signify the uniqueness and gravity of adultery.

To whom is the commandment addressed? Despite use of the masculine verb form (which the rest of the Decalogue also employs), the nature of the Hebrew verb, *na'af*, has led me to the view that the commandment is not limited to free male Israelites but includes women as well. As in the previous case of "honoring parents," so here, the originally implied male addressee serves only as the starting point of reference in determining the audience intended.

Nevertheless, the implicit rationale of the commandment, as Patrick suggests, seems to be, to use modern terms, sanctity of marriage. Miller offers some helpful insights on the marital sanctity within the Israelite tradition: First, there exists within marriage a commitment to an intimate and mutually exclusive relationship as well as to a partnership between husband and wife (Genesis 2:18, 24). Physical union that reflects such intimacy is central to this relationship. Second, there is a subsequent, procreative goal within marriage in which children are crucial to the continuity and preservation of the family line (Genesis 1:28). Third, it is through marriage that family is formed and supported and its stability and wholeness maintained. This in turn secures the economic and physical needs of the individual members and the order of Israel's society, for family is the nucleus of the community.

Therefore, adultery signifies a violation of the fidelity between two married persons. The adulterer also infringes on the other person's exclusive right with one's spouse that is given in the bond of marriage. In the case of incest, it further confuses family relationships and disrupts the social order (e.g., Leviticus 18:16–18). It is a great crime against individuals, the family, and the entire Israelite community.

This could explain why adulterers and adulteresses caught in the act are sentenced to death (e.g., Leviticus 20:10). We also learn from early Jewish documents that pestilence and the death of the unborn child of the adulterer are perceived as consequences of adultery and forms of punishment (e.g., 2 Samuel 12:14). However, despite what is written elsewhere, the sixth commandment does not pronounce any sanctions at all.

As far as the function and significance of the commandment for the Israelites is concerned, the prohibition clearly protects the institution of marriage.[4] However, some, like Miller, insist that it specifically protects the marriage of *one's neighbor*. They explain that since the previous commandment is concerned with the neighbor's life, it is logical that this commandment aims at protecting the neighbor's marriage. Only when the marriage of the neighbor is protected will one's own marriage be protected as well. This makes sense if we focus on the male adulterer alone. In also turning to the adulteress, the commandment protects her own marriage. Based on our understanding of the nature of the Hebrew verb, I take the more inclusive view that the commandment protects one's own marriage *as well as* that of the other against which adultery would represent a violation. Furthermore, since marriage is never a private, casual matter for Israelites, the prohibition also helps preserve the family and the order of the society.

A third function of the prohibition is a theological one. We have already recalled that in the prophetic literature, adultery is often employed as a metaphor to describe Israel's idolatry and disloyalty to YHWH (e.g., Hosea 1–3). 20:14 could serve as a warning against the Israelites' violation of their covenantal relationship with YHWH (Exodus 34:15–16). As a whole, this warning is, then, a twofold one: it warns against infidelity and calls for faithfulness in marriage, and it warns against idolatry and highlights the importance of faithfulness in Israel's covenantal relationship with YHWH.

Finally, the commandment offers important moral insights to individual Israelites and the entire community. Adultery is not just a crime within the society but also a grave personal sin against God and a source of personal guilt. We learn this directly from the reactions of those involved. Among these, the emotional words of David are the example par excellence: "I have sinned against the Lord" (2 Samuel 12:13). These stories of adultery become, using Miller's words, a "communal memory" for Israel's moral life that reminds the community of the destructive power of unapproved sexual relations. In positive terms, the commandment calls for certain attitudes among Israelites, such as fidelity, that help sustain and protect their marriages. The protection of the marriage of one's neighbor further emphasizes the need for justice and charity. Using the language of "respect," the commandment thus calls for respect in different levels of "exclusive" spousal relationships that both the individual and the neighbor have; therefore, more than one virtue seems necessary.

THE JOINT VIRTUE OF CHASTITY AND FIDELITY

Many Christians would naturally refer to Jesus's teaching on lust as the core moral teaching of this and the ninth commandments (Matthew 5:27–28). While this interpretation rightly focuses on internal attitudes and thoughts rather than acts, few would explore in detail what the needed positive dispositions and attitudes for married life would be. Among them some highlight the need for forgiveness between the spouses; others innovatively suggest the respect for the human body. The exposition of the verse shows, however, that moral values and attitudes that respect corresponding relationships in one's own marriage and that of the neighbor are crucial. I consider chastity and fidelity as such fundamental virtues.

The Changing View of Marriage and Sex

In many modern metropolitan areas marriage is only one of many possibilities for having sex and children. Consensual sex is often accepted without much debate. Even some married couples perceive consensual sex outside marriage as permissible "as long as the people involved understand why they are doing it and as long as nobody gets hurt."[5] This kind of "don't ask, don't tell" strategy, as some ethicists rightly note, risks the danger of self-deceit and exploitation.

Changing views toward marriage and sex, nonetheless, influence the prevalence of divorce and infidelity in our society. I agree with Klinghoffer that among factors that contribute to their growth, the role of mass media cannot be ignored. As seen in popular TV shows like *Sex and the City* and *Desperate Housewives*, adultery is often portrayed as a commonplace. What virtues can we learn from the sixth commandment in order to counteract this unhealthy trend and safeguard marriages?

The Meaning of Chastity and Fidelity

Aquinas taught that Christian marriage is a sacrament contracted before the Church, has God as the witness to the bond of fidelity, and legitimates conjugal intercourse between a man and a woman.[6] In order to protect and sustain their marriage, spouses have to respect both the marriage bond they freely made and the conjugal act proper and exclusive to them. This points to the relationship with one's own spouse as well as to one's own sexuality. These two aspects are inseparable within the context of marriage.

For Catholics, the bond of marriage is grounded in the covenant the spouses freely contracted—the promise they give to each other, definitively and totally. This covenant imposes upon them the obligation to preserve it as indissoluble (*CCC* #2364). To do so means husband and wife have to be faithful to each other. It must also be "the willingness to go on growing in a relationship."[7] Marital fidelity thus enables the couple to live a more flourishing life and can be seen as "a practice *intrinsic* to" the happiness and wholeness of marriage.[8]

Moreover, it is in and through our bodies and our bodily expressions that we "communicate the truth of our relationships" and become aware that we are faithful to the one in relationship.[9] Therefore, fidelity in the conjugal act is the bodily expression of faithfulness toward one another. For Christians, as one writer remarks, since this covenant is made in front of the Church and witnessed by God, marital fidelity also points to living out the married life with trust and commitment to God.[10]

Regarding sexuality, the claim of the *Catechism of the Catholic Church* that it "affects all aspects of the human person in the unity of his body and soul" (#2332) seems to be welcomed by both Christians and non-Christians. It is concerned with one's affectivity and the capacity to love and to procreate, which pertain to the person's innermost being (#2362). In short, as many note, sexuality is at the core of a person's humanity. In order to attain this unity of body and soul, the *Catechism* turns to the vocation to chastity.

For Luther, chastity is associated not only with external conjugal acts but also with our thoughts, words, and the entire body (*LC* #203). Calvin further noted that one may still be "inwardly inflamed with lust" even without an outward sexual act (*ICR* 2.8.43). He thus claimed that we also need to attain purity, for chastity is the purity of mind and of body. In contemporary terms, it is depicted as "the successful integration of sexuality within the person" (*CCC* #2337).

Chastity and Fidelity as a Joint Virtue

Aquinas also taught that chastity is a special virtue. It is the moderation of "the concupiscence relating to venereal pleasures" by reason (*ST* II.II. 151.2). It comes under the virtue of temperance, which is "chiefly concerned with those passions that tend towards sensible goods, viz. desire and pleasure" (*ST* II.II. 141.3). Aquinas further clarified that purity regards external signs such as impure looks or touches while chastity regards sexual union. Thus the virtue of purity can be seen as a form of chastity and "as expressing a circumstance of chastity" (*ST* II.II. 151.4). Despite these categorical differences, Calvin insisted that all three virtues (temperance, chastity, and purity) are needed to restrain our indulgence (*ICR* 2.8.43, 44). The *Catechism* further suggests the acquisition of the virtues of integrity and friendship—chastity finds expression in one's friendship with the neighbor (#2347).

The virtue of fidelity, on the other hand, points to faithfulness and trust toward one another in the first place. It also calls for exclusiveness as well as justice and perseverance, for marital fidelity is possible only between two equal lovers who keep the covenant for their entire life. It is the "least natural of virtues" and an "alien ideal" because lifelong commitment demands enormous effort.[11] Nevertheless, for Christians it is also an expression of obedience to God. And the virtue of charity is needed, for it is the foundational source of mutual growth and fidelity.[12] As a whole, though this joint virtue focuses on specific relationships, it shares certain dispositions with its preceding commandments.

The Practice of Chastity and Fidelity

Calvin thoughtfully proposed a list of things that we should avoid doing for the sake of preserving the purity of chastity: we should not let "[our] mind burn within with evil concupiscence, [our] eyes wanton after corrupting objects, nor [our] body be decked for allurement; let neither [our] tongue by filthy speeches, nor [our] appetite by intemperance, entice the mind to corresponding thoughts" (*ICR* 2.8.44). Unfortunately, this detailed list is still focused on prohibitions.

The *Catechism*, in contrast, offers some constructive suggestions: one needs to "[acquire] self-knowledge, practice of an ascesis adapted to the situations that confront him [*sic*], obedience to God's commandments, exercise of the moral virtues, and fidelity to prayer" (#2340). It also requires the practice of self-mastery. For a married couple, the cultivation of chastity is not a private practice but can benefit from mutual help. The couple thus needs to "see in this time of testing a discovery of mutual respect . . . and the hope of receiving one another from God. . . . They will help each other grow in chastity" (#2350). Here, the *Catechism* rightly reminds us of the role of spiritual practices of which we seldom think.

The practice of fidelity, in comparison, is an explicit mutual practice that is "the-other-oriented" and motivated by love. It is because "a person committed to the practice of sexual fidelity can be severely hurt by the infidelity, the violence, the emotional abuse or even the loveless indifference of the partner."[13] Hence both the husband and the wife should be sincere toward one another. Calvin further proposed that both spouses have to acquire sobriety in their conjugal love so as to safeguard the dignity of the married life (*ICR* 2.8.44). In other words, the practice of marital fidelity implies certain modesty in sexual intercourse so that one is not driven by an indulgence of sexual pleasure that leads one to seek self-satisfaction inside and outside the bond of marriage. I find this proposed practice most urgent in today's society, which is often driven by wants rather than needs. Finally, the spouses need to trust each other and be open and honest to one another totally.

The Exemplars

One wonders if Jesus can be an exemplar here: although Jesus lived a life of chastity, he does not say much about married life except to warn against the danger of lust. Paul, in contrast, has written rather extensively on the issue of married life in a straightforward manner, especially in 1 Corinthians 6–7 and Ephesians 5:21–33. Although 1 Corinthians 6–7 has been one of the most controversial sections of his writings, some scholars today claim that Paul seems to echo much of the positive Israelite appreciation for the body and sexuality, and the principle of reciprocity runs throughout his entire writings.[14]

Within the Catholic tradition, we note that two couples were beatified in recent centuries. The first couple was Luigi Beltrame Quattrocchi and Maria Corsini of the twentieth century. Pope John Paul II praised them for "their fidelity to the gospel and their heroic virtues . . . as spouses and parents."[15] The second were Louis Martin and Marie Celine Guerin, who lived in the nineteenth century. The Martins are praised as "exemplary witness of conjugal love, which is bound to stimulate Christian couples in practicing virtue."[16] We heard from their daughter St. Theresa that their virtue of purity was most outstanding. However, they are the *only* two cases where married couples are honored by the Church (and neither couple is canonized). I admit that Church beatification might not be the best source of modeling in today's challenging married life.[17]

By turning to some American married couples in real life, I find that fidelity, chastity, and holiness are expressed in various ways. For example, within the field of academia, Denise and (the late) John Carmody are remembered for their companioned dedication to the Church and to theology. *Together* they authored and edited many books, lectured widely, and traveled around the world. They were honored together, time and again.[18]

Beyond the academic circle, I recall meeting Christian couples and families who went to Cambodia as lay missionaries. I was edified by how they lived out their love of God and of each other at the same time as they sacrificed a comfortable lifestyle and served the needs of others. And I find their examples have an impact not only on those they serve but also on society itself.

The Social, Communal Aspect of the Virtues of Chastity and Fidelity

Since the structure of a society is built upon families that are properly formed through marriage, the joint virtue of chastity and fidelity would logically have an impact on both familial and social levels.

On the societal level, the virtues challenge the above-mentioned un-healthy mentality toward marriage and sex by denouncing infidelity and extramarital affairs, which disturb relationships on all levels. Paul Ramsey rightly points out that extramarital sexual intercourse, for example, raises the concrete questions of contraception and abortion, as well as the legitimacy of the child born outside wedlock, all of which are at the same time ethical and social issues.[19] Subsequently, society and its government have to protect the marriages of its citizens and prevent and tackle those ethical and social issues by appropriate means.

The virtue of chastity, though primarily focused on the integrity of the person, involves "a *cultural effort*, for there is 'an inter-dependence between personal betterment and the improvement of society'" (CCC #2344). For instance, when citizens live more chaste, integrated lives, social issues such as prostitution and pornography might be more comprehensively addressed. Therefore, society might seek constructive measures (such as education) that assist its citizens to grow in sexual integrity. In brief, the sixth commandment and its virtues are needed for today's society as much as they were for the Israelite community.

NOTES

1. Thomas B. Dozeman, *Commentary on Exodus* (Grand Rapids, MI: Eerdmans, 2009), 494.

2. J. J. Stamm and M. E. Andrew, *The Ten Commandments in Recent Research*, SBT 2.2 (London: SCM, 1967), 100, as cited in Brevard S. Childs, *The Book of Exodus* (Philadelphia, PA: Westminster Press, 1974), 422.

3. For further discussion on the question of double standard, see David Klinghoffer, *Shattered Tablets* (New York: Doubleday, 2007), 150–53.

4. Surprisingly, Harrelson claims that adultery in ancient Israel may not destroy marriages as much as one would imagine. See his Walter J. Harrelson, *The Ten Commandments and Human Rights* (Macon, GA: Mercer University Press, 1997), 109–10.

5. Stanley M. Hauerwas and William H. Willimon, *The Truth about God: The Ten Commandments in Christian Life* (Nashville, TN: Abingdon Press, 1999), 100.

6. Aquinas, "Explanation," http://dhspriory.org/thomas/TenCommandments.htm; *ST* Supplementum III. 42.4.

7. Joan Chittister, *The Ten Commandments: Laws of the Heart* (Maryknoll, NY: Orbis Books, 2006), 84.

8. Gregory L. Jones, "Fidelity Makes You Happy," *Christian Century* 115, no. 24 (September 9–16, 1998): 832. See also John Grabowski, *Sex and Virtue: An Introduction to Sexual Ethics* (Washington, DC: Catholic University of America Press, 2003).

9. James F. Keenan, *Commandments of Compassion* (Franklin, WI: Sheed & Ward, 1999), 34.

10. Ernest J. Lewis, *Light for the Journey: Living the Ten Commandments* (Waco, TX: Word Books, 1986), 117.

11. Gilbert Meilaender, "Touched by the Eternal," *Theology Today* 50, no. 4 (January 1994): 539, 541.

12. See John J. Snyder, "Love as the Source of Growth and Fidelity: A Philosophical Discussion," *Christian Marriage Today* (1985): 89–109.

13. Jones, "Fidelity Makes You Happy," 832.

14. See Raymond F. Collins, *First Corinthians, Sacra Pagina* (Collegeville, MN: Liturgical Press, 1999), 224–305.

15. Claire Schaeffer-Duffy, "Models of Holiness and Married Life: Couple's Beatification Spotlights Marital Sanctity—Luigi and Maria Beltrame Quattrocchi," *National Catholic Reporter*, December 28, 2001, http://findarticles.com/p/articles/mi_m1141/is_8_38/ai_82066335.

16. Pilgrims of St. Michael, "Beatification of Louis and Zelie Martin, the Parents of St. Theresa of the Child Jesus," *Michael* (November–December 2008), www.michaeljournal.org/martins.htm.

17. For example, some wonder "why the church would put forth, as its first example of matrimonial holiness, a couple who lived more than half their life together as celibates?" See Schaeffer-Duffy, "Models of Holiness and Married Life."

18. See Mark Ralkowski, "Memorial Mass for Theologian John Carmody," *The Santa Clara*, January 18, 2011, http://www.thesantaclara.com/2.14535/memorial-mass-for-theologian-john-carmody-1.1874651#. I am in debt to Lisa Sowle Cahill for identifying the Carmodys and other Christian couples as present-time models for holiness.

19. Paul Ramsey, "A Christian Approach to the Question of Sexual Relations outside of Marriage," *Journal of Religion* 45, no. 2 (1965): 106.

Chapter Eleven

The Seventh Commandment in Exodus 20:15

You shall not steal.

WHAT DID THE TEXT COMMAND?

We now turn to the third and last of the commandments that contain only two Hebrew words. The seventh commandment, like the previous two, seems to be so self-evident that it hardly elicits much scholarly interest by specialists. For example, even prominent scholars such as Miller spend only half the number of pages they normally do with the other nine commandments. [1]

However, there is still much we can learn about the commandment. In the first place, the crime of stealing appears in those "lists" of the prophets, and its prohibition finds important parallels in Exodus and Deuteronomy (e.g., Deuteronomy 24:14). These parallels provide useful information about sanctions and clarify the scope of the matters touched on by this commandment—for example, restitution (Exodus 21:37).

We also find a number of passages where stealing is actually narrated (e.g., Genesis 27). The most famous story, however, is the plot of Jezebel and King Ahab to take possession of Naboth's vineyard by deceit and abuse of power, and Naboth's eventual murder (1 Kings 21). The narrative highlights the rich stealing from the poor, and the cry of the victims is often heard (e.g., Nehemiah 5:1–5).

Here, although stealing as a crime may appear insignificant, these scriptural texts reveal that it is understood by the prophets and the community as a serious issue that connects with other grave crimes, such as murder.

When we turn to the Decalogue itself, Exodus 20:15 seems to overlap with the tenth commandment, just as the sixth commandment does with the ninth. Yet Miller demonstrates how it is related to the rest of the Decalogue: both scriptural texts and human experiences show a mutual affinity among stealing, false witnessing, and coveting. The seventh commandment is thus related to the commandments that follow. Specifically, there are extensive connections between stealing and false witnessing: they are mentioned side by side in the Bible (e.g., Leviticus 6:1–5). Similarly, their positive corollaries are also mutually dependent (e.g., a good reputation is essential to the acquisition of property, which in turn builds up one's good name). Additional connections might be made with other commandments—for instance, when the first commandment warns against worshipping idols, it also implicitly joins 20:15 in renouncing an improper attitude and attachment to material things. All in all, these connections confirm that stealing is not a light matter, as the term might otherwise imply.

The Hebrew verb *ganab* ("steal") refers to the "unlawful secret taking of another person's property without the owner's knowledge and permission."[2] Childs clarifies that it differs from other inappropriate acts of taking in that it is characterized by secrecy. However, the usage of the verb in the Hebrew Bible is not limited to denote taking something away secretly but includes all kinds of deceptive behavior commonly practiced in ancient Israel, such as the use of inaccurate scales and weights (Deuteronomy 25:13–16). The general goal of these practices is the enrichment of the self at the expense of others. In other words, one steals for economic gain.[3] These actions, as mentioned above, are criticized by the prophets and writers of wisdom literature.

In order to resolve the matter of the overlap between the seventh and the tenth commandments, some propose to distinguish the two by giving a restricted interpretation of the object of the seventh commandment.[4] They declare that the original form of the prohibition contains a concrete object—human beings. In this view, 20:15 was directed against kidnapping free Israelites (e.g., Exodus 21:16).[5] These authors further claim that because the sanction attached to acts prohibited by the previous two commandments is the death penalty, the seventh one should likewise refer to a grave matter, such as the stealing of a human being.

Those who disagree argue that although kidnapping happened in ancient Israel, it was such a rare practice as to be easily detected. However, if kidnapping does not refer to the secret imprisoning of a free person but rather is a metaphor for the practice of slavery (and the slave trade), then one has to admit that it was widely practiced in the society of that time. People could be seized and sold into slavery in foreign lands through certain agents, as in the case of Joseph (Genesis 37:26–28, 36; 39:1).

While understanding the seriousness of stealing, the lack of particularity of the Hebrew verb and its actual usage convince me that the final form of the commandment presents a much broader scope regarding what should not be stolen from others, from personal property to free Israelites to what belonged to YHWH directly, such as the spoils of war that Achan stole in Shinar (Joshua 6:18–7:26).[6]

As far as personal property is concerned, it would normally be animals that could be used for food, work, and clothing, although money is also considered (Exodus 21:28–22:15). As Miller remarks, they are the means for livelihood and production. Still, these goods and property were crucial to the survival of one's family as well (especially the poor). A cloak, for example, is more than outer clothing; it is what preserves the life of a poor person in ancient Israel (e.g., Exodus 22:26–27). Moreover, property was also a guarantor of one's freedom: property becomes "an extension of the 'self' of the individual or family or community."[7] Stealing not only violates someone's wealth or ownership but also attacks the dignity of the person. Therefore, even if the goods belong to one's enemy, one should not take them but instead protect them (e.g., Exodus 23:4–5).

Regarding the specific addressees of the commandment, they are often the wealthy and powerful Israelites, and those who take advantage of the poor and the weak. Of course, we do not deny the reality that the poor also steal, often because of poverty (e.g., Proverbs 6:30). In this latter case, the writers of wisdom literature claim that while it is understandable, it is still unacceptable for anyone to steal, and a penalty is imposed.

Such a firm view could be grounded in the implicit rationale of the prohibition, which regards the right to property and liberty even though one's property, wealth, and freedom are gifts from God and we are stewards of these gifts. Another possible, secondary rationale is grounded in the sanctity of work:[8] we are dignified by God by receiving the fruits of our labor. Stealing, on the other hand, implies the rejection of God's will. In this sense, a person steals so as not to work, and this reflects an unwillingness to live as God has created us.

In a society like ancient Israel, compensation for the thing stolen is therefore crucial, and the thief is usually punished with a fine or the like according to the law of restitution (e.g., Exodus 21:37). To reflect its seriousness, the compensation may at times exceed the original value of the good stolen (e.g., Proverbs 6:30–31). In fact, as a crime stealing could even lead to the death penalty, such as in the case of kidnapping a free person (e.g., Deuteronomy 24:7) or stealing things devoted to God (as seen from the fate of Achan).

Taken together, the general function of the prohibition, as in the earlier commandments, is to protect the well-being of the neighbor. Specifically, it aims to preserve the neighbor's property, which is needed for sustaining life and family, as well as safeguard the freedom and dignity of the Israelites.

The commandment also seems to be explicitly intended for the protection of the poor and, by implication, becomes strongly critical of the misconduct of wealthy Israelites and their unjust treatment of slaves. From a communal perspective, Harrelson remarks that it implicitly criticizes the uneven allocation of the goods within Israelite society. The prohibition then underscores a moral and social obligation for all Israelites: stealing can be a grave sin in the eyes of God.

Positively speaking, the commandment calls for a variety of attitudes and practices for individuals and for the entire community. First, each needs to show respect for another's property and freedom, and to do so fairly and inclusively (i.e., without favoritism or prejudice). Second, 20:15 calls for charity and generosity toward the poor. Elsewhere, the Hebrew Bible offers specific regulations and practices for the sharing of wealth and goods with the poor and those marginalized in society. For example, the edges of the field and fallen grapes are reserved for the poor to glean and gather (e.g., Leviticus 19:9–10). During the sabbatical and jubilee years, both the slaves and the land will revert to their original status and ownership (e.g., Exodus 21:2). Third, the commandment indirectly encourages the Israelites to lead productive lives by means of labor.

In sum, we see that, on the one hand, stealing can cause great damage to the victim (and the family) and, on the other hand, there is much an Israelite can and should do to value and promote the right to property and liberty of other members of the community, especially those of the poor.

VALUING THE PROPERTY AND LIBERTY OF OTHERS

Some interpret the contemporary ethical teaching of the commandment to be respect for the liberty and dignity of the person. Others highlight respect for ownership and the consequent right of possession and use of goods. Our study suggests that *both* the material possession *and* the freedom of the neighbor, especially that of the poor and the powerless, are to be respected.

When Stealing Is Not Stealing Anymore

Luther once said that stealing is "quite a wide-spread and common vice, but so little regarded and observed" (*LC* #224). His observation is still valid today. On the personal level, we can steal and cheat by shoplifting, tax evasion, plagiarism, and so on. On the professional and corporate level, apart from white-collar and corporate crimes, there are many unchallenged malpractices, such as monopoly in providing goods and services. Moreover, in the age of cyberspace, we encounter new forms of stealing, especially in terms of identity theft and the secret selling (or exposure) by service providers of restricted personal user information to others.[9] From the viewpoint of global and ecological ethics, many authors and ethicists raise the concern that our disproportionate consumption and control of natural resources should be perceived as stealing from poorer countries and from the Earth itself.

Sadly, as one author accurately observes, for many of us the question is no longer "Is it wrong?" but "How can I get away with it?"[10] We consider ourselves clever opportunists rather than thieves, and we justify our acts by all kinds of excuses. In addition, we have become insensitive to the problem of unfair distribution in our world. Luther rightly warned that we should not treat the commandment lightly (*LC* #246). In contemporary society, we have to respect and value the property and liberty of others even more eagerly.

The Meaning of Valuing the Property and Liberty of Others

Aquinas pointed out that stealing is both a crime and a sin against justice: valuing the property and liberty of others is fundamentally a matter of treating them justly.[11] Luther held a similar point of departure but offered a more forceful definition of stealing: the acquisition of anything by any unjust means, especially those unjust practices in trade that "skin and scrape to the bone" of the poor (*LC* #247). Lehman further remarks that, for Luther, "the function and the use of property . . . are concretely expressed for everyone in the exercise of his or her calling."[12] Therefore, respecting another's property also means valuing that person's vocation.

Moreover, Luther's attention to moral character throws light on our subsequent discussion of the virtues and vices that are attendant to matters covered by the seventh commandment (*LC* ##226–34). First, he characterizes those who overcharge as being lazy, unfaithful people. Conversely, valuing another's property points to diligence and faithfulness in our own enterprise. Second, he observes that there is the inner contradiction of those who pretend to be "great noblemen [*sic*], and honorable, pious citizens, and yet rob and steal under a good pretext" (*LC* #229). Therefore, we need to be honest and constantly maintain the integrity of our thoughts and actions. Third, stealing often reflects defiance and arrogance in the thief. Respecting the property/liberty of others, on the contrary, is an expression of humility and obedience. Finally, in Luther's view, when we respect what belongs to others, we more faithfully preserve and advance what belongs to us.

Calvin agreed with Aquinas and Luther that justice is crucial for valuing another's property. However, justice has to mean more than legal entitlement, since even legal means and court actions can be a form of theft (*ICR* 2.8.45). Rather, justice is defined by the particular vocation that people have toward each other (*ICR* 3.10.6).[13] Our respect for the property of others is therefore based on the reciprocal duty of each to the other. Calvin also expanded the scope of "property" to embrace a wide range of rights that a person can possess. Consequently, to value the property and liberty of others is also to respect their rights. Like Luther, Calvin correlated respect for the property and liberty of others with promotion of their interests, especially those of the poor. He thus preached that we should be ready to sacrifice some of our rights, share our abundance, and contribute to the relief of the poor (*ICR* 2.8.46).

Calvin's call for sharing our abundance is taken up by modern scholars. Barclay, for instance, says that "private property is a kind of theft when a man uses it for nothing but his own pleasure and his own gratification, with never a thought for anyone else. It is not the property but the selfishness which constitutes the theft."[14] Today Chittister similarly calls the commandment a law of sharing.

Apart from advocating sharing as a crucial aspect of respecting the property of others, the Catholic Church would also emphasize the necessity of respecting human dignity and the integrity of creation. The latter focuses on the natural world and calls for gentleness and reasonable use of it (*CCC* ##2415–18). In conclusion, these insights reveal not only the needed virtues of the commandment but also its social significance.

Valuing the Property and Liberty of Others as a Virtue

Considering respect for the property and liberty of others as a virtue begins with and opens the door to a range of personal virtues, such as honesty, diligence, and gratitude, which Luther and Calvin identified. Still, among them all, justice is foundational. Aquinas offered a systematic exploration of this virtue: justice, in simple terms, is "rendering to each one his right" (*ST* II.II. 58.1). It is a cardinal virtue and is directly concerned with external human actions. What is distinctive about justice is that it is the greatest of the moral virtues and, anchored in the will, it directs all our activities (*ST* II.II. 58.4, 12). As a virtue it can be general, particular, and legal. It is a general virtue when it has the common good of the community as its object (*ST* II.II. 58.5, 6). It is a particular virtue when it is directed toward others and concerns actions instead of passions (*ST* II.II. 58.2). Justice in its legal sense does not pertain to positive law per se but to what is in accord with the common good.[15]

Justice as an act can be classified into two major types: *commutative justice* refers to the order between two persons and considers restitutions; *distributive justice* points to "the order of that which belongs to the community in relation to each single person" and hence refers to proportionate distribution of goods (*ST* II.II. 61.1). For Aquinas, stealing violates commutative justice; the unfair distribution of goods violates distributive justice (*ST* II.II. 61.3).

Apart from being just, we have to be aware of the needs of those who, in certain circumstances, have a claim upon our wealth and possessions. The virtue of vigilance is, however, not sufficient. We further need to acquire the virtue of charity and its specific dispositions, especially solidarity, in our relationship with the needy.[16] Therefore, the virtue corresponds to the seventh commandment, which, though strongly rooted in justice, demands the cultivation and practice of other personal virtues as well.

The Practice of Valuing the Property and Liberty of Others

The *Catechism of the Catholic Church* has offered some good practical suggestions in the area of economic activities, such as regulating exchanges "between persons and between institutions in accordance with a strict respect for their rights" (#2411).

In our contemporary world, practices that are specifically directed toward the poor and disadvantaged are far more urgent. Some authors suggest sharing and being hospitable, grounded in the understanding that we "all depend on someone else somehow to provide what we each need."[17] Besides sharing, we also need to manage our own property appropriately, especially through detachment and moderation. In short, we need to be responsible stewards, as Calvin advised (*ICR* 3.10.4–5).

Among the various Christian traditions, the practices of tithing and offerings, as well as the corporal works of mercy and self-sacrifice—both spiritually (e.g., piety) and materially—are commonly recommended.

However, today, the concept of "preferential option for the poor" as advocated by liberation theology in the 1960s is crucial. As one pioneer explains, the term "preference" points to "who ought to be the first . . . objects of our solidarity," while the often misunderstood word "option" focuses on our "free commitment of a decision" with the poor (and by the poor as well).[18] It is a prophetic and theocentric option because it is an option for God and has God as the core reason of our preference and commitment. And it is best manifested in the experience of the Israelites and in the life and mission of Jesus.

The Exemplars

During his earthly ministry Jesus not only cares for the poor but also encounters and welcomes a number of people who steal! For instance, Matthew and Zacchaeus are popularly reviled as tax collectors for making profits by assessing taxes greater than people should pay Rome. Judas Iscariot, in contrast, steals from the common purse of his community (John 12:6). Jesus also deals with the rich indiscriminately, teaching them how to use their possessions properly, and he warns them against the danger of wealth (e.g., Matthew 19:16–22; Luke 12:13–21). In these encounters Jesus respects their liberty by inviting them to change.

In modern American society, Dr. Martin Luther King Jr. was known for promoting freedom and equality of African American people. Within the Catholic tradition, liberation theologians—among them Gustavo Gutiérrez, Leonardo and Clodovis Boff, and Jon Sobrino—played an important role in the evolution of liberation theology and promoted social justice through their writing. Gutiérrez, in particular, "awakened the world to the experiences and voices of those long ignored."[19] He insisted that theology is "the critical reflection on the Christian praxis in light of the word of God,"[20] and he actively participated at the historic Medellín meeting in Colombia in 1968.

While the Medellín meeting was an initiative by the local church, the social doctrine of the Catholic Church formulated at the international level is also well known for inspiring "right attitudes with respect to earthly goods and in socio-economic relationships" (*CCC* #2420). These are promoted in various encyclicals, including *Rerum Novarum*, which deals with the right to property, just wages, and the just distribution of capital, and *Centesimus Annus*, which critiques capitalism and consumerism and insists on the freedom of participation. The Catholic Church acknowledges the right of individual ownership, not as an absolute, but in relation to the universal destination of all goods. It thus turns our focus to the poor and the communal and social levels.

The Social, Communal Aspect of the Virtue of Respect for Property and Liberty

Catholic social teaching echoes our own reflection that respect for the property and liberty of others is not concerned so much with fair exchange between two persons as with the role of the community and society in safeguarding the welfare of its members, especially of the poor and the disadvantaged. Imaginative initiatives are needed on all levels.

Within the sector of economics and trade, therefore, the legitimate authority inspired by this respect could monitor and regulate the marketplace to prevent malpractice and maintain order (e.g., through proper taxation). In the related sector of work and employment, society will promote the right of economic initiative, access to employment, just wages for ordinary people, and so on (*CCC* ##2426–36).

In the broader public domain, ethicists such as Hauerwas and Willimon claim that a virtuous society as such could promote the common good and thus counteract prevailing practices of privatizing what belongs to the community. It could also advance the civil liberties of each citizen (such as movement and lifestyle). Moreover, it could question the inequitable distribution of wealth and the presence of social injustices on both the national and international levels. On the international level, in particular, the virtue calls not only for cancellation of debts but also for the provision of direct aid as a sign of solidarity and justice toward poorer nations.

In policies related to human liberty, the virtue urges nations to secure the freedom of immigration and emigration and to provide measures to prevent involuntary migration and the trafficking of women and children.

Finally, on the global level, respect for the property of others could urge collaboration among nations in the conservation and sharing of the Earth's limited resources, and call for responsible stewardship (*CCC* ##2415–18). Indeed, the seventh commandment and its affiliated virtue are the most socially oriented in nature.

NOTES

1. Ironically, Miller himself makes the same criticism about the work of Werner Schmidt, Holger Delkurt, and Axel Graupner, *Die zehn Gebote im Rahmen alttestamentlicher Ethik*, Erträge der Forschung 281 (Darmstadt: Wissenschaftliche Buchgesellschaft, 1993). See Patrick D. Miller, *The Ten Commandments* (Louisville, KY: Westminster John Knox Press, 2009), 318.

2. Cornelis Houtman, *Exodus*, vol. 3, trans. Johan Rebel and Sierd Woudstra (Kampen, Netherlands: Kok, 1993–2000), 63–64.

3. Childs observes that an exceptional case is the stealing of the son of Ahaziah so as to prevent him from being killed (2 Kings 11:2); Brevard S. Childs, *The Book of Exodus* (Philadelphia, PA: Westminster Press, 1974).

4. For a discussion of the various views among these scholars, see Cheryl B. Anderson, "The Eighth Commandment: A Way to King's 'Beloved Community'?" in *The Ten Commandments: The Reciprocity of Faithfulness*, ed. William P. Brown (Louisville, KY: Westminster John Knox Press, 2004), 284–85.

5. See Albrecht Alt, "Das Verbot des Diebstahls im Dekalog," in *Kleine Schriften zur Geschichte des Volkes Israel*, vol. 1 (Munich: Beck, 1953), 333–40, as referenced in Childs, *The Book of Exodus*, 423.

6. Patrick and others exclude real estate, like land and buildings, claiming that it is explicitly prohibited by the eighth and tenth commandments. See Dale Patrick, *Old Testament Law* (Atlanta, GA: John Knox Press, 1985), 56.

7. Walter J. Harrelson, *The Ten Commandments and Human Rights* (Macon, GA: Mercer University Press, 1997), 113. See also Terence E. Fretheim, *Exodus* (Louisville, KY: Westminster John Knox Press, 1991), 235.

8. See Fretheim, *Exodus*, 236.

9. Emily Steel and Geoffrey A. Fowler, "Facebook Apps Transmit, Sell Personal Info," *Wall Street Journal*, October 18, 2010, http://online.wsj.com/article/ SB10001424052702304772804575558484075236968.html.

10. Ernest J. Lewis, *Light for the Journey: Living the Ten Commandments* (Waco, TX: Word Books, 1986), 126.

11. Yet Aquinas added that it is also a protection of the spiritual goods of oneself and one's family. See Aquinas, "Explanation," http://dhspriory.org/thomas/TenCommandments.htm.

12. Paul L. Lehmann, *The Decalogue and a Human Future: The Meaning of the Commandments for Making and Keeping Human Life Human* (Grand Rapids, MI: Eerdmans, 1995), 196. Luther's view differs from that of the capitalist in that the right of possession is not exclusive— that is, the right of use determines the right of possession. See Lehmann, 192–93.

112 Chapter 11

13. For example, employees should "pay all due honor to their rulers . . . [while employers should] take due charge of their people" (*ICR* 2.8.46). Here, Calvin's reading of vocation could be misinterpreted as justifying the economic status quo (*ICR* 2.8.45–46). See Allen Verhey, "Calvin and the 'Stewardship of Love,'" in *The Ten Commandments for Jews, Christians, and Others*, ed. Roger E. Van Harn (Grand Rapids, MI: Eerdmans, 2007), 159.

14. William Barclay, *The Ten Commandments* (Louisville, KY: Westminster John Knox Press, 1998), 168.

15. See Jean Porter, "The Virtue of Justice (IIa IIae, qq. 58–122)," in *The Ethics of Aquinas*, ed. Stephen Pope (Washington, DC: Georgetown University Press, 2002), 272–86.

16. The virtue of solidarity will be discussed in chapter 18.

17. Joan Chittister, *The Ten Commandments: Laws of the Heart* (Maryknoll, NY: Orbis Books, 2006), 90.

18. Gustavo Gutiérrez, "Option for the Poor," in *Mysterium Liberationis*, ed. Ignacio Ellacuría and Jon Sobrino (Maryknoll, NY: Orbis, 1993), 239–40.

19. James F. Keenan, *A History of Catholic Moral Theology in the Twentieth Century* (New York: Continuum, 2010), 199.

20. Gustavo Gutiérrez, *A Theology of Liberation*, 2nd ed., trans. and ed. Sister Caridad Inda and John Eagelson (Maryknoll, NY: Orbis Books, 1988), xxix.

Chapter Twelve

The Eighth Commandment in Exodus 20:16

You shall not bear false witness against your neighbor.

WHAT DID THE TEXT COMMAND?

After a series of three terse, two-word commandments, the eighth returns to a more detailed style by adding a qualification and an object. We also see a shift of focus—Exodus 20:16 is concerned primarily with what we say that may harm others, rather than what we do.

Like the previous three commandments, the prohibition against false witness appears in those "lists" of the prophets. But more explicit and parallel texts are found in Exodus 23:1–9, Deuteronomy 17:2–7, and Deuteronomy 19:15–21. Miller points out that the first text is significant in that it reflects the primary context in which the commandment operates—the administration of justice. It also spells out the worst possible consequence of uttering false and harmful words—namely, killing of the innocent. The texts in Deuteronomy 17 and 19 further provide explicit instructions about giving witness in the court, especially the need for sufficient witnesses and thorough inquiry so as to avoid wrongful conviction. Above all, there is punishment for whoever testifies falsely. We further find in Deuteronomy statutes that illustrate the explication of the eighth commandment in relation to the protection of the poor and the marginalized (e.g., 24:17–25:3). These statutes are concerned with proper administration of justice to the vulnerable, particularly with respect to their dignity and reputation in the community. [1]

Apart from these important legal texts, we also identify some Old Testament stories in which false witness is involved. The first is the false accusation of Potiphar's wife against Joseph that leads to his unjust imprisonment (Genesis 39). Another case is the false testimony of the two scoundrels against Naboth that costs his life and the loss of his vineyard (1 Kings 21). Within the Catholic canon, we hear the story of Susanna, in which Daniel disclosed the false testimony of two elders against her (Daniel 13).

These stories share the same themes of coveting or stealing the neighbor's property or dignity or life by means of false witness. They confirm the earlier comment that there exists a close interaction among the commandments against killing/murder, adultery, stealing, false witness, and coveting. Specifically, the eighth commandment could serve as the final protection of those who are wrongfully accused of killing/murder, adultery, and stealing.

Still, 20:16 and the second commandment are also related in a unique way: as noted in chapter 6, the Deuteronomy version of the eighth commandment and Exodus 20:7 use the same Hebrew term, *shawe'* ("in vain"). This connection echoes the fact that testifying in the name of YHWH is both permitted and practiced (and at times abused) in ancient Israel (e.g., Exodus 22:10–11).

On the other hand, the story of Naboth's vineyard and other similar accounts (e.g., 2 Samuel 11) highlight the role of the prophet. Indeed, we regularly hear prophets give judgment to those who speak falsely in public (e.g., Isaiah 59:3–4). They also attack those prophets who prophesy falsehood and illusionary assurance to the people (e.g., Jeremiah 23:9–40). Elsewhere the writers of the Psalms and the wisdom literature similarly criticize those who give false testimony (e.g., Proverbs 25:18).

Taken together, these legal texts, narratives, and criticisms highlight the seriousness of the matter—it can be a very dangerous and powerful means to injure another Israelite. However, by the same token, the above exploration also hints that the observance of this commandment can be an important means to protect the neighbor from wrongful charges.

In general, the commandment does not present any major translation problem. However, some think the employment of two different Hebrew words in the Exodus and Deuteronomy versions commands our attention. The Hebrew word used in 20:16 is *sheqer* ("falsehood"). This term is concerned with "utterance which distorts or misrepresents or skews."[2] The Deuteronomy version, in contrast, employs the term *shawe'* that, as discussed before, has a broad and complex meaning. Some exegetes see the two terms as synonyms, while others suggest that the use of a broader term in Deuteronomy 5:20 reflects certain editorial developments and the subsequent expansion of the scope of the prohibition. As we shall see, however, this difference does not affect the core understanding of the commandment.

Another issue that draws our attention concerns the actual object of the commandment. Cassuto notes that elsewhere in the Torah the Hebrew term *re'ahka* ("your neighbor") is used in two different ways: it may refer to Israelites alone (e.g., Leviticus 19:18) or include whoever resides in the community, such as the alien residents (e.g., Leviticus 19:34).[3] Now since the Israelites during the exile often addressed the surrounding peoples, such as the Egyptians, as neighbors, it makes sense to us to take a more inclusive view of the object of the commandment.

Nevertheless, the major discussion among scholars seems to be the scope of prohibition. Many note that the nature of the Hebrew noun *'ed* ("witness") and verb *'aneh* ("answer"/"bear") implies that the commandment is set in a judicial context:[4] it was a common practice in the ancient Near East for elders to call for public hearings in front of the gates to handle certain regulated public affairs (e.g., Ruth 4:1–12). Witnesses are summoned to testify for or against another person. The accused parties in trial should answer to the charges. In this way, the prosecutor can speak falsely or honestly (e.g., Proverbs 14:25). If the prosecutor chooses to speak falsely, the subsequent damage is severe. It does great harm to the life, property, or reputation/dignity of the other, as well as to the order of the judicial system and of the society. In order to prevent abuse, the people of Israel set up certain regulations, such as the rule that no one can be put to death on the testimony of one witness alone (e.g., Deuteronomy 19:15). Sadly, false witnessing continued to be a rather common happening in ancient Israel, as hinted at in those above-mentioned charges in Psalms and the wisdom literature.

However, should the commandment restrict itself to a narrow legal usage or embrace a broad interpretation, one that prohibits not only lies and falsehoods but also the use of distorted words? While the implied judicial context of the commandment cannot be denied, for several reasons I take the view of those who consider a broad interpretation of the prohibition:[5] In the first place, the two terms *sheqer* and *shawe'* basically share the same intention and concern for uttering words that have harmful consequences. Second, the damage done to the wrongfully accused within or without the judicial setting could be equally huge. Third, both the one who testifies falsely and those who lie, deceive, and slander are referred to as "malicious witness" or "witness of violence" to emphasize the power of words to injure a person severely (e.g., Psalm 35:11). Fourth, biblical accounts of speaking falsely often appear alongside (and even serve) those texts that deal with false witness directly (e.g., Proverbs 6:16–19). Fifth and last, a broader interpretation does not diminish the commandment's primary force, which is against the use of false and/or deceptive words that do violence to the neighbor. The juridical setting thus serves as a starting point of reflection.

Consequently, the primary rationale of the prohibition could be the inviolability of personal reputation and dignity as required by justice; and the secondary rationale could be the inviolability of truth. The socio-communal dimension of the commandment is also emphasized. However, Exodus 20:16 does not mention any sanction if one breaches the commandment. The writer of Deuteronomy, in contrast, makes it clear that those who testify falsely deserve the same punishment they intended for others—although the exact form of punishment may vary (e.g., 22:18–19). The penalty is grounded in the principle of justice expressed in *lex talionis* (19:19–21). Some scriptural texts further indicate that if one fails to come forward to speak against the wrongdoers of an injustice he has witnessed, the person likewise will be punished (e.g., Leviticus 5:1).

Grounded in this rationale we can further propose that the basic function of the prohibition is to protect the reputation and dignity of each member of the community against injustice, especially the threat of false accusation by another member, both inside and outside the judicial context. Such protection is particularly important to the poor and the marginalized in the community who possess nothing but their reputation.

Within the judicial context, the commandment seeks to secure a reliable and independent inquiry of the case. Walter Brueggemann reminds us that the protection of the judicial system of Israelite society is crucial, for the court is the last resort for seeking justice.[6] Specifically, as Patrick comments, the prohibition addresses the issue of the inadequacy (and abuse) of the trial system, which relied heavily on the testimony of witnesses rather than physical evidence: the witness is often also the accuser and normally does not need to testify under oath. The witness thus plays the role of deciding the fate of the accused.

Based on the above-cited arguments for a broad interpretation of the text, it seems logical to perceive the commandment, outside the legal framework, as concerned not so much with lying or truth-telling in general, as with harming one's neighbor directly or indirectly by words. In other words, 20:16 is a guard more against the destructive power of false testimony than against lying per se.

In sum, the prohibition highlights the importance of justice for the good of the Israelite community, especially of the poor and the vulnerable members. It also points to the need for the protection of the reputation of the neighbor. In addition, the commandment reminds all Israelites to be careful and responsible in their use of words, especially when judging others, so that they may not harm the other in any way. It is a matter of respect. They should, instead, speak constructively for the advancement of the neighbor's reputation and dignity in the society.

VALUING THE REPUTATION AND DIGNITY OF OTHERS

Many writers, like Barclay and Keenan, center their ethical reflection on the positive meaning of the eighth commandment, such as truth-telling in the light of our professional roles and creating space in interpersonal relationships where truth can be heard. However, our work shows that its core moral value lies in the protection of the reputation and dignity of our neighbors through our spoken (and unspoken) words. It is explicitly oriented for the good of others in the society.

Hurting Others by Our Spoken and Unspoken Words

As Brueggemann claims, most of us live in a society basically ruled and protected by law. In the United States, for instance, the courts safeguard the constitutional vision of civil and human rights. However, by recalling the false allegations against Assistant District Attorney Steven Pagones in the late 1980s, the Wenatchee sex abuse cases in the 1990s, and other such cases, many Americans realize that false witness against others continues to occur and that the legal system is sometimes unable to prevent false accusations and wrongful punishment of the innocent.[7] Therefore, in recent years states have begun to abrogate capital punishment statutes in light of DNA evidence of the wrongful conviction of many accused in capital cases.[8]

Still, what is most disturbing is when the leadership is involved. On both national and international levels we encounter investigations of administration officials or politicians who falsely witness and lie about certain policies that lead to wrong decisions, sociopolitical unrest, and even the death of many innocent people.[9]

Another common form of false witness outside the judicial context that causes damage in society, as a couple of theologians suggest, is stereotyping or racial profiling: we consciously or unconsciously project our prejudices against another group through statutory policies, mass media, and insensitive words. These prejudices are often "false and injurious judgments we have slipped into making without even thinking whether they are based on sufficient knowledge or justified grounds."[10]

Here, no matter whether we set the context in the ancient Israelite community or in a highly civilized twenty-first-century society, false witnessing and dangerous words continue to pose serious harm to others. In and outside the legal system, we thus need to be careful of our speech and gestures so as to respect and safeguard others' reputation, dignity, and even life.

The Meaning of Valuing the Reputation and Dignity of Others

By observing how the people involved in a court case could violate the commandment according to their distinctive roles, Aquinas implied that it is the duty of *all* to respect and safeguard the reputation and dignity of the wrongfully accused.[11] Luther, who perceived the primary context of the commandment as pertaining to the legal system, further emphasized the need to defend the poor—to maintain, guard, and promote the legal rights of the powerless (*LC* ##257–61). We have to make legal judgment truly and uprightly, without favoritism but with courage even to the point of offending the rich and the powerful. This duty is in and of itself a matter of justice and the actual carrying out of justice.[12]

How does this play out in ordinary conversation? For Aquinas, respecting another's reputation and dignity meant listening to rumors or accusations about others with discernment, repeating what one has heard only when necessary, not speaking in an unflattering manner, and being ready to promote or praise another's name.[13] For Luther, false witness is the tongue's work. Consequently, one should speak only the best words and use speech that "benefits everyone, reconciles the discordant, excuses and defends the maligned . . . [with] a manner of speech which is truthful and sincere."[14] It is an act of charity.

Luther further claimed that we should not publicly judge and criticize others unless we are authorized to do so (*LC* ##264–66). For him, at times, we even have to cover up their faults (unless it is quite public already), for it is very difficult to restore what is damaged (*LC* ##273, 284–85).[15] We must be careful here, however. The current scandal caused by Catholic Church officials who "covered up" charges and allegations of sexual abuse is a case in point. We must always remember that the primary context of the commandment is the administration of justice, so we may cover up the faults of others *if and only if* other people are not the victims of those faults.

On the other hand, Calvin highlighted vicious detraction and lying as the two main components of false witness. Thus, he insisted on maintaining and cultivating unfeigned truth (*ICR* 2.8.47). Still, in line with the view of Aquinas and Luther, Calvin also stressed the integrated role of our speech, listening, and judgment. It is out of true fear and love of God, as well as charity toward others, that we value the reputation and dignity of our neighbor.

By far, the insights of Aquinas and Luther remind us of the two important values in juridical matters: equality and defending the vulnerable. Moreover, their concrete, practical suggestions are not just doable in today's context but also help us acquire the needed virtues.

The Virtue of Valuing the Reputation and Dignity of Others

Based on what has gone before, we may likewise perceive valuing the reputation and dignity of others as a virtue from two different perspectives. As a virtue for the legal system, it points, in the first place, to the related virtues of justice, fairness, and impartiality for the sake of safeguarding the rights of the accused to fair hearings.[16] If the accuser is someone who is powerful, the virtue of courage is also called for so that the legal process may not be compromised by the powerful. Here, as in the previous commandment, justice is the key. Yet the eighth commandment assigns it to a particular setting.

As a virtue beyond the judicial context, respect for the reputation and dignity of others further highlights the virtue of charity: it is out of love for our neighbors that we tell the truth and praise and speak highly of them. Still, it is also out of love for what is true that we speak the truth. Here, speaking the truth directs us to the virtue of truthfulness. The *Catechism of the Catholic Church* suggests, "[Truthfulness] consists in showing oneself true in deeds and truthful in words, and in guarding against duplicity, dissimulation, and hypocrisy" (#2468). Specifically, it "keeps to the just mean between what ought to be expressed and what ought to be kept secret: it entails honesty and discretion" (#2469). Therefore, prudence is essential. The virtue of prudence, as Aquinas understood it, is an intellectual virtue that trains and directs practical reason by determining and pursuing the right cause for one's deeds (*ST* II.II. 47.7). In today's understanding, it seeks the mean and resolves the possible tension between two conflicting values.

Finally, many would agree that it is a common human weakness that we prefer speaking and hearing evil of our neighbors and are often envious when hearing good of them. Thus, we need to be humble as well.

The Practice of Valuing the Reputation and Dignity of Others

Along with those suggestions of Aquinas, Luther, and Calvin, one contemporary author offers a very useful practice for our ordinary conversation: to ask ourselves three basic questions—"Is it true? Is it helpful? Is it kind?"—before uttering any word.[17] To answer the first question, we need to acquire sufficient knowledge before making a statement. The second question points to the idea of simplicity of speech, which is often the prudent thing to observe. The last question points to the habit of speaking the truth in charity, which does not mean sacrificing the truthfulness of the speech or exercising a pretentious humility.

Within Christianity, the practice of praise and adoration to God "embodies the tongue's restored splendor."[18] Augustine was very serious about this Christian practice; he claimed that failing to do so is a sin and that lying is incompatible with the adoration of God.[19] Among many other Catholic practices, the sacrament of reconciliation provides the needed forum and space where the penitent can speak the truth deep inside and make appropriate reparation demanded by God's justice and legal justice. In fact, I see that creating a safe forum for people to speak honestly is a much-needed practice in our secular world as well.

The Exemplars

Many observe that Jesus is the perfect model of how and what we should speak. He teaches us to speak truthfully (Matthew 5:37). Whenever he speaks, he speaks only the truth (e.g., Luke 21:3–4). He also values the reputation and dignity of others, as indicated in his words about the sinful woman who wipes his feet (Luke 7:44–47). In addition, Jesus makes it clear that his earthly mission is to "testify to the truth" (John 18:37). And it is because of this that he is falsely accused and put to death (Matthew 26:59–60). Last but not least, Jesus is the truth itself (John 14:6). Moreover, the words of the Old Testament prophets are equally exemplary, especially in challenging social injustice.

I find the late American Jesuit Robert Drinan a contemporary model of the virtue. He was best known for introducing the initial resolution demanding the impeachment of former president Richard M. Nixon. Drinan's involvement demonstrated what this virtue in the arena of legal justice would demand—namely, justice, impartiality, and courage for the sake of the truth and the good of the society. Moreover, Drinan practiced what he preached by committing himself to the promotion of legal ethics, professional responsibility, and justice through scholarship.[20]

The Social, Communal Aspect of the Virtue of Valuing the Reputation and Dignity of Others

Drinan's exemplary role highlights the social aspect of the virtue in the context of the legal system. The virtue safeguards the trustworthiness of this particular instrument of justice in the society. Harrelson rightly points out that it strengthens our public confidence toward the leadership, whose role is to secure society's order. In addition, since the wealthy and the powerful members of society have a better chance at full justice than those who are poor, I agree with Holbert that the virtue urges society to provide sufficient resources for the disadvantaged to have access to better legal services.[21]

Many ethicists like Harrelson agree that outside the courtroom, the virtue is important for creating and maintaining reliable relationships that are crucial for building and sustaining social structures, especially relationships in professional sectors, from the doctor-patient relationship to interfaith relationships, and so on. Brueggemann further suggests that the virtue challenges the use of euphemism (or "doublespeak") in our society, such as the use of so-called free market economy as a camouflage for greedy business ethos.[22] While honoring the freedom of speech, it also confronts the abuse of communication and mass media in manipulating and misrepresenting information.

Lastly, Hauerwas and Willimon rightly remind us that the Church itself is called to be a testimony to the truth in our world. The virtue thus urges us—both the leadership and the faithful—to live out our Christian discipleship faithfully in our relationships with God, our aged parents, our spouses, and our neighbors.[23] This brings us back to the earlier commandments.

NOTES

1. Dennis Olson, *Deuteronomy and the Death of Moses: A Theological Reading*, Overtures to Biblical Theology (Minneapolis: Fortress Press, 1994), 108, as cited in Patrick D. Miller, *The Ten Commandments* (Louisville, KY: Westminster John Knox Press, 2009), 355.

2. Walter Brueggemann, "Truth-Telling as Subversive Obedience," *Journal for Preachers* 20, no. 2 (Lent 1997): 2.

3. Umberto Cassuto, *A Commentary on the Book of Exodus*, trans. Israel Abrahams (Jerusalem: Magnes Press, Hebrew University, 1967), 247.

4. Ludwig Köhler, "Justice in the Gate," in *Hebrew Man* (London: SCM, 1958), 149–75, as cited in Brevard S. Childs, *The Book of Exodus* (Philadelphia, PA: Westminster Press, 1974), 424. See also Dale Patrick, *Old Testament Law* (Atlanta, GA: John Knox Press, 1985), 56; Walter J. Harrelson, *The Ten Commandments and Human Rights* (Macon, GA: Mercer University Press, 1997), 120.

5. See Brueggemann, "Truth-Telling as Subversive Obedience," 2; Patrick, *Old Testament Law*, 57; Patrick D. Miller, "Ten Commandments," in *The New Interpreter's Dictionary of the Bible*, vol. 5 (Nashville, TN: Abingdon Press, 2006–2009), 522; Miller, *The Ten Commandments*, 344, 355, 381.

6. Brueggemann, "Truth-Telling as Subversive Obedience," 2.

7. See Paul L. Lehmann, *The Decalogue and a Human Future: The Meaning of the Commandments for Making and Keeping Human Life Human* (Grand Rapids, MI: Eerdmans, 1995), 200–201; David Klinghoffer, *Shattered Tablets* (New York: Doubleday, 2007), 206–8.

8. See Death Penalty Information Center, *Facts about the Death Penalty*, www.deathpenaltyinfo.org/FactSheet.pdf.

9. See Bernd Debusmann, "The U.S. War in Iraq Is Over. Who Won?" *Reuters*, September 3, 2010, http://blogs.reuters.com/great-debate/2010/09/03/the-u-s-war-in-iraq-is-over-who-won.

10. Miroslav Volf with Linn Tonstad, "Bearing True Witness," in *The Ten Commandments for Jews, Christians, and Others*, ed. Roger E. Van Harn (Grand Rapids, MI: Eerdmans, 2007), 184.

11. Aquinas, "Explanation," http://dhspriory.org/thomas/TenCommandments.htm.

12. See Volf with Tonstad, "Bearing True Witness," 182–83.

13. Aquinas, "Explanation."

14. Martin Luther, *Luther's Works*, vol. 43, ed. Harold J. Grimm (Philadelphia: Fortress Press, 1957), 23, as cited in Volf with Tonstad, "Bearing True Witness," 186.

15. See also Martin Luther, "The 7th, 8th, and 9th Commandments," in *Luther's Works*, vol. 51, 158, as cited in Volf with Tonstad, "Bearing True Witness," 186.

16. We need to extend fairness toward those in power as well, for the powerless also have their own way of false witness against the powerful (as in the case of Pagones).

17. Ernest J. Lewis, *Light for the Journey: Living the Ten Commandments* (Waco, TX: Word Books, 1986), 134–35.

18. Reinhard Hütter, "The Tongue—Fallen and Restored: Some Reflections on the Three Voices of the Eighth Commandment," in *I Am the Lord Your God: Christian Reflections on the Ten Commandments*, ed. Carl E. Braaten and Christopher R. Seitz (Grand Rapids, MI: Eerdmans, 2005), 203.

19. Paul Griffiths, "The Gift and the Lie: Augustine on Lying," *Communio: International Catholic Review* 26 (1999): 30, as cited in Hütter, "The Tongue—Fallen and Restored," 203.

20. Carrie Menkel-Meadow, "A Tribute to Robert F. Drinan, S.J.: A Deeply Ethical Man," *Georgetown Law Journal* 95 (2007): 1713. See also Raymond Schroth, *Bob Drinan: The Controversial Life of the First Catholic Priest Elected to Congress* (New York: Fordham University Press, 2010).

21. John C. Holbert, *The Ten Commandments* (Nashville, TN: Abingdon Press, 2002), 116.

22. See Brueggemann, "Truth-Telling as Subversive Obedience," 295, and Hütter, "The Tongue—Fallen and Restored," 200.

23. Stanley M. Hauerwas and William H. Willimon, *The Truth about God: The Ten Commandments in Christian Life* (Nashville, TN: Abingdon Press, 1999), 118.

Chapter Thirteen

The Ninth Commandment in Exodus 20:17

You shall not covet your neighbor's wife . . .

WHAT DID THE TEXT COMMAND?

As noted earlier, one of the main discrepancies among the different Christian traditions is whether Exodus 20:17 is a single commandment or two. For Roman Catholics and Lutherans, 20:17 contains two commandments against coveting, for the verse presents two prohibitions with different objects. Still, the Roman Catholic tradition differs from the Lutheran tradition in its order of the two commandments. Roman Catholics follow the word order of Deuteronomy 5:21 as Augustine did. Thus, the ninth commandment is literally about coveting the neighbor's wife and the last commandment is concerned with coveting another's property.

While adopting the Roman Catholic tradition's view on the order of these last two commandments, we continue to focus on Exodus 20:17 for the sake of consistency in our exegesis.

As a whole, the two commandments in 20:17 do not contain any motivation clause or sanction. They differ from the other eight commandments in that the explicit subject matters of the other eight commandments are concrete actions. Still, the two prohibitions are often referred back to the commandments against adultery and stealing, respectively. They are also connected with other commandments in one way or another. The commandment on the observance of the Sabbath, for instance, can be a concrete implementation of the prohibition against coveting: apart from noting a similar list of

123

content, some scholars explain that regularly taking rest on certain days is a sign of Israel's refusal to covet the seemingly attractive ways of the neighboring peoples, such as their lifestyle.

Within the Hebrew Bible, although the two commandments do not appear in those "lists" of the prophets as the previous commandments do, similar prohibitions can be found, such as the prohibition on coveting the gold of the enemy in Deuteronomy 7:25. On a number of occasions the prophets and the writers of wisdom literature criticize the problem of coveting in their societies (e.g., Micah 2:2).

As a whole, these connections and references reveal the fact that coveting affects our relationships not only with our neighbors but also with God. And the departure from talking about concrete actions explicitly does not lighten the gravity of the issue, for it is still criticized by the prophets.

Coveting

We now turn to what is common to both commandments—namely, the prohibition on coveting itself. The nature of the Hebrew verb *chamad* ("covet") used in 20:17 has caused scholarly dispute: Does the verb imply concrete and practical actions or simply speak about attitudes and emotions? Literally, *chamad* itself has a number of meanings, such as "delight in" and "desire" (e.g., Genesis 2:9; Psalm 19:10). Both Dozeman and Miller point out that it is often translated as "covet" when an object follows.[1] Moreover, it tends to refer to a desire stimulated by seeing a delightful object, from the fruit of the tree in Eden to a beautiful mantle from Shinar (Joshua 7:21). In this way, *chamad* could imply the possession of the desired object.

Those who claim that *chamad* denotes the simultaneous taking of concrete action argue further that ancient Israelite laws address actions and not inner thoughts. They also turn to ancient texts and Hebrew passages that deal with coveting (e.g., Joshua 7:21) to argue that desiring and taking possession are almost one and the same thing.

Others insist that the opposite is true of these scriptural passages: the texts simply imply that desire precedes action, and so action and desire are two different things. They note that there are other scriptural passages in which *chamad* is not followed by a corresponding action (e.g., Deuteronomy 7:25) and that not all Hebrew verbs for "desire" have links with their subsequent actions. Moreover, the use of another verb (*'awweh*, "desire") in the Deuteronomy version (5:21b) makes more explicit the prohibition's focus on desire rather than action: *'awweh* denotes a desire that has emerged from one's inner needs/appetites, such as craving food (e.g., Numbers 11:4).[2] Harrelson further points out that both ancient Near Eastern literature and the Hebrew commandment of love of neighbor are concerned not only with deeds but also with inner feelings and motivations (e.g., Leviticus 19:18, 34). Lastly, if the prohibition of coveting designates an action, then there is redundancy between the last two commandments and the earlier prohibitions against adultery and stealing.

Here I find the last argument most compelling, for it puts the debate within the context of the Ten Commandments itself. In other words, coveting seems to be concerned with the attitude of the mind and heart. Yet the above-mentioned stories as well as our concrete human experience indicate that coveting is a needed driving force from which planned actions are produced. That means, coveting is "a disposition of the self in the direction of the deed."[3] As a result, we conclude that the prohibition on coveting highlights that inner dispositions and desires are as important as the prohibited acts themselves and are *inseparable* from the acts. They are the first step to these forbidden acts and are responsible to the act that follows. Exodus 20:17 thus could play the role of supplementing the sixth and seventh commandments. It also internalizes the teachings of the entire Decalogue.

In this fashion, coveting is more of a moral issue than a legal one, for it does not transgress any particular Israelite law in the strict sense. The two prohibitions draw the community's attention to the powerful role that inner movement of the heart and desire play in one's behavior: the desire for something often grows to a point that is beyond control, and subsequently one will plan on getting the desired thing not just by legal but also by illegal measures that are against the will of the neighbor (e.g., 1 Kings 21). There is thus an urgent need to cultivate self-control in one's desire.

Moreover, Fretheim's suggestion that the two commandments throw new light on the moral meaning of obedience is insightful:[4] true obedience involves not just avoiding specific prohibited actions but also the submission of one's desires. In this way, 20:17 invites individual Israelites to a change of inner attitude in living out their obedience to God. Specifically, the prohibitions call for an attitude of pure desire toward YHWH.

Consequently, "purity of heart and mind" is foundational to the two commandments. Indeed, the Hebrew Bible spells out the truth that YHWH desires a pure heart and pure desire from the Israelites (e.g., 1 Samuel 16:7).

Coveting the Neighbor's Wife

Regarding the specific content of the ninth commandment (verse 17b), we need first to understand the meaning and place of "wife" in relation to other objects in the verse. This is because the Exodus version does not single out the wife from the rest of the list as the Deuteronomy version does.[5] Some scholars are convinced that, by placing the wife among other possessions of the neighbor in the second prohibition, the writer of Exodus was in accord with the traditional view that the wife is part of what is owned by her free Israelite husband. Coveting the neighbor's wife is thus in the first place an

offense against the neighbor's property. Other scholars, such as Patrick, however, argue that a married woman is not considered in biblical law as the
property of her husband. Even if the wife were counted as part of her husband's possessions, she would not be *simply* a piece of property: the wife is a
crucial member of the house owner's workforce that contributes to his well-
being economically.[6]

Still, one scholar points out that, if this prohibition is related to the sixth
commandment, it would not make sense at all for anyone to "sexually" lust
after other property on the list. In order to resolve this puzzle, he counterproposes that the whole prohibition points to coveting the "dowry" of the wife.
Indeed, it was a common practice of the ancient Near East to provide a dowry
that could include both servant girls and land (1 Kings 9:16). Ancient Israel
was aware of such a practice and at times followed it, as in Jacob's marriage
and that of Acsah, where some kinds of gifts are mentioned (e.g., 1 Samuel
25:42).[7]

Unfortunately, such a proposal would risk the danger of completely denying any possible relationship between the sixth and the ninth commandments;
many of the stories of adultery told in the Hebrew Bible are in general also
stories of coveting the neighbor's wife, such as that of King David (2 Samuel
11). Wisdom literature also explicitly points out that coveting the neighbor's
wife often leads to violation of the sixth commandment and deserves the
death penalty (e.g., Proverbs 6:25–26).

The discussion thus far reveals that there is as yet no coherent view
regarding the meaning and the place of the wife in the formulation. By not
singling out the wife in the prohibition I suspect that the writer of Exodus
was not so much concerned about the neighbor's wife per se. Yet, as an
individual commandment that is related to the sixth commandment, coveting
the neighbor's wife seems not to focus on violation of the neighbor's property right either. Therefore, I propose that the least we can say is that the
commandment prohibits coveting a woman lustfully no matter whether one
perceives her as primarily the neighbor's possession or his human partner.

The immediate and explicit addressees of the commandment are therefore
male Israelites. In this fashion, I agree with Patrick that the commandment
differs from the rest of the Decalogue through having a gender-specified
addressee.[8]

Consequently, the commandment warns against unrestrained sexual inclinations that could otherwise lead to unlawful acts. It also attends to and
protects the well-being of women, which could be the specific rationale of
the prohibition. One scholar thus claims that it throws new light on the
understanding of the ancient Israelite custom of levirate marriage (Deuteronomy 25:5–10):[9] it is not so much an institutionalized exception to the prohibition on coveting the neighbor's wife as actually an obedience to the com-

mandment and protection of the woman, for the levir loses more than he gains. I find this claim further reflects society's role in protecting its female members, especially widows.

Finally, the commandment and its rationale raise the concern about immoral practices that may not be directly rooted in those unrestrained sexual desires but equally harm the well-being of Israelite women and their families, especially by means of violence and abuse of power, such as sexual assault and rape (Genesis 34). Positively, the commandment joins other commandments to underscore the need for Israelites to "respect" other community members. In the case of women, they are reminded to show proper esteem for them.

SHOWING ESTEEM FOR WOMEN

Many Christian ethicists, past and present, attend to the issue of taming lustful desires of men toward women when commenting on the ninth commandment. Some contemporary American writers, for example, cite former president Jimmy Carter's confession that he had lusted after some women in his heart.[10] Others, including the Pontifical Biblical Commission, claim that the commandment is all about degradation of humankind and hence its value lies in respecting all members of the community. Our exposition suggests that the commandment is concerned about *both* aspects, with special focus on the well-being of women.

Our Perception of Women

In the past century we have seen a growing recognition of the status and dignity of women in society. Still, women continue to be treated or portrayed as mere sexual objects and as subservient to men. For instance, women are often shown in sexually provocative poses/clothing in advertisement and media, presenting the message that what is important for women (and men) is their appearance alone. The situation is even worse in the porn industry, where women are simply objects for the satisfaction of men's lust.

Apart from being treated as objects of lust, women also suffer from all kinds of discrimination and ill treatment. The situation in Asia is particularly illustrative:[11] in South Asia, one in every four women is abused by men either physically or otherwise. The wide acceptance of male promiscuity, the stereotyping of women as burden bearers, and growing sex tourism in Southeast Asia have robbed many women of their basic dignity. In East Asia, although women are rather well educated, they are still subject to harassment and violence in their workplace and blocked from taking leadership roles in

the society.[12] As a whole, women in Asia do not receive the esteem and
dignity they deserve. Yet the situation of women in Asia is not a singular
case.

The Meaning of Showing Esteem for Women

The twofold concern of the commandment implies that showing esteem for
women likewise can be understood from two perspectives. First, it points to
the proper discipline of sexual desires toward women. Aquinas asserted that
it is primarily the question of concupiscence of the flesh.[13] Concupiscence is
"the movement of the sensitive appetite contrary to the operation of the
human reason" (*CCC* #2515). It can lead to sin when consent is given in the
heart, is expressed in words, and serves iniquity. In simple terms, concupiscence of the flesh is equated with lust. Still, lust is not just about desire but
also about power and control because, as Chittister rightly puts, it attempts to
consume all that we see (including ourselves).

Calvin claimed that in order to gain control of our sexual desires, charity
is crucial for regulating the thoughts of the mind and guarding it against
those harmful desires: when the mind is filled with a love of neighbor, it
leaves no room for cupidity (*ICR* 2.8.49, 50). The *Catechism of the Catholic
Church* further suggests that it points to the purification of the heart in the
area of sexual rectitude (#2518).

Second, showing esteem for women directs us to the protection and promotion of the well-being and dignity of women. Luther's view is helpful
here. In the context of marriage, he perceived the morality of the commandment as concerned with how any Israelite male can easily endanger his wife
by putting her away publicly and then estranging his neighbor's wife from
her husband. Specifically, men could manipulate the legal system so as to
satisfy their lustful desires (*LC* ##299, 305). Therefore, for Luther, to show
esteem for women is to protect their juridical rights and promote their equality.

However, how can the well-being of women be promoted outside the
juridical setting? Apart from advocating for and showing solidarity with
them, I am convinced that women need to take part in protecting their rights
and in showing esteem for themselves as well. One feminist remarks that
women should learn "not to be subservient to the wishes of their fathers,
husbands and partners."[14] They need to have the courage to protect themselves in their relationships with men and to promote their own cause, though
in many societies an individual woman can hardly do this on her own. Hence,
we all need to acquire certain relevant virtues.

Showing Esteem for Women as a Virtue

The above understanding brings about two groups of virtues that are relevant to showing esteem for women. First, the need to control one's sexual desire calls for the virtues of temperance and modesty. As Aquinas defined it, temperance denotes a kind of moderation that protects reason against the rebellious passions (especially those toward sensible goods like desire and pleasure of touch and taste). The virtue of modesty, theoretically, is an integral part of temperance (*ST* II.II. 141.3, 5; 160.1). It regards our outward presentation such as clothing and posture. In contemporary terms, modesty "protects the intimate center of the person . . . [and] guides how one looks at others and behaves toward them in conformity with the dignity of persons and their solidarity" (*CCC* #2521). Other virtues to be acquired here include the virtue of purity of heart and its related virtues of charity and chastity; both are hinted at in Calvin's (and the *Catechism*'s) interpretation.[15]

Second, in terms of protecting and promoting the well-being of women, showing them esteem again calls for the cultivation of the virtues of charity and justice (as "respect" would require) that assist in recognizing their dignity, and as equal to their male counterparts. In addition, both women and men have to acquire the virtue of courage in order to defend against any kind of gender discrimination, violence, and abuse of power, and to promote the well-being of women in society. Finally, the virtue of solidarity with women would do us all good.

The Practice of Showing Esteem for Women

Since desire is rooted in the mind and heart, keeping concupiscence under control requires both exterior and interior practices. We continue to find insights from the major figures of the past and of the present. Exteriorly, Aquinas suggested that one should preoccupy the self with other business so as to avoid whatever circumstances that may become an occasion to sin. Interiorly, one acquires the habit of prayer and mortification of the flesh, for there is an ongoing combat between the spirit and the flesh.[16] For Calvin, the practice of true piety—that is, a good conscience—and an unfeigned faith is significant (*ICR* 2.8.51). These interior practices in turn help nurture the virtue of purity of heart. While modern psychology would prefer more active measures, the *Catechism* simply proposes the discipline of feelings and imagination in our daily life (#2520). Nevertheless, as is the case of the sixth commandment (regarding chastity and fidelity), these practices highlight the role of spiritual practices of which we seldom think.

Practices that promote the well-being of women and attend to the issues of equality and dignity require equal opportunities in the world of education and work, and provisions for legal (and nonlegal) channels for reporting and challenging gender discrimination, harassment, violence, or abuse of power. It is also important to provide safe forums for women so that their voices can be heard and cultures transformed.

The Exemplars

In the gospels, Jesus turns our attention to the sinfulness of those inner thoughts and desires rather than the exterior acts (Matthew 15:19). In the specific area of sexuality, he is aware of the great impact of lust and goes so far as to even suggest that we should rid all possible sensations that cause such desires (Matthew 5:28–30). Still, as Stoppel rightly claims, Jesus does not only teach how we should cope with the lust of the flesh but also models a healthy and fitting relationship with women. Throughout his earthly mission, Jesus encounters women on many occasions—such as befriending the two sisters Martha and Mary (John 11:5) and engaging in conversation with the Samaritan woman (John 4:4–26)—with appropriateness, care, and concern no less than in his dealing with men. One scholar rightly says, "Jesus treated women with dignity and respect and he elevated them in a world where they were often mistreated."[17]

In the contemporary world, we see a growing number of Christian and non-Christian organizations promoting the dignity and well-being of women by means of education, advocacy, and academic writings. Within the U.S. Catholic Church, for example, we encounter feminist theologians who promote the cause of women through scholarship, such as biblical theologian Sandra Schneiders and ethicist Margaret Farley. Farley, in particular, clarifies that feminism, being a disputed term, "represents a position, a belief, a perspective, a movement, that is opposed to discrimination on the basis of gender."[18]

Beyond the Western world I note the example of the Ecclesia of Women in Asia, a forum of Asian Catholic women theologians that "seeks to develop theologizing from Asian women's perspectives and the recognition of Asian Catholic women theologians as colleagues in theological discussions within the Church and the Academe."[19] They address various issues related to the well-being of women, such as violence, Church structures, and the Bible, and call for greater integrity and justice on gender relationships in the Church.

The Social, Communal Aspect of the Virtue of Showing Esteem for Women

Although some of the virtues (like purity of heart) seem to be concerned with the character formation of individuals, they actually have an explicit impact on social attitudes toward women and sex. For instance, the virtue of modesty "protests . . . against the voyeuristic explorations of the human body in certain advertisements, [and] the solicitations of certain media that go too far in the exhibition of intimate things" (*CCC* #2523). Showing esteem for women also challenges the kind of moral permissiveness in society that encourages eroticism and pornography, which is a social manifestation of the lust of the flesh (*CCC* #2525). In this way, it indirectly criticizes the pervasive mentality that sex is simply a good to be consumed.

The virtue of showing esteem for women likewise has a clear social and communal tone in the promotion and protection of the well-being of women. It challenges society's recurring tolerance of polygamy that treats women as the property of husbands.[20] It also counteracts those existing institutional, societal, and international practices that discriminate and exploit women, especially women migrant workers. On the contrary, the virtue invites society to provide education and effective legislative (and sociopolitical) measures that assist women to stand on their own feet with confidence. From my limited privilege of encountering some of the above-mentioned feminist theologians and organizations, I would hope that the larger society can continue to show greater support to these initiatives.

NOTES

1. Patrick D. Miller, *The Ten Commandments* (Louisville, KY: Westminster John Knox Press, 2009), 390; see also Thomas B. Dozeman, *Commentary on Exodus* (Grand Rapids, MI: Eerdmans, 2009), 495.

2. Moshe Weinfeld, *Deuteronomy 1–11* , AB 5 (New York: Doubleday, 1991), 318, as cited in Michael D. Matlock, "Obeying the First Part of the Tenth Commandment: Applications from the Levirate Marriage Law," *Journal for the Study of the Old Testament* 31, no. 3 (March 2007): 302.

3. Walter J. Harrelson, *The Ten Commandments and Human Rights* (Macon, GA: Mercer University Press, 1997), 124. For Aquinas, the commandments on coveting likewise contain both the intention and the subsequent action taken. See Aquinas, "Explanation," http://dhspriory.org/thomas/TenCommandments.htm.

4. See Terence E. Fretheim, *Exodus* (Louisville, KY: Westminster John Knox Press, 1991), 239.

5. The writer of Deuteronomy held firmly that the wife is a woman and an equal partner to her husband. Consequently, the commandment in Deuteronomy 5:21 logically prohibits any kind of sexual and lustful desire after another's wife.

6. These scholars further employ this hypothesis to explain why children are not mentioned in the list.

7. See Robert Ivan Vasholz, "You Shall Not Covet Your Neighbor's Wife," *Westminster Theological Journal* 49, no. 2 (Fall 1987): 397–401.

8. Dale Patrick, *Old Testament Law* (Atlanta, GA: John Knox Press, 1985), 59.

9. Dennis T. Olson, *Deuteronomy and the Death of Moses*, OBT (Minneapolis: Fortress Press, 1994), 111, as cited in Matlock, "Obeying the First Part of the Tenth Commandment," 307. See also Stephen Kaufman, "The Structure of the Deuteronomic Law," *Maarav* 1 (1979): 143; Patrick D. Miller, *The Ten Commandments* (Louisville, KY: Westminster John Knox Press, 2009), 403.

10. See Joan Chittister, *The Ten Commandments: Laws of the Heart* (Maryknoll, NY: Orbis Books, 2006), 117; John C. Holbert, *The Ten Commandments* (Nashville, TN: Abingdon Press, 2002), 127.

11. See Elaine Ann Charles, "Promoting the Dignity of Women in Asia," www.laici.org/charles.pdf.

12. Asian women theologians are writing on this phenomenon. See Agnes Brazal and Andrea Lizares Si, eds., *Body and Sexuality* (Quezon City: Ateneo de Manila University Press, 2007).

13. Aquinas, "Explanation."

14. Chittister, *The Ten Commandments*, 119.

15. The virtue of purity of heart will be discussed in Part III.

16. Aquinas, "Explanation."

17. Thomas R. Schreiner, "Women in Ministry," in *Two Views on Women in Ministry*, ed. James R. Beck and Craig L. Blomberg (Grand Rapids, MI: Zondervan, 2001), 184.

18. Margaret A. Farley, "Feminist Ethics," in *Feminist Ethics and the Catholic Moral Tradition*, ed. Charles Curran, Margaret Farley, and Richard A. McCormick (New York: Paulist Press, 1996), 5.

19. Ecclesia of Women in Asia, "EWA Home," http://ecclesiaofwomen.ning.com/.

20. See Jan Shipps, "Polygamy Returns," *Religion in the News* 9 (2006): 7–10.

Chapter Fourteen

The Tenth Commandment in Exodus 20:17

You shall not covet your neighbor's house . . . or male or female slave, or ox, or donkey, or anything that belongs to your neighbor.

WHAT DID THE TEXT COMMAND?

After treating the prohibition on coveting the neighbor's wife, we now turn to the remaining prohibition in Exodus 20:17 that deals with the neighbor's property. We find a parallel Hebrew text that informs us what goods are coveted: fields, houses, people, and inheritances (Micah 2:2). Elsewhere, there are stories about coveting property, such as the classical example of King Ahab's desire to take hold of Naboth's vineyard. Although the text does not literally mention that King Ahab "coveted," most scholars agree that the presence of a consuming desire is very explicit. We read, "He lay down on his bed, turned away his face, and would not eat" (1 Kings 21:4). In Joshua 7 we also hear Achan's own confession that his stealing was a result of an unrestrained desire for the beautiful mantle that he had seen (v21). In sum, these texts show that coveting the property of others was a common phenomenon among these ancient people.

Within the Decalogue, the prohibition on coveting the neighbor's property is often referred back to the commandment against stealing. Cassuto notes that it shows connections with other commandments, too. For example, it forms an *inclusio* (that is, a bracketed passage) with the first commandment, both literally and theologically: the first commandment begins with and is about the God of the Israelites, while the last begins with and is concerned with their neighbors. The sin of idolatry is also identified with that of greed. In this way, the tenth is not only the last of the commandments but also affirms the view that the entire Decalogue is a carefully structured text.

Regarding the specific content of this second prohibition, three observations can be made. First, the lists of the two versions of the Decalogue are different: besides singling out the "wife" instead of the "house" from the formulation, the Deuteronomy version also adds the "field" to its list right after the "house." In addition, as mentioned in the previous chapter, Deuteronomy 5:21b uses a different Hebrew verb (*'awweh*, "desire") for coveting.

Second, there are in all seven kinds of goods (including the wife) that one should not covet. The list is similar to the one found in the third commandment on observing the Sabbath and, according to Cassuto, is common to ancient Near Eastern literature. Specifically, the first category in these lists could be understood as a general term. In light of this understanding, the categories listed after the "house" could be referred to as what the house owner would have. This partially explains why the "field" is not mentioned by the author of Exodus—the house is more than just a dwelling place, for it also has a broader interpretation, one that already includes the field. Deuteronomy's list, as Houtman explains, seems to highlight that the house, just as the field itself, is what is eyed greedily by one's brethren.

Third, the last category is a general expression to include what is not listed here. As Childs suggests, it gives the impression that there are just too many things that one could covet; it also shows that the list is meant to be all-inclusive. However, by making reference to other Hebrew texts, such as Leviticus 27:1–25, 28–29, one exegete wonders if the list could have a particular purpose:[1] its items could represent three important types of goods over which one has some claim—namely, real estate, people under one's authority, and animals. Though different in function, these three property groups essentially constitute one's personal economic life, as well as the lives of the family and of the community. Consequently, the house "signals both a family's means of sustenance and shelter and the network of human nurture that could grow only once these survival needs had been met securely."[2] It deserves special protection.

Summarizing, the above discussions point to a smooth conclusion of what else there is that belongs to our neighbor and that needs to be respected: we begin with the neighbor's life and move to one's wife, then to one's liberty and reputation, and finally to *all* that one possesses. Inversely, they also reveal what a greedy person would desire from the neighbor—almost *everything* that one's neighbor possesses.

Consequently, the rationale in this commandment seems to be the concern for one's desire to possess. On the one hand, the prohibition, like that of the seventh commandment, protects what belongs to an individual Israelite and sustains one's life and family. On the other hand, it aims at inhibiting the untamed inclinations that lead one to obtain illegally whatever possession belonged to other members of the community.

We remember that the Fall is precipitated by the uncontrolled desire to possess (Genesis 3:6), a desire which so often reflects a lack of trust in YHWH and an overreliance on what we possess (Job 31:24–28). Still, the commandment has an important moral aspect, too. The desire to possess raises the question of greed, prevalent in the community:[3] people covet beautiful things and precious metals/gems that are often used to make idols (Deuteronomy 7:25–26). In the marketplace, they use inaccurate weights and scales to take advantage of others (e.g., Deuteronomy 25:13–16). Our understanding of the content of this commandment further implies that greed seems to have no bounds!

Moreover, the commandment warns against the avarice of the rich and the powerful (such as the royalty), who already have more than what is adequate to sustain themselves and their families. The prohibition also helps prevent Israelites from excessive accumulation of (and attachment to) wealth, frequently the object of criticism by the prophets (e.g., Isaiah 3:16–26). Nonetheless, the last commandment, like the previous one, bears the positive value of calling Israelites to cultivate attitudes that help control excessive desire. As far as one's desire to possess is concerned, apart from "respect," the commandment suggests other inner values, such as satisfaction with what we are and what we have.

SATISFACTION WITH CONTENTMENT

Some contemporary writers, like Klinghoffer, are concerned with the issue of jealousy and envy, with the conviction that they are the source of covetousness. Others claim that the value promoted by the commandment is noninterference in the property of another. Still, there are writers whose interpretation is in line with what our exegesis suggests—that is, the need for positive attitudes regarding what one already has.

The More the Merrier?

The history of European colonization during the last few centuries, especially in Asia and Latin America, as Stoppel reflects, was often promoted by the desire for access to natural resources, and the means used often exploitative. Greed prompted not only the acquisition of gold, silver, spices, and silk, but also human beings for cheap labor.[4] He and others rightly note that such desire for things continues to find expressions in different levels and sectors in our contemporary world: consumerism and materialism encourage us to desire ever more and to accumulate as much as possible. Advertising and the media are designed to awaken the desire to possess well beyond need. The advancement of technology similarly leads us to desire what is the latest and most advanced. Certain practices within the business world, like credit card loans and second mortgages, co-opt our desire for more and tempt us to spend more than we should or have. Aren't the recent economic and ecological crises generated by the same illusion: consuming beyond our means?

Harrelson, Hauerwas, and others argue that the root problem of our human desire for more is not so much having a lot of desires but of yearning without limits (just as our exegesis implies) and not being content with what we already have at our disposal. Some authors even see it as a "spiritual disease" and the consequence of our restless dissatisfaction.[5] It deludes us into believing that getting what we desire will bring us satisfaction and happiness. However, the sad reality is that it will only make our desire stronger and more difficult to satisfy. Thus, even ancient Greek philosophers and Eastern religions have long pointed out that the only way to be happy is to still those desires.[6] Barclay further observes that competition and comparison may lead us to desire even what we do not have the right to have.[7] Consequently, we are strongly tempted to acquire inappropriately. In any event, when are we able to say "enough"?

The Meaning of Satisfaction with Contentment

Augustine once said, "You have made us for yourself, and our heart is restless until it rests in you."[8] Only God can fully satisfy our ultimate desire. Aquinas likewise understood our desire as endless and dissatisfied until we find rest in God. In this way, Christian contentment has a theological and teleological aspect—we should set our desire on the ultimate happiness, God. Aquinas further offered us important insights on the meaning of contentment.[9] First, it brings satisfaction to our hearts without inhibiting human flourishing. Second, it restores to the heart the peace that covetousness can destroy. Third, it treasures the riches that one has. Fourth, it safeguards the equality of justice. Fifth, it strengthens our love of God and of neighbors. Sixth, it prevents the emergence of all kinds of wickedness and the possibility of committing sins.

Luther was concerned about the use of seemingly lawful means by rich and pretentious people (*LC* ##296–310): they manipulated the legal system and cunningly practiced their trade irrespective of fairness and the needs of others. Therefore, justice, responsible relationships that go beyond following the letter of the law, and purity of heart are crucial to counteract unrestrained desires and to achieve contentment.

Calvin found unacceptable the acquisition of wealth with excessive eagerness even by lawful means. He thus demanded temperance and contentment (*ICR* 2.8.46). The latter "is gained by faith in God . . . , [points to] the nonchalance, the freedom from anxiety . . . [and] enables us to be patient in adversity and grateful and generous in abundance."[10]

Finally, the *Catechism of the Catholic Church* follows the teaching of Augustine and understands envy—which represents a particular form of sadness, comes from pride, and denies charity—as the capital sin and root cause of covetous desire (##2539–40). Contentment, on the contrary, has a claim on joy, humility, and charity.

Taken together, the understanding of contentment by major Christian figures of the past shows that it is not enough to do what the law and the society allow; rather, one needs to acquire certain inner values that attend to our inner self so as to bring lasting contentment.

Satisfaction with Contentment as a Virtue

The invitation to contentment reveals a nest of virtues, some of which are also found in other commandments. First, the teleological characteristic of contentment points to the theological virtues of faith and hope in God. Second, it directs us to the virtue of temperance in moderating our desire for and actual acquisition of goods. Third, contentment invites us to cultivate the virtue of tranquility that brings inner peace in accepting who we are and what we have. Fourth, by treasuring the riches we have, we show gratitude to the one who satisfies us (especially God). Indeed, gratitude is a significant key toward contentment. Fifth, contentment motivates us to promote the virtues of justice and honesty in interpersonal relationships and in trade, for avarice can move under the guise of prudence.[11] Sixth, it calls for charity, which is the great safeguard against greed and urges us to acquire the virtue of generosity toward those in need. Seventh, contentment requires the virtue of purity of heart just as the virtue of showing esteem for women does. Lastly, it counteracts those envious and jealous feelings by calling for humility.

The Practice of Contentment

Since gratitude is a major key to achieving contentment, a basic practice of contentment points to giving thanks to God and others for all that we have received. We also learn to enjoy and rejoice in our own little accomplishments and, as Stoppel suggests, say no to endless acquisition of wealth and goods.

Moreover, in joy we become more generous and charitable toward our neighbors, especially by joyously giving away and sharing our material goods and money. However, these practices alone do not address the temptation of covetousness within us. We need to acquire a peaceful, pure, and humble heart. In so doing, it is important first to acknowledge the presence of jealousy and envy within us. We also discern what is within and beyond our ability to acquire, and appreciate the goods that we can never own as well as the success of others.

On the spiritual level, the practice of meditation helps prevent the mind "from its continual striving and helps us experience the fullness of the present moment."[12] For example, one writer points out that the practice of the contemplation of death ("Memento Mori") in the late medieval and Renaissance periods reminds us of the reality of death and hence helps us to overcome the false attraction of the world and its wealth.[13] In the Christian funeral, as well as the Catholic celebration of Ash Wednesday, the recitation of Genesis 3:19 ("You are dust, and to dust you shall return") likewise reminds us of our humble origin and urges us not to cling to our earthly life. Concrete practices of mortification as well as living a simple lifestyle, as recommended by the *Catechism*, also help overcome the seductions of pleasure and power, and detach ourselves from those earthly goods (##2548–49).

Finally, contentment and happiness are found in healthy personal relationships with self, others, and God. As a result, the practices of self-respect, fidelity in human relationships, and obedience out of the love of God are recommended.

The Exemplars

As an ordinary Israelite who lived a simple lifestyle, Jesus of Nazareth teaches us how we should deal with material goods and wealth; we need not accumulate, worry about, or strive for earthly belongings, for God the Father will provide (Matthew 6:19, 25–34). His conversation with the rich young man further challenges us to give up our earthly possessions for the sake of discipleship (Matthew 19:16–30). Jesus also warns against greed and the danger of endless accumulation of wealth and possessions in our earthly life (Luke 12:13–21). Last but not least, Jesus is very aware of our inner desires and thus invites us to change and not to imitate the scribes and Pharisees who desire status and power (Matthew 23:1–12).

Throughout the history of Christianity, the example of the Desert Fathers is noteworthy. Among them was fourth-century John Cassian, who introduced the idea of monastic life to the West. He was convinced that living a life of radical renunciation of the world could help people to put covetousness behind them.[14]

Today we continue to see religious men and women who follow a monastic style of life as a counterexample to the values promoted by our secular society—Cistercians and Poor Clares, for example, whose lives are marked by solitude, contemplative prayer, renunciation, and labor. There are also members of secular institutes, single men and women who have chosen consecrated lives in the world witnessing to the simplicity of the Gospel. They demonstrate that finding satisfaction in God rather than in our possessions and wealth is not just possible but also necessary in our materialistic world.

Although these saints and models may seem impossible for most of us to follow today, we can begin with simple living. Perhaps imagination and self-reflection will be required here. for example, is it possible that we not only resist the impulse to consume more but also live with *less* in order for there to be both fair distribution of resources and sustainable development? Perhaps in order to get started, we might try a little prayer. The Irish Jesuits have developed a wonderful website precisely for busy people like us: www.sacredspace.ie.

The Social, Communal Aspect of the Virtue of Satisfaction with Contentment

The above description of monastic life and self-reflection gives the impression that the virtue of satisfaction with contentment is a personal virtue. Yet it does have a social, communal dimension. In the first place, it urges society to be self-critical of its consumerist and materialistic view that neglects other aspects of our human society, such as interpersonal relationship and spiritual lives of its citizens. It also reminds us that our self-worth, dignity, and identity are never determined by what we have.

Moreover, Lehmann and others are rightly concerned that capitalism, which emphasizes the economic function of the society, has turned human beings into commodities. Today, in many ways, the market not only tolerates but actually promotes exploitation in the workplace and disregards human welfare. Quality of life cannot be measured by an economic yardstick. Thus, the virtue of contentment challenges the rich and society itself to restore and respect the value and dignity of human beings. It indirectly promotes the rights of workers and protects them from exploitation.

Achieving contentment also invites us to shed our "rugged individualism" on both the societal and international levels, so that we become more ready to provide for the material needs of the poor and marginalized communities and nations. This might entail revamping the world's financial systems. [15]

Finally, the virtue counteracts certain lifestyles—especially in terms of the rate of consumption of nonrenewable natural resources—that are simply not sustainable. This points to international cooperation and global strategy in the conservation of the Earth.

As we saw in the previous chapter, coveting, as an appetite, is almost inseparable from the actions that flow from it. As a result, coveting another's possession has concrete implications in many aspects of our daily life. The comprehensive nature of the commandment reveals that, although it is the last of the Decalogue, the scope of its impacts on the levels of the individual and of society is no less significant than the other commandments. Moreover, the virtue of satisfaction with contentment is as much needed as those identified in the other nine commandments. In the concluding chapter, I will briefly comment on how these virtues are related. For now, I will turn to the Beatitudes.

NOTES

1. Erhard Gerstenberger, *Leviticus*, The Old Testament Library (Louisville, KY: Westminster John Knox Press, 1996), 441, as referenced in Patrick D. Miller, *The Ten Commandments* (Louisville, KY: Westminster John Knox Press, 2009), 393–96. Miller himself claims that in the case of the male and female slaves, the right of possession is only a temporary one.

2. Marvin L. Chaney, "'Coveting Your Neighbor's House' in Social Context," in *The Ten Commandments: The Reciprocity of Faithfulness*, ed. William P. Brown (Louisville, KY: Westminster John Knox Press, 2004), 313.

3. See Miller, *The Ten Commandments*, 398–406.

4. The acquisition of the Philippines, Hawaii, Cuba, and Puerto Rico by the United States at the turn of the twentieth century is also seen as an example of greed for territory and resources.

5. See Joan Chittister, *The Ten Commandments: Laws of the Heart* (Maryknoll, NY: Orbis Books, 2006), 112–13, 128; William Barclay, *The Ten Commandments* (Louisville, KY: Westminster John Knox Press, 1998), 191–92; James F. Keenan, *Commandments of Compassion* (Franklin, WI: Sheed & Ward, 1999), 56.

6. Buddha's Four Noble Truths see that craving and clinging lie at the heart of suffering.

7. Augustine rightly claimed that we specifically desire what is forbidden. See Augustine, *Confessions*, II.4.9.

8. Augustine, *Confessions*, I.1.1.

9. Aquinas, "Explanation," http://dhspriory.org/thomas/TenCommandments.htm.

10. Allen Verhey, "Calvin and the 'Stewardship of Love,'" in *The Ten Commandments for Jews, Christians, and Others*, ed. Roger E. Van Harn (Grand Rapids, MI: Eerdmans, 2007), 167.

11. See Russell R. Reno, "God or Mammon," in *I Am the Lord Your God: Christian Reflections on the Ten Commandments*, ed. Carl E. Braaten and Christopher R. Seitz (Grand Rapids, MI: Eerdmans, 2005), 225.

12. Donna Cunningham, "Gratitude: A Key to Contentment," *Vibration Magazine* 3, no. 4 (February 2001), www.essences.com/vibration/feb01/gratitude.html.

13. Reno, "God or Mammon," 232.

14. Ibid., 221.

15. Cf. the Pontifical Council for Justice and Peace, "Towards Reforming the International Financial and Monetary Systems in the Context of Global Public Authority," October 2011, http://www.vatican.va/roman_curia/pontifical_councils/justpeace/documents/rc_pc_justpeace_doc_20111024_nota_en.html.

III

Exegeting and Interpreting the Beatitudes in Matthew 5:3–12 for Ethical Living

The Beatitudes in Matthew 5 is as popular as the Decalogue and holds a significant place in both theology and Christian ethics. As seen in the prologue, both Catholic leaders and theologians often cite the two texts together. Biblical scholars further point out that the Decalogue and the Beatitudes are related to each other in a special way: they are set in the background of a mountain. The travel notice in Exodus 19:2–3 indicates that Moses went up to the mountain to meet YHWH. No matter whether Mount Sinai and Mount Horeb are the same mountain, it provides the necessary setting for the revelation of YHWH. In the case of the Beatitudes, the Matthean Jesus went up to the mountain and addressed the disciples and the crowds from there (Matthew 4:23–5:1). Similarly, although scholars disagree about which mountain it was, the symbolic-theological setting in Matthew is more important than the historical-geographical setting.

Indeed, the Beatitudes and the Decalogue are closely compared theologically: as Raymond Brown puts it, the Decalogue expresses God's will while the Beatitudes reveals the values Jesus prioritized.[1] Moreover, from a Christological point of view, just as Moses is the conveyer of the Law, the Matthean Jesus is the new lawgiver who calls for a deeper observance of the Law and thus is more authoritative than Moses.

Grounding itself in the narrative of the dialogue of Jesus with the rich young man in Matthew 19:16–21, *Veritatis Splendor* further attempts to depict the connection between the two texts:

> The Sermon on the Mount begins with the proclamation of the Beatitudes, but also refers to the commandments (cf. *Mt* 5:20–48). At the same time, the Sermon on the Mount demonstrates the openness of the commandments and their orientation towards the horizon of the perfection proper to the Beatitudes. [The Beatitudes] are above all *promises,* from which there also indirectly flow *normative indications* for the moral life. (##12, 16)

With these connections in mind, I now treat the Beatitudes in Matthew 5 in a manner parallel to the Ten Commandments.

NOTE

1. Raymond E. Brown, *An Introduction to the New Testament* (New York: Doubleday, 1997), 178.

Chapter Fifteen

The Beatitudes in History

As noted earlier, early Church Fathers like Gregory of Nyssa and John Chrysostom produced commentaries on the Beatitudes. Their Western counterpart, Augustine, also offered his own commentary on the Sermon on the Mount.[1] One of his insights is that the Sermon as a whole holds "all the precepts needed for our guidance in the Christian life" and thus has a "complete, perfect teaching on Christian morality."[2] For Augustine, the Sermon poses a perfectionistic ethics. It is intended for all followers of Christ, although some of the imperatives can be kept by only a few disciples.

Augustine held fast to the biblical language because it was for him rich in spiritual and moral content. As in the case of the Decalogue, Augustine interpreted Scripture with Scripture. For example, he turned to Isaiah 11 to make it clear that there are seven beatitudes, just as there are seven gifts of the Holy Spirit.[3] Moreover, he evoked personal experiences in his interpretation of the text, and he perceived the Beatitudes as a description of his own journey of conversion. Pinckaers notes that Augustine understood the Beatitudes as representing seven stages in the Christian life, as the principal part of and keystone that governs and divides the entire Sermon, and as the perfect answer to the question of happiness. Thus, Augustine's approach does not exactly belong to the work of exegesis or hermeneutics in today's understanding. Nevertheless, his reading of the Beatitudes has had a strong impact on the Church even until the thirteenth century.

During this long period, some theologians began to interpret the Beatitudes in the light of the virtues.[4] Ambrose claimed that the four beatitudes common to Luke and Matthew reflect the four cardinal virtues (justice, temperance, fortitude, and prudence). The medieval Dominican William Peraldus wrote a theological treatise on the relationship between the virtues and the Beatitudes. Francis of Assisi interpreted the text literally and physically, underlining a trend that claims that one's outward action manifests the inner disposition of the person.

Aquinas also related the Beatitudes to the virtues and claimed that the Beatitudes plays as significant a role in the New Testament as the Decalogue does in the Old Testament. His first detailed interpretation of the Beatitudes, as Jeremy Holmes notes, is found in the *Lectura in Matthaeum*.[5] Aquinas carried out the interpretative work by commenting word by word and with numerous biblical citations. For instance, Aquinas cited both Genesis 19:17 and Isaiah 2:2 to point out the link between the term "high mountain" and contemplation. He also divided the eight beatitudes to correspond to the three stages of the development of virtuous perfection—avoiding evil, pursuing good, and seeking perfection.

Holmes comments that Aquinas's interpretation is a kind of monastic exegesis that "focused on the reality described rather than on the text describing it."[6] One philosopher adds that "Aquinas's scholarly concerns seem more focused on appropriating the insights and arguments of earlier philosophers and theologians than on engaging in historical investigation of the biblical text."[7]

Later, in the *Summa Theologiae*, Aquinas returned to the Beatitudes and offered a more mature interpretation and division of the text (I.II. 69.3). Here, Aquinas seemed to agree with Augustine's view that in the Beatitudes is "the culmination of a succession of human responses to the question of happiness."[8] It became the primary source for his treatise on human happiness and our ultimate end.

Moreover, Aquinas associated each beatitude with a virtue acquired through a corresponding gift of the Holy Spirit, and he connected the three together in a systematic way (I.II. 68–70). He claimed that the beatitudes are not virtues. Carolyn Muessig comments that Aquinas thus departed from the Augustinian view that the seven beatitudes are gifts of the Holy Spirit and extensions of virtues (that indicate dispositions); rather, they are, for Aquinas, the subsequent perfect actions of these gifts.

Muessig also notes that it was the fourteenth-century Observant Franciscan Bernardino of Siena who first specifically interpreted the eight beatitudes in light of virtue: the Beatitudes is a grace that indicates one's soul is purified. Each beatitude is at the same time an extension of the virtues and an action disclosing one's inner and proper disposition. For example, the fourth beatitude pertains to righteousness with God, self, and neighbor. As a result, the virtues of self-discipline and honoring God, together with obedience, concord, and beneficence (toward neighbors), are needed for the realization of this righteousness. Moreover, as a preacher, Bernardino's interpretation focuses not only on individuals but also on the community.

During the Reformation, Luther also produced a commentary on the Beatitudes through a series of sermons on the Sermon on the Mount. It was basically an exegesis that had a polemical nature. Church historian Susan Schreiner notes that, for Luther, "the Bible spoke immediately to his own time."[9] She also observes that Luther rejected the traditional interpretation of the Beatitudes—that the beatitudes are evangelical counsels for the perfection of the spiritual "elite"—which leads to a two-level ethics of minimalism for most and perfection for a few. Rather, Luther held the Augustinian view that the Beatitudes is a command for all Christians—for instance, the call to be "pure in heart" addresses ordinary husbands and wives and children alike.

Calvin likewise preached on the Beatitudes in the form of short sermons.[10] Commentators generally agree that these sermons reveal the other side of Calvin: a passionate preacher who is critical of the spiritual interpretation of the text.[11] In this work, Calvin comments on the texts of both Matthew and Luke.

The interpretations of the Beatitudes by these major Christian figures are primarily homiletical and pastoral, much the same as the interpretations of the Decalogue. Yet we also see the emergence of reading the Beatitudes in the light of virtue.

Unfortunately, this trend to interpret the Beatitudes in light of virtue has lost some ground against the rise of other ethical approaches. For example, during the twentieth century, in his meditation guidebook Häring offered a performance-oriented interpretation of the text that is set within the context of the songs of the suffering servant in Isaiah. He claimed that Christian life is in essence a manifestation of the Beatitudes. Similarly, Gutiérrez uses the text in light of the Last Judgment in Matthew 25:31–46. He points out that the teachings of Jesus "begin with the blessing of the poor (Matt. 5); they end with the assertion that we meet Christ himself when we go out to the poor with concrete acts (Matt. 25)."[12] Gutiérrez is basically more concerned with the call for social transformation and social justice found in the text than the texts themselves.

Still, the recent resurgence in attention to virtue has led to a growing interest among ethicists to revisit the relationship between the Beatitudes and virtues.[13] Benjamin Farley identifies several virtues that are extolled in the Beatitudes, such as absolute renunciation and docility. Glen Stassen also turns to the Beatitudes for guidance in the search of virtues needed for peacemaking. He concludes that the Beatitudes (and other biblical traditions) are a better source than those traditional Greek virtues for a virtue ethics of peacemaking.[14] Verhey turns to the Beatitudes for his own agenda: for him, the Beatitudes is a kind of eschatological wisdom. Verhey concludes that this wisdom has practices that express the virtues and values that form our character.

Despite these notable exceptions, William Mattison rightly comments that a real lacuna still exists and that the recent resurgence of virtue ethics seems not to draw enough attention to the importance of the Beatitudes.[15] Mattison argues that the Beatitudes is appropriately understood in the context of the classical ethical reflection on the question of happiness and is a rich resource in answering virtue-focused questions. Furthermore, since the Beatitudes is all about happiness, it is only appropriate to employ virtue ethics that similarly seek happiness. However, Mattison himself is more concerned with arguing for an intrinsic relationship (or continuity) between the qualifying condition of the individual beatitude and the state of reward/happiness obtained by it. He basically presents a patristic view of the Beatitudes and specifically follows Augustine's approach. With my emphasis on the need for the prior work of exegesis, however, I am convinced that the chapters to follow and the schema employed here can lead us to a truer grasp of the meaning and therefore a better grounded interpretation of the Beatitudes.

NOTES

1. See Augustine, *The Lord's Sermon on the Mount*, trans. John James Jepson (New York: Newman Press, 1948). Servais Pinckaers has offered a very good review of Augustine's works on the Sermon. See his *The Sources of Christian Ethics*, trans. Mary Thomas Noble (Washington, DC: Catholic University Press, 1995). See also Robert Louis Wilken, "Augustine," in *The Sermon on the Mount through the Ages*, ed. Jeffrey P. Greenman, Timothy Larsen, and Stephen R. Spencer (Grand Rapids, MI: Brazos Press, 2007), 43–57.

2. Pinckaers, *The Sources*, 136.

3. Augustine's coordination of the Beatitudes and the gifts of the Holy Spirit can be traced back to the Cappadocian Fathers. See Hans Dieter Betz, *The Sermon on the Mount*, ed. Adela Yarbro Collins (Minneapolis, MN: Fortress Press, 1995), 46. However, Pinckaers notes that Augustine removed the eighth one, arguing that it is a recapitulation of the first, and the sum and fulfillment of the others.

4. See Carolyn Muessig, "Preaching the Beatitudes in the Late Middle Ages: Some Mendicant Examples," *Studies in Christian Ethics* 22, no. 2 (2009): 136–42.

5. Raphaelis Cai, ed., *Super Evangelium S. Matthaei Lectura*, 5th ed. (Rome: Marietti, 1951), as referenced in Jeremy Holmes, "Aquinas' *Lectura in Matthaeum*," in *Aquinas on Scripture: An Introduction to His Biblical Commentaries*, ed. Thomas G. Weinandy, Daniel A. Keating, and John P. Yocum (New York: T&T Clark, 2005), 74–76.

6. Holmes, "Aquinas' *Lectura in Matthaeum*," 84.

7. Eleonore Stump, "Biblical Commentary and Philosophy," in *The Cambridge Companion to Aquinas*, ed. Norman Kretzmann and Eleonore Stump (Cambridge: Cambridge University Press, 1993), 256.

8. Pinckaers, *The Sources*, 148.

9. Susan E. Schreiner, "Martin Luther," in *The Sermon on the Mount through the Ages*, ed. Jeffrey P. Greenman, Timothy Larsen, and Stephen R. Spencer (Grand Rapids, MI: Brazos Press, 2007) , 110.

10. See John Calvin, *Sermons on the Beatitudes*, trans. Robert White (Edinburgh: Banner of Truth Trust, 2006).

11. Paul Helm, "John Calvin on the Beatitudes," *Banner of the Truth*, June 12, 2007, www.banneroftruth.co.uk/pages/articles/article_detail.php?1291.

12. Gustavo Gutiérrez, "The Irruption of the Poor in Latin America and the Christian Communities of the Common People," in *The Challenge of Basic Christian Communities*, ed. Sergio Torres and John Eagleson, trans. John Drury (Maryknoll, NY: Orbis Books, 1981), 121.

13. However, this does not mean that reading the text through the lens of virtue is the only methodological approach. As I noted in the first chapter, Schockenhoff attempts to relate the theological-ethical interpretation of the Sermon on the Mount with natural law.

14. Glen H. Stassen, "The Beatitudes as Eschatological Peacemaking Virtues," in *Character Ethics and the New Testament: Moral Dimensions of Scripture*, ed. Robert L. Brawley (Louisville, KY: Westminster John Knox Press, 2007), 245–57.

15. William C. Mattison III, "The Beatitudes and Christian Ethics: A Virtue Perspective," paper presented at the annual meeting of the Society of Christian Ethics, San José, California, January 4–7, 2010.

Chapter Sixteen

Some Preliminary Questions

The Beatitudes is part of the Sermon on the Mount, which is widely known as the first of the five major discourses ascribed to Jesus in Matthew's gospel. Just as in the case of the Ten Commandments, many would point out that neither the Beatitudes nor the Sermon on the Mount is intended to stand by itself.[1] Therefore, in order to offer an exposition of the text that is faithful to the gospel, we need to look at both the Sermon and the gospel as a whole and attend to certain issues that may serve as exegetical guidelines.[2]

WHAT IS THE PLACE OF THE BEATITUDES IN THE GOSPEL OF MATTHEW?

Although Matthew's gospel is traditionally associated with Matthew the tax collector turned apostle, more and more scholars are suspicious of this identification.[3] Nonetheless, the linguistic structure, the style of writing, and particularly the evangelist's knowledge (and frequent use) of the Hebrew Scripture and his awareness of Jewish debates about certain legal issues have convinced many scholars that the author was beyond doubt a member of the Jewish community.[4] The evangelist's audience (and community) was likewise Jewish Christians who "were involved in an ideological and theological struggle over which movement best preserved and represented the heritage of Israel after the capture of Jerusalem and the destruction of its temple in 70 CE."[5] It is widely suggested that the community was situated in Antioch of Syria—a large Greek-speaking city where a substantial Jewish community had settled. Both the evangelist's apparent references to the destruction of the

Temple of Jerusalem (e.g., 22:7) and other external allusions indicate that the gospel was written after 70 CE but before the turn of the century, most probably around 85 or 90 CE.

This period was a time of crisis for the whole Jewish community. Judaism was in its early stage of transition during which various movements/communities emerged. As far as Matthew's community was concerned, its relationship with the broader Jewish community was complicated.[6] Moreover, the community adopted a policy of distancing itself from the Gentile world. It also seemed to have had difficulties with those "law-free" Christians.

Alongside the destruction of the Temple and the presence of Roman control, Matthew's community inevitably sought its own identity and continuity (within discontinuity). The fundamental purpose of the gospel was to point out that Jesus is "the authoritative interpreter of the Torah and the fulfillment of Israel's hopes."[7] The best way to preserve the heritage of Christian Jews is to follow Jesus's teaching and example and to recognize him as the Son of David and the Lord.

These observations lead us to consider the gospel as fundamentally a Jewish text "in its conceptual and rhetorical assumptions, in its sociological setting, and in its theological message."[8] It is thus seen as the most Jewish gospel. However, the gospel is sometimes misinterpreted as anti-Jewish for its polemical tone in certain texts (e.g., 27:25).[9]

Regarding the source of the gospel, most scholars accept the so-called two-source hypothesis: the evangelist apparently employed the materials from Mark, the Sayings source Q,[10] and other oral (and/or written) traditions peculiar to Matthew. As will be discussed shortly, while there is no firm evidence that Matthew depended directly on any particular Jewish apocalypse (and vice versa), Matthew at least shared their apocalyptic theology.[11]

Scholars generally divide the gospel into sections even though the divisions are themselves debatable. Many continue to adopt Benjamin Bacon's principle—that there are five major speeches (chapters 5–7, 10, 13, 18, 24–25), each containing a discourse and a narrative, and ending with a phrase like "when Jesus had finished saying these words."[12] Nevertheless, some remark that the gospel is structurally mixed despite its apparent unity, and Matthew's "plan" was "much less systematic and much richer in variety than most scholars have thought."[13]

Finally, Ulrich Luz, William Davies, and Dale Allison observe that Matthew used many different literary techniques to construct his gospel. He also demonstrated a penchant for numbers (especially the triad), as learned Jews did. In addition, the evangelist was inclined to suggest his themes by repeating key words (e.g., "righteousness") or summarizing statements (e.g., 7:12).

Is It for the Future?

Due to the influence of Jewish messianic and eschatological apocalyptic movements on the Sayings source Q, we may assume that the synoptic gospels are colored by an apocalyptic worldview.[14] In the case of Matthew, it is noted that all the characteristics of Jewish apocalyptic theology and eschatology are present in the gospel (e.g., 19:28).[15] Indeed, Matthew had been seen as "the most thoroughly 'apocalyptic-eschatological' of the gospels in its general outlook."[16]

One scholar turns to the sociohistorical setting of the community to explain why Matthew took recourse to apocalyptic eschatology:[17] for instance, its characteristics allowed the community to legitimate their existence and sectarian inclination in times of isolation. Furthermore, the fear of punishment generated from apocalyptic literature could offer the community pragmatic ethical value—especially "[the] demand for a committed life in the face of fierce opposition and conflict."[18]

WHAT IS THE PLACE OF THE BEATITUDES IN THE SERMON ON THE MOUNT?

Matthew's Sermon on the Mount is situated toward the beginning of the gospel. If we take the view that the gospel consists of five major speeches, then the Sermon is the first of these five discourses. Nevertheless, most scholars agree that the Sermon is by no means an independent speech. The broader context must be considered, for it is part of the story of Jesus and an integrated part of the gospel as told by Matthew.

In light of this, no one would deny that the Sermon plays an important role in the gospel. However, there is no consensus among scholars regarding its exact place and role: some suggest that the Sermon is simply "the example par excellence" of Jesus's teaching; others claim that the entire gospel is a commentary on the Sermon. A more nuanced path suggests that "most of the topics covered in the Sermon come up again elsewhere in Matthew, where they are often treated at further length."[19]

On the other hand, the designation of the notion of "sermon" can be traced back to Augustine. However, Matthew's use of οἱ λόγοι ("sayings") and ἡ διδαχή ("teachings") implies that the Sermon, strictly speaking, is not really a speech. Betz thus proposes that the specific literary genre of the Sermon is one of "epitome"—"a condensation of a larger work, made . . . [with] brevity and precision in selection and formulation . . . intended to be a systematic synopsis."[20]

Still, Allison and others are convinced that the Sermon is partially a poetic text that is both dramatic and pictorial. Specifically, it employs hyperbole, which is common among Semitic literature. Harrington, from a different perspective, suggests that the Sermon is closest to the instructions found in the wisdom literature, such as Sirach. [21]

While much of the Sermon on the Mount could be originated from the Q sayings, Warren Carter insists that Matthew also carried out redactional work like expansions and reordering. Yet the evangelist also might rely on materials peculiar to Matthew alone (e.g., 6:16–18). One Jewish writer even argues for the presence of Jewish influence by recalling Tertullian's words that the Sermon is "in agreement with the spirit and teaching of the Hebrew Scriptures." [22]

Despite these diverse views, one can still claim that either the anonymous redactor or the evangelist creatively shapes and interprets those materials passed on to him by the early Christian community. It could be formulated "in direct confrontation with Pharisaic Judaism." [23] Still, based on our earlier discussion of the settings of the gospel, I take the view that the Sermon is meant to "[proclaim] the definitive and authoritative teaching of Jesus for [the] community . . . [and provide] guidance on how disciples of Jesus are to live and [sustain] the community's self-understanding in a situation of transition and marginality." [24]

This leads to the inquiry about the basic theme of the Sermon. One popular viewpoint is "greater righteousness"—it refers not just to a righteousness that is greater than that of the Jewish Pharisees and scribes but also to the lifestyle of those who devote themselves to God wholeheartedly by doing God's will. [25] However, others, like Luz, counterpropose that the notion of "Father" is the core subject matter of the Sermon and hence argue that the Lord's Prayer (6:9–13) is the heart of Matthew 5–7.

In either case, Allison rightly claims that the themes identified often determine the structure of the Sermon. For those who focus on the theme of "greater righteousness," the Sermon can be divided into parts that specify those who practice the greater righteousness and the kinds of practices Jesus demands. Those who claim the centrality of the Lord's Prayer either center it on other units (such as the Beatitudes) or divide the Sermon into symmetrical parts. Carter notes that there are a few scholars who even suggest that the Beatitudes provides the structure for the Sermon—the rest of the Sermon is basically an expansion in reverse order of the Beatitudes. Again, there is no real agreement among scholars. What is sure, as Joseph Fitzmyer claims, is that Matthew's Sermon on the Mount is better structured than Luke's Sermon on the Plain, for it is constructed around a single core theme. [26]

Is It a Radical Ethics for All?

No matter whether one considers the Sermon as an epitome or not, Matthew 5–7 has an explicit ethical function. Davies and Allison claim that the Sermon on the Mount is the summation of Jesus's moral demand that implies the motif of the imitation of Jesus Christ. Harrington, from a different perspective, highlights that the Sermon is concerned with both principles and attitudes and that it has personal and communal ethical implications. Charles Talbert likewise comments that the Sermon "[serves] as a catalyst for the formation of character."[27]

While its ethical function is undeniable, one still wonders whether Matthew 5–7 contains radical ethics or not, and whether they are meant for all people. We have already seen that there is a spectrum of views throughout history, ranging from exclusiveness to inclusiveness. Again, grounded in the apocalyptic-eschatological nature of the gospel, I take the view of those (such as Davies, Allison, and Jack Dean Kingsbury) who argue that the determining factor of Jesus's ethics is the reality of God's eschatological kingdom. Only when reading the Sermon in light of its eschatological orientation can its radical demands be explained. Even if one cannot achieve moral perfection, one builds up one's character through earnest striving. Moreover, the ideal posted by the Sermon is a necessity—it has the ultimate end in view and sets forth the means to that end.[28] By adopting Climacus's view on virtue, the Sermon's ethical demand can be perceived as a ladder or as a challenge to Christians to become better over the course of time.

WHAT DOES THE TERM "BEATITUDE" MEAN? IS THERE ONLY ONE BEATITUDES IN THE BIBLE?

The term "beatitude" is derived from the Latin word *beatitudo* and is equivalent to the Greek term μακάρισμος ("macarism"), which refers, as we shall see, to a literary genre. It is derived from the adjective μακάριος meaning "blessed" or "happy." Another Greek adjective that has a similar meaning is ευδαιμων, the same adjective employed by Aristotle in his discussion of human happiness.[29] The evangelist, however, opted for μακάριος for a specific reason: it points toward the divine happiness that is intended by Jesus for his followers.

As a literary genre, "macarism" refers to a living, multisided form of speech when used in the predicative form.[30] Betz notes that ancient macarisms were ritual in function, declarative in nature, and present-and-future in orientation and in relation with morality. Later on, macarisms were employed to formulate a philosophical idea in a succinct way, or to serve as an introduction to the instructions that follow.

Macarisms are also found in the Bible, and the adjective is commonly translated into "blessed" and "happy" to denote the happiness bestowed by God upon those who receive God's blessings.[31] Although some biblical scholars find these translations either inadequate or unsuitable, I follow the English translation adopted by the *New Revised Standard Version* (i.e., "blessed").

In the Hebrew Bible, the macarisms usually appear either in pairs or in series (e.g., Sirach 14:1–2). Specifically, they first appeared in wisdom literature and later were employed in apocalyptic writings (e.g., Daniel 12:12). In the wisdom literature, some macarisms pronounce blessings on ethical conducts that are offered as models (e.g., Proverbs 3:13) and point to moral exhortation; others speak of the happiness that is granted and indicate the nature of these blessings (e.g., Psalm 144:12–15). In addition, they assumed that good deeds are rewarded in the present. Those macarisms found in apocalyptic literature, in contrast, focused on assurance and the proffering of hope in the future. Blessings are pronounced in the present and promises are to follow, as in Tobit 13:14. As a whole, they are employed to "create, or recreate, an apocalyptic vision in the imagination of the reader."[32]

In the New Testament, macarisms are usually found in Matthew and Luke, and they are all used to express religious joy. Similar to what is observed in the Old Testament macarisms, New Testament macarisms are also diverse in forms and types, and they are divided into sapiential and eschatological macarisms, as in Romans 14:22 and Revelation 19:9, respectively. They also appear either in isolation (e.g., Matthew 11:6) or in series. The Beatitudes is a typical example of the latter form.

WHAT ARE THE CHARACTERISTICS OF THE BEATITUDES?

The Background, Source, and Origin of the Beatitudes

While the genre of macarism might have ancient Egyptian and Greek origin, Betz is convinced that the macarisms in 5:3–10 share the tradition of Jewish wisdom literature.[33] George Wesley Buchanan further claims that the Beatitudes seems to be closely related to certain Hebrew biblical texts, especially passages from Isaiah (57, 61, 66), and Psalm 37. However, Buchanan warns that "in dealing with the Beatitudes . . . it is not enough to recognize the quotations of scripture included in them. These texts must be understood against their entire background."[34] The Babylonian Jews expected that they would be redeemed by their Lord, who also redeems Jerusalem, proclaims good news to the afflicted, and comforts those who mourn. It was "this mythological background upon which the author of the Beatitudes appealed, assuming that his readers were in the same situation as the captive Jews in Babylon."[35]

Regarding the origin of the Beatitudes, most scholars assume that at least the three common beatitudes of Matthew (5:3, 4, 6) and Luke (6:20b, 21) are dependent on Q. Based on this assumption, some claim that the differences between the two versions (such as the additional beatitudes of Matthew and the woes in Luke) are simply due to the redaction of the evangelists. Subsequently, the stages of redactional development of the Matthean Beatitudes can be proposed as follows:[36] there were three original beatitudes (vv3, 4, 6) found in both Matthew and Luke. They were expanded with the addition of a fourth beatitude (v5) and all of them employ the "π" alliteration.[37] Matthew added three beatitudes that he found in the tradition that reflect the concerns for greater righteousness (vv7–9). Finally, he rearranged the order and added the eighth one (v10) so as to form two balanced sets of beatitudes.

However, this entire claim is not without challenges, especially by those who think that Luke used Matthew. As a result, there is no overwhelming consensus regarding the exact relationship between the two versions.

The Unity and Structure of the Beatitudes

Borrowing Luz's words, a first glance at the Beatitudes gives the impression that they are "self-contained and compactly composed."[38] Indeed, many agree with Luz that such a unity is found: the first and the eighth beatitudes enclose the texts with the same, long concluding clause to form a single unit.[39] Buchanan concludes that the consistency and unity of the eight beatitudes lies in their shared meaning, repetition, scriptural background, and stylistic composition.

However, there is no consensus among scholars on how they are structurally united. One dominant view is that there are two sets of four beatitudes:[40] the first four beatitudes are grouped together for they employ adjectives that begin with the Greek "π" sound. Both sets conclude with the use of righteousness and contain an equal number of words (thirty-six). Moreover, if the first set focuses on the persecuted (passive) condition of the disciples or their relationship to God, then the second set treats the ethical qualities that lead to persecution or their relationship to others.

The other dominating view claims that the Beatitudes is comprised of *inclusio*, where the first and the eighth beatitudes employ the enveloping present tense of the verbs as well as the same concluding clause. A "chiastic" structure (that is, a symmetrical ABBA pattern) is proposed, and within that framework certain structural characteristics, such as parallels, rhyme, and alliteration between individual beatitudes, are identified. Based on these structural characteristics, others add that the Beatitudes demonstrates the kind of poetic structure defining Hebrew poetry. In conclusion, although a universally agreed-upon structure of the Beatitudes may not be possible, we may still claim that the Beatitudes is one of the most carefully crafted passages and that there is a sophisticated web of relationships between the individual beatitudes.

Internally, each macarism is comprised of a two-line statement: the first line is introduced by μακάριοι while the second one begins with ὅτι ("for/ that/because") and contains a promise. In other words, each beatitude has a pronouncement concerning who the blessed is, as well as a promise concerning why one is blessed.

Augustine argued that there are seven beatitudes.[41] Many other scholars, however, insist that there are eight of them. Still, there are some scholars like Davies, Allison, and Harrington, who would include verses 11 and 12 as well, making the beatitudes nine; these two verses, though different in form from the preceding verses, are thematically closer to the eighth beatitude than to 5:13–16. Having a much longer concluding text of a series also seems conventional. The changes in verses 11 and 12 could be simply a result of literary design. Convinced that there are nine macarisms, they note that this fits the tripartite number. A few scholars would even opt for ten beatitudes solely based on the numerical popularity in Jewish symbolism and employ the Decalogue as a model.

Finally, it is noted that some scholars attempt to show correlation of the Beatitudes with the Sermon by rearranging, pairing up, and dividing the Beatitudes in such a way that shows coherence with 6:19–7:12. Others adopt a kind of arbitrariness in searching for connections (e.g., the first beatitude corresponds to 7:7–11).[42] Although these strategies are diverse, they affirm that the Beatitudes is closely related to the Sermon and plays a unique role in revealing the teaching of the Sermon. What, then, is the function of the Beatitudes in the Sermon and the gospel?

The Function of the Beatitudes

There are different proposed views with regard to the function of the Beatitudes.[43] I classify these perspectives into three basic types. First, the Beatitudes is primarily hortatory in nature. It is an ethical imperative calling for cultivation of certain character traits and for regulations for the community life. Specifically, it is perceived as entrance requirements for the kingdom.

Second, the Beatitudes points to a kind of eschatological ethics. Some argue that the beatitudes are primarily declarative promises and are moral imperatives only secondarily. They are offered as eschatological blessings and hope for the oppressed. The Beatitudes is therefore conciliatory and implies the notion of grace.

The third view is a more nuanced one. Scholars like Betz are convinced that the Beatitudes must be seen as both a series of ethical virtues and promises because they are at the same time future-oriented and pronounced in the present. Luz, who thinks that they continue to express God's grace, concludes that these different approaches are complementary to each other. Harrington, in a similar way, says, "The [b]eatitudes function not as 'entrance requirements' but rather as a delineation of the characteristics and actions that will receive their full and appropriate eschatological reward."[44]

Last but not least, a related debate regarding the function and ethics of the Beatitudes is whether it offers reversals or rewards. Those who insist on seeing the eight beatitudes as statements of reversal for the unfortunate would argue that Jesus proclaims a revolutionary nature of the kingdom of God.[45] Others like Luz suggest that each beatitude should be allowed to be interpreted on its own terms even at the expense of diminishing unity. In order to resolve this problem, one writer suggests that the first half of the Beatitudes "speaks of reversals for the unfortunate" while the second half "describes rewards for the virtuous."[46] However, such an attempt risks dichotomizing and segregating the Beatitudes.

MY OWN APPROACH

The above exploration reveals that many of these critical issues, just like those of the Decalogue in Exodus 20, do not have a definitive solution. Yet this discussion helps lay the foundation that will guide my exegesis.

In the first place, the Beatitudes, though structurally formed into a single unit, is related to the Sermon and the gospel as a whole. Specifically, the apocalyptic-eschatological nature of the gospel plays an important role in our understanding of the Sermon and the macarisms. Thus, though our exegesis is focused on the eight beatitudes, it is done in light of the Sermon and the gospel.

Second, the reason for taking up the translation adopted by the *New Revised Standard Version* Bible is that, just as μακάριος implies a divine characteristic that ευδαιμων lacks, it seems that "blessed" likewise offers a stronger religious tone than the term "happy" does and highlights its source, God. Its direct reference to prosperity can also be particularly helpful for cross-cultural dialogue. Nevertheless, I adopt the translation "blessed" without diminishing the original meaning of the Greek term.

Third, I too assume the majority view that certain beatitudes are rooted in the Sayings source Q and the remaining ones are a result of redaction by the evangelist. Therefore, our exegesis will attend to the redactional differences between the Matthean and Lukan Beatitudes.

Fourth, insofar as Matthew 5:3–12 forms a sophisticated unified whole with a specific structure, I decline to divide them into two sets of beatitudes for the same reason I argue in treating the Decalogue: it risks segregation and undermines their interconnectedness. Thus, I will explore the relationship among the beatitudes in the examination of each of them.

Fifth, I would adopt the traditional view that there are eight beatitudes, for they form a more unified structural unit. Their structural coherence also fits the genre of macarism better. Moreover, the cultural factor is considered here: the traditional view of "eight beatitudes" is widely known and accepted by Christians and non-Christians alike. Considering eight instead of seven or nine beatitudes may be more helpful to engage dialogue with them. Verses 11 and 12 can be well integrated into the exposition knowing that they are thematically close to verse 10 (and therefore can be an elaboration of the eighth beatitude).

Sixth and finally, I too perceive the Beatitudes as neither a set of solely moral demands nor as one of eschatological promises. This perception is in line with the "already-but-not-yet" nature of the kingdom of God, which calls for both active response within the community and attentiveness toward the ultimate end. Furthermore, the blessings need not be construed exclusively as either reversals or rewards. They both point to the effects of God's grace to those who follow Jesus's teaching and example.

After stating my own approach, a subsequent question yet needs to be raised: Who, then, are the blessed in the Matthean Beatitudes? Thus, I now turn to the exposition of each of these eight beatitudes with the hope that some hints can be found during the process.

NOTES

1. William D. Davies and Dale C. Allison Jr., "Reflections on the Sermon on the Mount," *Scottish Journal of Theology* 44, no. 3 (1991): 299.

2. For instance, it is noted that "the Sermon's connection to the rest of Matthew's gospel [highlights] the relationship of God's gift and demand, of law and grace." See Warren Carter, *What Are They Saying about Matthew's Sermon on the Mount?* (New York: Paulist Press, 1994), 2–3.

3. In deference to convention, I refer to the evangelist as Matthew.

4. See William D. Davies and Dale C. Allison Jr., *A Critical and Exegetical Commentary on the Gospel according to Saint Matthew*, vol. 1 (New York: Continuum, 1988), 9–33, 58. John Meier counterproposes that Matthew was either a learned Gentile scholar or a Greek-speaking Diaspora Jewish Christian. See his *The Vision of Matthew: Christ, Church, and Morality in the First Gospel* (New York: Paulist Press, 1991), 22–23.

5. Daniel J. Harrington, *The Synoptic Gospels Set Free: Preaching without Anti-Judaism* (Mahwah, NJ: Paulist Press, 2009), 8.

6. Charles H. Talbert argues that Matthew's separation is one *within* Judaism and not *from* it. See his *Reading the Sermon on the Mount: Character Formation and Ethical Decision Making in Matthew 5–7* (Columbia: University of South Carolina Press, 2004). Ulrich Luz, however, claims that Matthew's community was no longer belonging to the Jewish system. See

his *Matthew 1–7: A Commentary*, trans. James E. Crouch (Minneapolis: Fortress Press, 2007), 54. See also Andrew Overman, *Matthew's Gospel and Formative Judaism: The Social World of the Matthean Community* (Minneapolis: Fortress Press, 1990), as referenced in Donald Senior, *What Are They Saying about Matthew?* (Mahwah, NJ: Paulist Press, 1996), 10. Nonetheless, many agree that Matthew's community obviously separated from the synagogue. See Carter, *What Are They Saying about Matthew's Sermon on the Mount?*, 62. See also David C. Sim, *Apocalyptic Eschatology in the Gospel of Matthew* (Cambridge and New York: Cambridge University Press, 1996), 181–221.

7. Harrington, *Synoptic Gospels*, 9.

8. Daniel J. Harrington, *The Gospel of Matthew, Sacra Pagina* (Collegeville, MN: Liturgical Press, 2007), 2.

9. For a detailed discussion, see Harrington, *Synoptic Gospels.*

10. The Sayings source Q (after the German word *Quelle*, meaning "source") is referred to as a collection of Jesus's sayings.

11. Apocalyptic theology or eschatology is concerned with the coming of the Messiah, a judgment with rewards and punishments, and the arrival of the new world in its fullness. See Adela Yarbro Collins, ed., "Introduction," in *Early Christian Apocalypticism: Genre and Social Setting, Semeia* 36 (Decatur, GA: Scholars Press, 1986).

12. Benjamin W. Bacon, *Studies in Matthew* (London: Constable, 1930), as referenced in Senior, *What Are They Saying about Matthew?*, 26.

13. Senior, *What Are They Saying about Matthew?*, 35. See also R. H. Gundry, *Matthew: A Commentary on His Literary and Theological Art* (Grand Rapids, MI: Eerdmans, 1982), 11; and James Moffatt, *An Introduction to the Literature of the New Testament* (New York: Scribner, 1911), 244, as cited in Davies and Allison, *A Critical and Exegetical Commentary*, 72.

14. See John S. Kloppenborg, "Symbolic Eschatology and the Apocalypticism of Q," *HTR* 80 (1987): 296, as cited in John J. Collins, *The Apocalyptic Imagination: An Introduction to Jewish Apocalyptic Literature*, 2nd ed. (Grand Rapids, MI: Eerdmans, 1998), 259.

15. See Sim, *Apocalyptic Eschatology in the Gospel of Matthew*, 75–177.

16. Frederick C. Grant, *The Gospels: Their Origin and Their Growth* (London: Faber and Faber, 1957), 137, as quoted in Sim, *Apocalyptic Eschatology in the Gospel of Matthew*, 2n.

17. See Sim, *Apocalyptic Eschatology in the Gospel of Matthew*, 3–4, 181–221, 241–42. See also B. H. Streeter, *The Four Gospels: A Study of Origins* (London: Macmillan, 1924), as referenced in Sim.

18. Lisa Sowle Cahill, "Gender and Strategies of Goodness: The New Testament and Ethics," *Journal of Religion* 80, no. 3 (July 2000): 447. See also Yarbro Collins, "Introduction," 8.

19. Dale C. Allison Jr., *The Sermon on the Mount: Inspiring the Moral Imagination* (New York: Crossroad, 1999), 9.

20. Hans Dieter Betz, *Essays on the Sermon on the Mount*, trans. L. L. Welborn (Philadelphia: Fortress Press, 1985), 13–14.

21. Daniel J. Harrington, "Problems and Opportunities in Matthew's Gospel," *Currents in Theology and Mission* 34, no. 6 (December 2007): 418. Luz, on the contrary, claims that there is no real analogy between the Sermon and other form structures and hence one should not seek any conclusion regarding the Sermon's genre. See his *Matthew 1–7*, 174.

22. Gerald Friedlander, *The Jewish Sources of the Sermon on the Mount* (New York: KTAV, 1969), 16.

23. William D. Davies, *The Setting of the Sermon on the Mount* (Cambridge: Cambridge University Press, 1966), as cited in Senior, *What Are They Saying about Matthew?*, 8.

24. Carter, *What Are They Saying about Matthew's Sermon on the Mount?*, 65.

25. Jack Dean Kingsbury, "The Place, Structure, and Meaning of the Sermon on the Mount within Matthew," *Interpretation* 41 (April 1987): 137.

26. Joseph A. Fitzmyer, *Gospel according to Luke*, Anchor Bible (Garden City, NY: Doubleday, 1981–1985), as referenced in Jan Lambrecht, *The Sermon on the Mount: Proclamation and Exhortation* (Wilmington, DE: Michael Glazier, 1985), 26.

27. Charles H. Talbert, *Reading the Sermon on the Mount*, 29.

28. Davies and Allison, "Reflections," 308.

29. Carl G. Vaught also points out that the nature of happiness found in the Beatitudes is not just divine but also relational. It also points to an inner condition "that can be achieved regardless of the circumstances in which we find ourselves." Vaught, *The Sermon on the Mount: A Theological Investigation*, rev. ed. (Waco, TX: Baylor University Press, 2001), 13–14.

30. M. Hengel, "Zur matthäischen Seligpreisungen," *TRu* 336, as cited in James W. Thompson, "The Background and Function of the Beatitudes in Matthew and Luke," *Restoration Quarterly* 41, no. 2 (1999): 109.

31. Thomas Hoyt Jr., "The Poor/Rich Theme in the Beatitudes," *Journal of Religious Thought* 37, no. 1 (1980): 34. According to Davies and Allison, the Hebrew word *ashre* ("happy"), though not applied to God, was the basis of the Septuagint/Greek translation of the Hebrew Bible (*A Critical and Exegetical Commentary*, 432).

32. Betz, *Essays on the Sermon*, 102.

33. Some exegetes thus conclude that the beatitudes are sayings of a sophisticated literary nature. For a detailed discussion of the complex web of the Beatitudes, see Andreij Kodjak, *A Structural Analysis of the Sermon on the Mount* (New York: Mouton de Gruyter, 1986), 41–74.

34. George Wesley Buchanan, "Matthean Beatitudes and Traditional Promises," in *New Synoptic Studies*, ed. William R. Farmer (Macon, GA: Mercer University Press, 1983), 162.

35. Ibid., 166.

36. This is the proposal of Christopher Tuckett. See his "The Beatitudes: A Source-Critical Study. With a Reply by M. D. Goulder," *Novum Testamentum* 25 (1983): 193–214.

37. Christine Michaelis noted that all the Greek forms of the subjects of the first four beatitudes begin with "π": πτωχοί, πενθοῦντες, πραεῖς, πεινῶντες. See her "Die π-Alliteration der Subjectsworte der Ersten 4 Seligpreisungen in Mt. v.s3–6 und ihre Bedeutung für den Aufbau der Seligpreisungen die Mt., Lk., und in Q," *Nov* 2 (1968): 148–61, as cited in Neil J. McEleney, "The Beatitudes of the Sermon on the Mount/Plain," *Catholic Biblical Quarterly* 43, no. 1 (January 1981): 13.

38. Luz, *Matthew 1–7*, 185.

39. See Alfred A. Plummer, *An Exegetical Commentary on the Gospel according to S. Matthew* (New York: Charles Scribner's Sons, 1910), 61; and John P. Meier, *The Gospel according to Matthew* (New York: W. H. Sadlier, 1983), 116. Both are cited in Buchanan, "Matthean Beatitudes and Traditional Promises," 172.

40. For further discussion on the two dominant views, see Buchanan, "Matthean Beatitudes and Traditional Promises," 174. See also David L. Turner, "Whom Does God Approve? The Context, Structure, Purpose, and Exegesis of Matthew's Beatitudes," *Criswell Theological Review* 6, no. 1 (1992): 29–42; Luz, *Matthew 1–7*, 185.

41. Augustine dropped the eighth beatitude. However, Betz notes that those who hold Augustine's view nowadays basically remove the textually disputed second beatitude (5:4).

42. H. Benedict Green, *Matthew, Poet of the Beatitudes* (Sheffield, UK: Sheffield Academic Press, 2001), 256–61.

43. See Thompson, "The Background and Function of the Beatitudes," 112–16; Luz, *Matthew 1–7*, 188; Turner, "Whom Does God Approve?," 38; Davies and Allison, *A Critical and Exegetical Commentary*, 439–40.

44. Harrington, *The Gospel of Matthew*, 83.

45. See W. R. Domeris, "Exegesis and Proclamation: 'Blessed Are You . . .' (Matthew 5:1–12)," *Journal of Theology for Southern Africa* 73 (1990): 68.

46. Mark Allan Powell, "Matthew's Beatitudes: Reversals and Rewards of the Kingdom," *Catholic Biblical Quarterly* 58, no. 3 (1996): 462.

Chapter Seventeen

The First Beatitude in Matthew 5:3

Blessed are the poor in spirit, for theirs is the kingdom of heaven.

WHAT DID THE TEXT PROCLAIM?

Matthew 5:3 is the first of the four beatitudes found also in Luke (6:20b). The main difference between the two versions is that Matthew qualifies the meaning of "poor": the poor are those who are "poor in spirit." Davies and Allison suggest that the insertion of the term "in spirit" is most probably the work of the redactor.[1] The reward/promise obtained by the beatitude is repeated in the eighth beatitude. This repetition, as said earlier, grounds the argument that 5:3–10 forms a single unit.

The first part of the beatitude mainly tells us that the "poor in spirit" are blessed by God. It finds direct reference in Isaiah 61:1, where the poor and the oppressed will receive God's good news. However, there are many other passages in the Old Testament that talk about God's command to care specifically for the poor, such as Deuteronomy 15:7–11. Harrington thus rightly reminds us about the need to read the beatitude in light of the Old Testament tradition.

Regarding the notion of "poor," the Greek term $\pi\tau\omega\chi\delta\varsigma$ employed here generally means "beggar." Exegetes inform us that there are several Hebrew equivalents, such as *ani* ("poor"/"afflicted"), *dal* ("weak"), and *ebyon* ("needy"). Thus, the term "poor" refers not only to those who are poor with few possessions but especially those who are socially and economically needy and dependent (such as those being forced to beg). Indeed, the condition of poverty is never regarded as a blessing—and yet the person who is in such a condition can be blessed. Moreover, the term also refers to those who

161

are in special need of God's help (e.g., Psalm 12:5) and have nothing to rely upon except God (e.g., Amos 2:6–7). There is, therefore, a religious aspect of poverty in the term that is affirmed in these Hebrew texts:[2] the oppressed and the poor are promised God's salvation when they turn to God in their need. They will experience eschatological blessing and be made rich.

We find this twofold meaning of "poor"—where the religious and economic meanings go together—in New Testament writings as well (e.g., Romans 15:26). The early Church community was aware of (or actually facing) the reality that those who suffer material poverty are at the same time experiencing religious poverty.[3] Still, Matthew's redaction tends to shift the emphasis from material to spiritual poverty for certain reasons.[4] Nonetheless, I think Betz is right that it would be a mistake to conclude that Matthew simply spiritualizes or softens Jesus's radical teaching; rather, the redaction could intend to forestall any misunderstanding of the meaning of "poor."

The phrase "poor in spirit" is not a new concept.[5] According to Davies and Allison, in Hebrew writings, it describes the fainthearted, those who opt for voluntary poverty, or those who are spiritually poor. Luz further understands the phrase as implying lowliness with reference to one's spirit. Talbert likewise claims that it is used to contrast those who have a "haughty heart" (Proverbs 16:18–19). In sum, the phrase essentially carries a positive meaning. Still, as an ethicist, I find Betz's view inspiring: the phrase refers more to an attitude than a condition. It specifically points to humility—one that is highly praised in Jewish circles.

Nevertheless, the literary composition of the beatitude deserves some clarification: First, it does not mean that the poor will possess the kingdom nor that the kingdom will be comprised solely of the poor.[6] Rather, it proclaims the eschatological outcome that the kingdom of Heaven will be given to (among others) the poor. Second, the phrase "kingdom of heaven" (19:23–24) is basically a synonym to "kingdom of God," which is also used in Luke's beatitudes and is referred to by Matthew as the "reign of God." The use of the term "heaven," as Harrington explains, is simply a Jewish substitute for "God" in order to avoid any abuse of the name "God."[7] Although Matthew uses the phrase in different ways throughout the gospel (e.g., 8:11, 12:28), many would agree that, as far as the first beatitude is concerned, it contains both eschatological and this-worldly implications. Third, the use of present tense ἐστιν ("is") signifies a sense of confidence in the emerging present—the kingdom is already being realized, and the corresponding blessing is already being bestowed. One of its immediate effects is that the evils that cause poverty at the present time are and will be eliminated.

These clarifications suggest that the poor and the "poor in spirit" are found in the community, and they are encouraged to keep up the spirit for they will soon experience some sort of blessing in the midst of current difficulties. From a different point of view, Betz further points out that the first beatitude was the center of interest in the New Testament period because poverty and wealth were subjects of debate since the time of antiquity. Yet it also offers valuable ethical materials for Matthew's community. The "poor in spirit," who often suffer from economic poverty, are those who acquire the internal attitude of humility. They will be made happy in the coming kingdom of God. As Davies and Allison comment, the beatitude overturns the popular, conventional macarism that the rich are those to be blessed and the poor forsaken.

THE VIRTUE OF HUMILITY

English Dominican Gerald Vann, in his interpretation of the first beatitude, focuses on its spiritual meaning without making much reference to material poverty.[8] Our exegesis, however, reveals that the "poor in spirit," who acquire the internal attitude of humility, are often those suffering from economic poverty. Therefore, one cannot talk about "poor in spirit" without looking into the reality of material poverty. Who, then, are the "poor in spirit" in our society?

Poverty as a Human Condition

Theologically speaking, human beings are created to share God's life. However, many would acknowledge that because of sin (especially pride) we lost the docility that makes oneness with God possible. Noting this, spiritual writer Susan Muto comments that there is poverty intrinsic to our humanity. In fact, German theologian Johannes Metz had identified, four decades ago, some concrete types of innate poverty within us, including poverty of our provisional nature in that our future is unknown, and poverty of finiteness in that the inescapable end is near.[9] Here, Metz highlighted the nonmaterial aspect of poverty. Nevertheless, Pinckaers rightly points out that the various forms of poverty are not isolated from one another, for poverty is experienced in both the body and the soul. He further identifies "the consciousness of our condition as creature"—that is, the fundamental emptiness which lies at the depths of our being, as the primordial poverty.[10]

I agree with Muto that the overall experience of poverty can awaken in us understanding both of our helplessness and total dependency on an unknown beyond, and our need to fuse with others in their poverty. These experiences help us become aware of both our place in creation and our need for redemption. Indeed, the late Jewish theologian Pinchas Lapide is right to claim that all the suffering and struggling from poverty, destitution, and marginalization will turn out to be meaningful, especially since God dwells among the poor.[11] Both his and Muto's claims encourage us to look beyond poverty itself and to embrace it with a positive attitude, like those who are "poor in spirit."

Expressing the Idea of "Poor in Spirit"

We find various expressions of the concept of "poor in spirit" throughout Christian history.[12] John Chrysostom, for example, perceived this poverty as an antidote of pride. For Luther, it means the detachment of one's heart from temporal things and reliance on God's grace. Modern Eastern Orthodox Christians call it a "spiritual emptying" that implies a total dependence on God's grace and has a childlike trust in God's providence. Metz depicts it as "obedient acceptance of our natural impoverishment."[13] Betz, on the other hand, defines it as "one's self-consciousness of the 'poverty' of the human condition."[14] These understandings, though diverse, are not contradictory to each other. In fact, a more comprehensive understanding of humility takes on all these aspects. In this way, in the language of virtue, "poor in spirit" correlates with the virtue of humility. Humility means accepting the complete poverty of our human condition.

Humility as a Virtue

Since the first beatitude is the starting point both of the Sermon and of one's journey to the kingdom of God, some scholars like Häring claim that it is the foundation of all the beatitudes (and the Sermon). Others similarly propose that humility is necessarily understood as the "lowest and most elementary virtue."[15] This proposal runs parallel with John Climacus's own metaphor of the life of holiness as a ladder and humility being the first step on that ladder. Saint Ambrose even saw it as "the parent and generation of the virtues."[16] This view implies that every virtue is a form of humility. Vann, for instance, says justice is the humility of the person who understands that every possession is at the same time a responsibility. In an analogous way, Metz perceives humility as the ground of the three theological virtues. He further claims that humility is not just a virtue among others but "a necessary ingredient in any authentic Christian attitude toward life" and through which imitation of Christ is possible.[17] This argument can be traced back to Chrysostom who claimed that the virtue of humility is an indispensable virtue for Christians at all times.[18]

On the other hand, according to Aquinas, humility is a part of temperance for it is a moderation of the spirit (*ST* II.II. 161.4). Still, humility as a Christian virtue implies the cultivation of other relevant virtues because of its foundational nature. Pinckaers suggests that a humble person will trust God, be patient for God's assistance, and put oneself completely at the disposal of God's command. I understand this suggestion as pointing to the need for the theological virtues of faith and hope in God and God's deliverance.

The Practice of Humility

Spiritual writer Michael Crosby highlights the necessity of the acknowledgment of God as our ultimate source and meaning of our lives. As an ethicist, I understand this as the first step for cultivating the virtue of humility. A second step is the renunciation of whatever separates us from God—especially spiritual pride. In practical terms, such renunciation or self-emptiness points to detachment. Within the Ignatian tradition, detachment does not mean "not caring"; on the contrary, it cares for things, though in a way different from how avaricious people do. We learn to see God in all things and love them in accordance with God's will. Thus, we are more than mere stewards of God's creation but lovers as well—yet that love as such is not a possessive one. Moreover, detachment does not simply mean the giving up of things but, more importantly, the giving up of the "obsessive" desire for them. When we are able to do so, we grow in freedom.

Some theologians further suggest the practice of sharing. Häring rightly claims that when we are ready to share all that we have received from God, we are able to rejoice and be happy, and we will not lose our equilibrium in the midst of poverty and hardships. Within the sphere of our liturgical and sacramental life, humility is further accompanied and expressed by Christian devotion as well as the Catholic sacrament of reconciliation, which help us recognize our sinfulness and hence remain humble in front of God. Finally, concrete practices of asceticism, self-denial, and obedience (particularly to the spiritual father) are rather common in the Eastern Church tradition. [19] Indeed, different traditions practice humility in rather different ways, some more externally and others more internally.

The Exemplars

In Matthew 11:29, Jesus says, "Take my yoke upon you, and learn from me; for I am gentle and humble in heart." These words tell us that we can turn to Jesus in our cultivation of Christian humility. Indeed, there are many narratives in the New Testament that portray Jesus as a model of humility—for example, he teaches us both by words (e.g., Luke 18:9–14) and by his own example (Philippians 2:6–8). As a whole, these narratives highlight certain traits of Jesus's humility: hiddenness, powerlessness, and self-emptying. [20] Specifically, many would agree that Christ's own humility and obedience to God the Father throughout his earthly life is the perfect example of humility. I agree with Häring that by making himself poor (and a humble servant) and dedicating his whole life to the lowly and the poor, Jesus enriches us all (2 Corinthians 8:9) and opens our hearts to a life in the service of God and others.

Besides Jesus, the person who comes to my mind as a model of humility is Mary, the mother of Jesus, whose humility is best manifested in her *Magnificat* (Luke 1:46–55) and her life (John 2:5). Still, there are many other notable saints throughout Christian history who exemplify this virtue. Francis of Assisi is well known for embracing poverty literally and concretely so as to lose pride and grow in humility. He spoke of having poverty as his bride, practiced strict poverty voluntarily, and insisted that one should "hate" oneself—especially the pride inside us. [21]

In our contemporary society, Mother Teresa of Calcutta and members of her religious congregation are known for living an extremely simple lifestyle and serving the poorest of the poor. They and other exemplary Christians take on voluntary poverty as a means to acquire spiritual poverty in imitation of Christ. They demonstrate that humbly living a simple life for the sake of the poor is possible for all. They also highlight the importance of solidarity (which will be discussed in the next chapter). Their simple lifestyle challenges our society's false beliefs that wealth and material possessions are the ultimate goals of human life. They effectively call for changes of mentality on both personal and social levels.

The Social, Communal Aspect of the Virtue of Humility

While the voluntary poverty of these Christians is praiseworthy, the reality of forced poverty in our contemporary society challenges the followers of Christ to look beyond personal spiritual growth. One specific aspect of this challenge is the sharing of our wealth—including the spiritual wealth—which is given "in the service of those who are worried and anguished." [22] Here, the practice is, more importantly, socially and internationally relevant: the virtue of humility challenges society and nation to share our natural resources, technological advancement, and financial wealth with developing countries. One concrete, immediate social action on the international platform could be the cancellation of international debts by the industrialized countries, perhaps along the line of the Heavily Indebted Poor Countries (HIPC) Initiative.

Häring rightly claims that human pride—manifested in our human lust to possess and to dominate (and manipulate) others—is often the cause of forced poverty and social injustice. We are called, then, not just to share but also to combat social injustice and promote social justice. Therefore, humility and the voluntary acceptance of poverty cannot mean "passivity in the face of the injustices which cause poverty." [23] On the contrary, the "poor in spirit" trust in God for their work to change the infrastructure that leads to a culture of domination/oppression.[24] In so doing, they see personal conversion and creation of alternative communities/societies as the first step of promoting changes.

Behind all of this is the humble insight that the "poor in spirit" are unable to change anything without God's grace.

NOTES

1. Davies and Allison propose the following reasons: (1) Matthew does not give qualification to the term "poor" in 11:5. (2) The subject of the first woe (the rich) in Luke does not have qualification either. (3) There would be perfect parallelism in Q without the qualification. See William D. Davies and Dale C. Allison Jr., *A Critical and Exegetical Commentary on the Gospel according to Saint Matthew*, vol. 1 (New York: Continuum, 1988), 442.

2. In order to explain this religious aspect, Mark Allan Powell points out that the Hebrew word *anawim*, which was translated into πτωχοί by the Septuagint, is a religiously nuanced term meaning "piety." It refers to a "socio-economic class of people in Israel who are noted as much for their piety as for their poverty." See Mark Allan Powell, "Matthew's Beatitudes: Reversals and Rewards of the Kingdom," *Catholic Biblical Quarterly* 58, no. 3 (1996): 463.

3. Therefore, some argue that the "poor" in Luke cannot be read as purely economical. Similarly, the rich include those who do not have a sense of need for God (Luke 12:16–21).

4. Powell, however, counterargues that since the Hebrew word *anawim* refers to those who have strong trust in God, Matthew's addition would be unnecessary. These people are actually spiritually rich rather than poor. Thus, the addition simply refers to those who have no reason for hope in this world.

5. Betz, however, notes that no other Greek usage of this phrase is found in the rest of the New Testament or other early Christian sources.

6. Davies and Allison point out that the term αὐτῶν ("of them") does not signify a sense of possession.

7. Some scholars, however, suggest that the term "heaven" is more than a substitute but an emphasis of God's transcendence and sovereignty. See H. Traub, "*Ouranos,*" *TDNT* 5 (1967): 522, as cited in Dennis Hamm, *The Beatitudes in Context: What Luke and Matthew Meant* (Wilmington, DE: Michael Glazier, 1990), 82.

8. See Gerald Vann, *The Divine Pity: A Study in the Social Implications of the Beatitudes* (New York: Sheed & Ward, 1946).

9. Johannes B. Metz, *Poverty of Spirit*, trans. John Drury (Paramus, NJ: Paulist Press, 1968), 37–48.

10. Servais Pinckaers, *The Pursuit of Happiness—God's Way: Living the Beatitudes*, trans. Mary Thomas Noble (New York: Alba House, 1998), 46.

11. Pinchas Lapide, *The Sermon on the Mount: Utopia or Program for Action?*, trans. Arlene Swidler (Maryknoll, NY: Orbis Books, 1986), 27–28.

12. See Liviu Barbu, "The 'Poor in Spirit' and Our Life in Christ: An Eastern Orthodox Perspective on Christian Discipleship," *Studies in Christian Ethics* 22, no. 3 (2009): 264–67.

13. Metz, *Poverty of Spirit*, 23.

14. Hans Dieter Betz, *The Sermon on the Mount*, ed. Adela Yarbro Collins (Minneapolis, MN: Fortress Press, 1995), 114–19.

15. Ibid., 108.

16. Ambrose, "*In Lucam* 5.51," in *Corpus Scriptorum Ecclesiasticorum Latinorum*, 32.4, ed. C. Schenkl (Vienna, 1937), 201, as quoted in Barbu, "The 'Poor in Spirit' and Our Life in Christ," 274.

17. Metz, *Poverty of Spirit*, 25.

18. John Chrysostom, "Homilies on St. Matthew (Homily XV)," in *The Nicene and Post-Nicene Fathers*, series 1, vol. 10, ed. P. Schaff (Edinburgh: T&T Clark/Grand Rapids, MI: Eerdmans, 1991), 89, as cited in Barbu, "The 'Poor in Spirit' and Our Life in Christ," 264. However, for Aquinas humility, as belonging to temperance, follows the theological virtues, the intellectual virtues, and justice. See *ST* II.II. 161.5.

19. Eastern Orthodox tradition believes that God's will for each of us is revealed in the advice of one's spiritual father.

20. See Ladislaus Boros, *Hidden God* (New York: Seabury Press, 1973), as referenced in Susan Muto, "Blessed Are the Poor in Spirit and the Pure of Heart," in *New Perspectives on the Beatitudes*, ed. Francis A. Eigo (Villanova, PA: Villanova University Press, 1995), 142.

21. See Jim Forest, *The Ladder of the Beatitudes* (Maryknoll, NY: Orbis Books, 1999), 25.

22. Bernard Häring, *The Beatitudes: Their Personal and Social Implications* (Slough, UK: St. Paul Publications, 1976), 16.

23. Pinckaers, *The Pursuit of Happiness*, 54.

24. Nathan E. Williams, "A Second Look at the First Beatitude," *Expository Times* 98 (1987): 40, as cited in Michael H. Crosby, *Spirituality of the Beatitudes: Matthew's Vision for the Church in an Unjust World*, rev. ed. (Maryknoll, NY: Orbis, 2005), 49–50.

Chapter Eighteen

The Second Beatitude in Matthew 5:4

Blessed are those who mourn, for they will be comforted.

WHAT DID THE TEXT PROCLAIM?

The second beatitude is also found in the gospel of Luke. However, the two versions are quite different in a couple of ways. First, they are ordered differently: for Matthew, this beatitude is put right after the one on the poor in spirit; Luke, in contrast, places it after the ones on poverty and hunger, and thus it becomes the third beatitude (Luke 6:21). Some suggest that Matthew's order is a result of redaction. Second, the subjects and promises stated by the two evangelists are also quite different: Matthew says that the mourners will be blessed and comforted; Luke, however, tells us that those who weep are promised laughter by God. These differences between the two texts, as we shall see shortly, could well be inspired by the Old Testament.

Besides the parallel verse in Luke, we notice that, like the first, the second beatitude in Matthew 5:4 also corresponds to Isaiah 61:2, which reads "to comfort all who mourn." Here, the order of the first and second beatitudes corresponds *directly* to the order of Isaiah 61:1–2. This close parallel between the two texts partly explains the above-mentioned differences; it also calls for our special attention to the ancient Jewish context in reading the second beatitude.

In the first place, according to certain ancient literature, mourning is an expected response to the reality of desperation and suffering. [1] Betz notes that in its most specific sense, πενθω (to "mourn") refers to the grief of death and great loss. It is contained in rituals and prayers, particularly in those practices related to the burial of the dead. By considering the present order of the two

169

beatitudes, Betz further suggests that the grieving in the second beatitude could be a natural response to the experience of the poor identified in the first beatitude. I find this suggestion logical and sound. Second, as Davies, Allison, and Luz remark, the Hebrew Bible tradition provides us with the contexts for Israel's mourning—for example, Isaiah 61:3–7 tells us that the returned Israelites were oppressed by their enemies (v3), their cities were in ruins (v4), and they were aware of their own shame and dishonors (v7). Elsewhere we also read that they mourned over Jerusalem, as YHWH had not acted to reverse this situation.

Davies and Allison then point out that in the New Testament, Matthew tells us that the situation is very much the same: the righteous are persecuted by the wicked (5:10–12); they have not seen the Twelve on their thrones (19:28); and the Son of Man has not come in his glory (24:29–31). In other words, they have not seen the kingdom of God in its fullness, and the eschatological promise has not yet taken place. As a result, the people of God mourn over the situation they are facing.

Still, Talbert and Luz note that certain writings in the Hebrew Bible (e.g., Joel 2:12–13) suggest that the people's mourning could be associated with repentance—they mourn for their own sins and the sins of others—and Matthew's use of the more general term "mourning" (rather than "weeping" in Luke's case) could open up a spiritualized interpretation. They add, however, that the close link with Isaiah 61 would discount this more spiritual view.

In the second half of the beatitude, we are told that the mourners will be comforted. With Davies and Allison, I too believe that this promise/reward can continue to be understood in light of the Old Testament tradition: the two Greek terms πενθοῦντες ("mourners") and παρακληθήσονται ("comforted") are paired up as catchwords to remind the audience of the prophet Isaiah who consoled the mourners of Zion (Sirach 48:23–25). It is a common theme within the Jewish tradition that God turns our sorrow into joy (e.g., Jeremiah 31:13).

How, then, are the mourners comforted? Exegetes point out that the linguistic nature of the beatitude reveals two distinctive features of this comfort. First, the use of the future tense makes it clear that the promised comfort is an eschatological prediction. Second, the use of the "divine passive"—which is a common Jewish way of avoiding the use of God's name—further indicates that God is the one who offers comfort, just as a mother comforts her child (Isaiah 66:13). Still, as Talbert observes, in the Old Testament tradition God's offer of comfort can be understood in various ways: it is equated with salvation and redemption (e.g., Isaiah 61:2; Jeremiah 31:13); associated with healing, pardon for iniquity, and nourishment (e.g., Isaiah 57:18; 40:1–2); and understood as freedom from and return from exile (e.g., Isaiah 49:13; 51:12). As a whole, God's comfort to the mourners converges on the experience of God's salvation and sustenance. However, Betz rightly clarifies that not all who mourn are called blessed—but only if their mourning is a sign of their waiting for the kingdom of Heaven.

In conclusion, many would agree that mourning over poverty, persecutions, and other losses are the concrete experiences of both the Old Testament Israelites and the people of God in the New Testament era. They will be comforted by God as God comforted their ancestors in the past. This is a divine act that brings salvation, pardon, and nourishment; the fulfillment of this eschatological prediction requires divine justice. The beatitude is therefore hardly an exhortation or imperative (no one is being told to mourn!). However, it does not mean that the second beatitude does not carry ethical values for Matthew's community. Specifically, I take the view of Davies and Allison that the emphasis is not on the state of mourning as such but rather on those members of the community who lament the grievous situation. In line with Betz's view, I also see that—in light of its ancient Jewish correspondence and closeness with the first beatitude—the practice of mourning points to a particular virtue.

THE VIRTUE OF SOLIDARITY

Some interpreters take a more personal and spiritual approach toward the beatitude and interpret it as resulting solely from one's sinfulness or personal suffering. Yet we have seen from the beginning that those who mourn are closely related to the "poor in spirit." The object of mourning is not so much one's own suffering or sins, but rather the concrete human experience of poverty and suffering encountered by community members. Mourning points to an other-oriented moral value.

The fulfillment of the eschatological prediction further requires, as we saw, divine justice. Such understanding guides us to grasp the moral value intended by the evangelist: we mourn over the suffering of others caused by injustice. Such is the lot of the disciples of Christ—when our brothers and sisters suffer, we cannot help but mourn. This is very different from other interpretations of the beatitude, such as "the call to console" proposed by Häring. The beatitude is not about that; it is about a certain disposition that genuine disciples have with one another, such that if one suffers, the other mourns as well.

Suffering and Mourning as Human Experience

Suffering and mourning often go hand in hand in our human experience, and it was especially the case for Matthew's community. Still, it is also the experience of our human family nowadays. Indeed, Jesus explicitly tells us that suffering, sorrow, and mourning are inevitable (John 16:20–22).

Like Matthew's community, a closer look at the reality in our contemporary world shows that the object of our grieving is not limited to individual suffering alone. There is massive suffering in every corner of human society—for instance, the discrimination experienced by the undocumented immigrants in our own countries, our alienating spirit toward HIV/AIDS victims, the severe poverty and political unrest in developing countries, and communal conflicts due to differences in religious belief. Even the despoliation of the Earth, as Crosby rightly claims, is another object of our mourning in the twenty-first century. Based on our earlier discussion on poverty in the first beatitude, we can claim that these people and this earth also suffer from being impoverished in one way or another.

As a whole, the object of our mourning is the various sufferings and predicaments of others caused by injustice in our society, and this suffering is especially but not exclusively the result of material/economic poverty and persecution.

The Meaning of Mourning

Pinckaers notes that Aquinas, in his commentary on the Sermon, systematically distinguishes the different kinds of grief experienced by human beings. But Aquinas seemed to overemphasize personal suffering and the spiritual dimension of the self. Vann, however, insists that "mourning" is, as we learned above, other-oriented: like mourning over one who has died, it has the other as the center of concern. In mourning, the self tries to identify with the other. Mourning is then the ready subordination of one's own comfort and well-being to the suffering of others in order to bring strength and courage to those who suffer. In this way, one allows one's private life to be touched by the pain and suffering of the other.

This openness and subordination to the other's suffering implies a certain degree of humility: while the arrogant person is simply "above it all," the humble person is able to sense the needs of the other. One writer thus claims that humility and mourning are inseparable. [2]

This other-centered attitude of grieving also points to the notion of solidarity—the sharing between the sufferer and the mourner in their experience of suffering, the oppression and sin that causes it, and the final redemption. Moreover, Vann rightly reminds us that mourning as such is not a kind of sentimentality made as an end in itself; it is not a kind of sensuality either, in which the sense-pleasure (of comforting/being comforted) is made an end in itself as well. Indeed, I see this other-centered solidarity as crucial to our understanding of mourning in today's suffering world.

Mourning as an Expression of the Virtue of Solidarity

Häring presumes that comforting is the core virtue ascribed in the second beatitude. However, our study discloses that mourning itself is the virtuous act to be practiced. Indeed, it is the necessary step *prior* to consoling others. Vann comments that, as a virtuous Christian act, mourning points to an attitude that identifies with God's will to accompany those who suffer and grieve. Thus, the act of mourning is a truthful expression of the virtue of solidarity.

The concept and virtue of solidarity, which was developed by Pope John Paul II, is foundational to Catholic social teaching (such as social encyclical *Sollicitudo Rei Socialis*) and gives the related concept "preferential option for the poor" greater claim. Sobrino understands it as "bearing one another" and, in the context of Christianity, "[a] type of communion generated by the church of the poor."[3] A Mexican theologian identifies some features of Christian solidarity.[4] It reveals the historical and practical dimensions of *agape* ("love") and *koinonia* ("communion"). Specifically, it implies a rich relationship with the victims of human sociohistorical injustice, takes their suffering on as one's own, and seeks and realizes effective actions to combat suffering. It further promotes hope for those who suffer and transformation of the society.

Besides expressing Christian solidarity, the inseparability between mourning and humility leads some like Vann to suggest that, in one sense, mourning is actually another form of the virtue of humility—a humility that is about and aimed toward the other and points to the surrendering of one's desires altogether for the sake of the other. In addition, mourning is related to the virtue of fortitude—the courage to face the reality of our world, as Pinckaers puts it. Crosby elaborates this point and adds that those who mourn over the sufferings of others first take the courage to accept the reality of sufferings and pains that they see rather than trying to deny them. In light of the recognition of the suffering, they can then address the causes of these sufferings.

Up to this point, our understanding of the virtue of solidarity likewise exposes the need for other relevant virtues, especially humility. Mourning is inevitably a necessary expression; yet what could we do so that our mourning is directed to solidarity with others?

The Practice of Mourning

Vann offers some concrete steps that help prepare our inner selves for the practice of mourning. First, we need to develop a sense of willingness in taking others' troubles to ourselves and in turn, actually sharing of our own selves. Second, we need to acquire an attitude of single-mindedness, so much so that we let go of our own desires even to the point of discomfort for the sake of bringing God's love to others. Here, then, is the practice of mortifying oneself in the best ascetical sense of that word. Third, this leads to the readiness to act by accompanying others.

By voluntarily suffering and choosing discomfort as love demands, we further learn about another's suffering and grief. Thus, such readiness also points to awareness. It is through such awareness that the sufferers around us can be recognized, and that our mortification becomes other-oriented rather than self-centered.

In concrete terms, Keenan highlights the importance of the act of listening. It allows and welcomes the sufferer to speak and to be heard,[5] for the voice of those who suffer is "their lifeline to the world from which they find themselves progressively isolated. Thus, through the voice the one isolated in suffering is able to reach out to others."[6]

Finally, as our exegesis shows, mourning is contained in rituals and prayers. Thus, in our Christian liturgy, the practice of intercession helps us be more aware of the sufferings and needs of those we know as well as those we don't know and strengthens our bonding with them. Indeed, as we shall see in the epilogue, similar rituals and prayers are found and emphasized in many other religions and cultures, such as Confucianism.

The Exemplars

Häring identifies Jesus as the consoler. However, Jesus is also one who exemplifies the real meaning of mourning: through his own suffering and death on the cross, Jesus is able to fully understand the grief of and listen to the voice of those who suffer. He also mourns and grieves as ordinary people do in witnessing loss and suffering, as in the case of the death of Lazarus (John 11:33–38). Moreover, he mourns not for his own suffering but that of others, including those of the evildoers (Luke 19:41–44).

Within the Catholic tradition, I find the life of Fr. Damien (the nineteenth-century Belgian missionary who was also called "The Apostle of the Lepers") a concrete example and model of the virtue of solidarity with the poor and the suffering. For a long time he was the only one who served the abandoned lepers in the Hawaiian Islands, comforted their suffering, and was in solidarity with them even to point of catching the same disease and dying of leprosy himself.

His example has subsequently inspired many missionaries and groups to be in solidarity with and care for especially those who are marginalized by our modern world. Not surprisingly, Fr. Damien has been named as the unofficial patron of those with HIV/AIDS.[7] His exemplary life has further challenged us to reflect upon our social practices that not only create inequities but also marginalize those so treated.

The Social, Communal Aspect of the Practice of Mourning and the Virtue of Solidarity

Häring rightly claims that mourning and sorrow can be authentic only when we open our hearts to the suffering of those around us in society. However, as we open our hearts and listen to their lament, we also become aware of the fact that we are part of the cause of their suffering: Have we thought of our global business practices and our overconsumption of goods as contributing to the causes of the shortage of basic needs in the developing world as well as directly creating poor working conditions there?

Hopefully, here we see that the practice of mourning is never a private matter. Thus, even when we grieve for our sins, it is not so much a sorrow for losing merit but rather for actually causing injustice to God's honor, to the community and the larger society.

Mourning that is other-centered is, then, a manifestation of our protest against the evil and injustice that causes the massive suffering of our human family, as well as our demand for restoration of justice. Mourning makes the voice of the sufferers heard and their unjust suffering known in the society. Solidarity then urges us to accompany them and take appropriate, courageous actions that challenge the society's unjust structure and policies. In this way, mourning and the virtue of solidarity becomes the first step to bringing about social change. By referring to the Second Vatican Council's Pastoral Constitution on the Church in the Modern World (*Gaudium es Spes*), one theologian rightly claims that mourning (and its corresponding beatitude) points to an ecclesial stance in that the Church commits itself to be involved in the pains and struggles of the human family.[8] I believe that such commitment is found in other religions as well. Mourning and solidarity thus become a ground for interfaith cooperation.

NOTES

1. Hans Dieter Betz identifies this ancient literature as consolation literature. For a more detailed discussion on this kind of literature, see his *The Sermon on the Mount*, ed. Adela Yarbro Collins (Minneapolis, MN: Fortress Press, 1995), 121–22.

2. Jim Forest, *The Ladder of the Beatitudes* (Maryknoll, NY: Orbis Books, 1999), 38.

3. Jon Sobrino, "Communion, Conflict, and Ecclesial Solidarity," in *Mysterium Liberationis*, ed. Ignacio Ellacuría and Jon Sobrino (Maryknoll, NY: Orbis, 1993), 632.

4. Javier Jiménez Limón, "Suffering, Death, Cross, and Martyrdom," in *Mysterium Liberationis*, ed. Ignacio Ellacuría and Jon Sobrino (Maryknoll, NY: Orbis, 1993), 706–8.

5. Keenan acknowledges that at times the sufferers are inhibited from communicating their pain by the suffering itself.

6. James F. Keenan, *Moral Wisdom: Lessons and Texts from the Catholic Tradition* (Lanham, MD: Rowman & Littlefield, 2004), 77.

7. See Catholic Online, "Saint Damien of Molokai," www.catholic.org/saints/saint.php?saint_id=2817#.

8. David P. Reid, "'A Strategy of Endurance': The Book of *Revelation* as Commentary on the Beatitudes, Blessed Are the Mourning and the Suffering," in *New Perspectives on the Beatitudes*, ed. Francis A. Eigo (Villanova, PA: Villanova University Press, 1995), as referenced in Michael H. Crosby, *Spirituality of the Beatitudes: Matthew's Vision for the Church in an Unjust World*, rev. ed. (Maryknoll, NY: Orbis, 2005), 74. See also Pope John Paul II, *Sollicitudo rei Socialis*, Encyclical Letter for the Twentieth Anniversary of *Populorum Progressio*, December 30, 1987, www.vatican.va/holy_father/john_paul_ii/encyclicals/documents/hf_jp-ii_enc_30121987_sollicitudo-rei-socialis_en.html.

Chapter Nineteen

The Third Beatitude in Matthew 5:5

Blessed are the meek, for they will inherit the earth.

WHAT DID THE TEXT PROCLAIM?

As noted earlier, the third beatitude in Matthew 5:5 does not have a parallel in Luke's version. Scholars suggest that it is probably a later addition by the redactor of the Sayings source.[1] Some further claim that verse 5 was inserted for the purpose of expounding the religious dimension of the term "poor" in the first beatitude.[2] From a different perspective, others comment that the third beatitude corresponds to the sixth in that they both use a future active verb with a direct object in the second half of the beatitude. However, is this beatitude also related to and influenced by the Hebrew Bible tradition as the first two beatitudes are?

We note that this beatitude does not follow the previous ones in making explicit correspondence with Isaiah 61. Rather, it makes direct reference to Psalm 37:11—the poor accept the present affliction, trust in the Lord, wait patiently for the Lord, and refrain from anger or envy.[3] They will soon be delivered by the Lord from the wicked and inherit the land. In this way, the direct reference foretells who the meek are in the beatitude.

Still, in order to understand better who they are, we examine the term "meek" from three different perspectives. First, the Greek term for "meek" is πραΰς. In the New Testament, it runs parallel with other Greek terms, such as ἡσυχίου ("quiet") and ἐπιεικεῖς ("gentle") in 1 Peter 3:4 and Titus 3:2, respectively. However, πραΰς appears in Matthew's gospel in a few more places (e.g., 11:29) to portray Jesus, like Moses before him, as a model and practitioner of meekness and gentleness.

Second, the Septuagint (a particular Greek translation of the Hebrew Bible) also employed πραΰς to translate the Hebrew word *anawim* as well. As we saw in 5:3, *anawim* has also been translated with πτωχοί ("poor").[4] Consequently, the term "meek" becomes a synonym and variation of the "poor (in spirit)." By recalling the Septuagint account of Isaiah 61:6–7, Davies and Allison further hint that the meek could at the same time be the "poor" and "those who mourn." Based on the Old Testament traditions of exodus and exile that speak of the disinherited receiving the promised land, they also propose that the term is associated with the particular human *condition* of the powerless or the oppressed.

Third and finally, the Greek term does not simply refer to a human condition but also to an ethical attitude. In Hellenistic culture, as Betz claims, meekness (πραότης) is an important ethical concept—a virtue closely related to philanthropy and a mark of the true philosopher, like Socrates. In Jewish piety literature, meekness is also a synonym for humility and a characteristic of the sage and the ruler.[5] Major figures like Moses serve as paradigms. Curiously, scholars note that although both the Greek and Jewish traditions praised meekness and gentleness, it was not widely practiced.

Taken together, while the term "meek" as a condition tends to refer to the poor, the powerless, and those who mourn, as a moral attitude it considers also the rich and the powerful. In this way, as far as its ethical dimension is concerned, the term has an inclusive nature.

The second part of the third beatitude tells us that the meek and the gentle will inherit the land. The Greek verb employed, κληρονομεῖν, originally means to "inherit"; however, Davies and Allison inform us that in the Septuagint it was translated as to "possess" or to "acquire." Still, it never means ownership; rather, in both the Old and New Testament traditions to "possess" or to "inherit" would imply eschatological hope and promise (e.g., Isaiah 60:21; Matthew 19:29).

Regarding the land to be inherited, the presence of the definite article τὴν ("the") could suggest that Matthew was referring to "the" land of Israel.[6] But various evidences show that the term γῆν ("land") tends to have a general meaning instead—it refers to the "Earth." For instance, Matthew seems to expect a broad cosmic renewal instead of a merely regional nationalistic hope (19:28).[7] The above examination of the verb "inherit" further supports an eschatological interpretation of this land. Still, by turning to 28:18–20, Betz points out that although the new earth might be given an otherworldly interpretation, this earthly world could still be a mission land for the disciples.

In conclusion, our exegesis clarifies who the meek are in the beatitude: they tend to be in line with the poor or those who mourn and are humble. They will inherit the land just as the "poor in spirit" will be given the kingdom of Heaven. Yet all members of the community (no matter whether they are the little ones or those in command) are called to cultivate this particular virtue. Although the promise of inheriting the new earth (and a new heaven) may be eschatological, the disciples have to reach out to the world as it is now.

THE VIRTUE OF MEEKNESS

The above examination of the text shows that the meek tend to be the poor and the mourners who accept the present affliction, wait patiently for the Lord, and refrain from anger or envy. Many interpreters similarly identify meekness with these powerless people, as Pinckaers does. Still, our exegesis shows that the term is also employed to portray the moral character of those in power. What, then, should the powerful in our contemporary world do?

Arrogance in the Human World

Sadly, we are living in a society that promotes individualism and competition in all sectors. We are always told how important we are and how much better we are than others. Within human relationships, such mentality is often expressed in terms of narcissism and arrogance. Still, such egoism and arrogance is also exercised on the communal and cultural level, especially in the form of movements of ethnic and racial discrimination, such as anti-Semitism, Islamophobia, and racism.

In the business sector, our economic policies on both corporate and national levels likewise are manipulated in a way that places our own benefits above all else: those international patenting and trade regulations, for instance, are often criticized as defending the profits of the wealthy at the expense of the poor and the weak. In this way, our arrogance manifests itself. Advancements in science and technology have prompted some to think that humankind is capable of resolving all the problems and achieving our own happiness.[8] Similarly, we act without any appreciation of limitations as we continue to expand our consumption of natural resources on earth despite the call for conservation by ecologists.

I agree with Crosby that a consequent and related issue here is the use of violence: for those in power, violence (in whatever form) is a means to control and "protect" their possessions, power, and prestige at the expense of others. And for those who are victimized and oppressed, it becomes their last resort in fighting for their cause. In order to counterbalance these trends, the virtue of meekness is clearly much needed.

The Meaning of Meekness

Meekness is sometimes used to signify a "spiritual sweetness," a quality that characterizes wisdom and is also attributed to God who is "slow to anger and abounding in steadfast love" (Nehemiah 9:17).[9] For Aquinas, it is a restraint or mitigation of anger according to right reason (*ST* II.II. 157.1). Either way, I agree with the view that this does not mean weakness or cowardice; rather, it refers to an attitude found among the poor: being humble and patient without resentment. It is also the proper attitude required of the powerful.

In both cases, meekness not only points to humility but also adds a unique quality to humility. For meekness is an attitude of human beings that is "the combination of open-mindedness, faith in God, and the realization that the Will of God for us is always something joyous and interesting and vital and much better than anything we could think of for ourselves."[10] One writer describes this attitude as trusting God above all other options including violence.[11]

Pinckaers claims that meekness relates to a spirit of peace. It signifies "the outcome of a long struggle against the disordered violence of our feelings, failings, and fears."[12] Some authors compare this struggle to taming a tiger and point to it as a form of self-control. Among them, one depicts meekness as "the secret of overcoming any kind of difficulty."[13] As a whole, we can interpret meekness as concerned with handling our anger in a positive manner so as to achieve inner calmness.

Meekness as a Virtue

According to Aquinas, meekness as a moderation of anger is a moral virtue annexed to the cardinal virtue temperance (*ST* II.II. 157.3). However, our exegesis shows that meekness as a Christian virtue for the poor and those who mourn basically bears those marks of true humility—awareness of one's helplessness, being patient for God's help, and seeking to be obedient to God's will. It counteracts personal vices such as envy, jealousy, and vengeance. For the poor and the suffering, Häring adds that meekness is connected to the virtue of fortitude in enduring the suffering.

Meekness as an important moral virtue for the powerful, such as rulers in our society, points to what humility demands: it calls for the acknowledgment of our insufficiency, even though we seem to be more than capable and sufficient. Vann rightly says that it allows us to "see" the reality of sin and our share of it. I find this self-awareness crucial in the recognition of what we call "structural sin" in today's society. The virtue of meekness helps transform our desire to dominate into a vital force to serve. Vann understands this energy as pointing to the loving service of God and God's people.

In sum, while accepting Vann's insight that meekness can be understood as an expansion of the virtue of humility to one's whole life, we need to emphasize it as a virtue needed by both the poor and the powerful.

The Practice of Meekness

As Christians, Vann suggests, the very first step to meekness is to acknowledge God as our ultimate source, which helps us achieve inner tranquility and peace. The poor and oppressed are further encouraged to practice self-control and restraint from violence and revenge. For those who are powerful, Monika Hellwig suggests that they are in turn called to practice the restraint of violent power and arrogance.[14] In so doing, they need to unlearn those patterns of behavior that control and dominate others and that "defend" their possessions and prestige at the cost of others.

Within the context of spirituality and human relationship, we (especially with power and prestige) are called to practice piety. For Aquinas, piety is giving due reverence and care to those to whom we are indebted, such as our parents (*ST* II.II. 101).[15] Vann describes this piety as rooted in a kind of justice that is concerned with those one cannot repay fully, especially God. In this way, the practice of piety begins with the family and expands to the society and, finally, to God. It points us back to the virtues grounded in the first and fourth commandments, and it helps us cultivate a life of worshipping God rather than self-worship.

The practice of meekness, by both the poor and the powerful, thus demands tremendous strength, both psychological and spiritual. We need God's grace to strengthen us. We also need the guidance of moral examples.

The Exemplars

In the gospels, Jesus invites us to learn from him to be gentle and humble (e.g., Matthew 11:29). There are a number of passages that illustrate Jesus's meekness toward others, including sinners. For instance, he treats the woman who is known as a sinner with this meekness (Luke 7:36–50). Still, Jesus's meekness is best revealed throughout his Passion: while suffering all sorts of physical pain, the betrayal and denial of his disciples, and unjust condemnation by the authorities, Jesus remains silent without anger. During his very last moment on earth, he continues to show kindness to those around him, especially by forgiving and praying for those who crucify him.

Within the Catholic tradition, Francis de Sales of the seventeenth century has been praised for being a model of Christian meekness in his renewal of religious life. He said, "Always be as gentle as you can, and remember that more flies are caught with a spoonful of honey than with a hundred barrels of vinegar."[16] Pope Pius XI, in his encyclical on the saint, described Francis de Sales as one who "excelled in meekness of heart, a virtue so peculiar to himself that it might be considered his most characteristic trait."[17]

In our contemporary era, James Allison, a gay Catholic theologian, demonstrates what meekness means on a personal level in his *Faith beyond Resentment*. A reviewer notes that for Allison—who reflects on the embittered experience and resentment of gay Catholics toward the official Church—"resentment on either side is complicity in the cycling of sacred violence . . . [and] most forms of resistance simply continue the cycle of sacred violence."[18] Allison thus urges the use of "fraternal dialogue" by both sides as a genuine Christian response.

In our secular world, one globally recognized exemplar of meekness is Mahatma Mohandas Gandhi, who employed the Beatitudes as a source of spiritual renewal. His meekness is best reflected in his insistence on nonviolence toward social and political injustice in his home country. Although Gandhi was never awarded the Nobel Peace Prize and was accused by some as not having been consistently pacifist, he has been identified as "the strongest symbol of non-violence in the 20th century."[19] His example in turn highlights the social dimension of the virtue of meekness.

The Social, Communal Aspect of the Virtue of Meekness

Häring rightly claims that the social and communal relevance of the virtue of meekness is rather obvious, for meekness is needed in all aspects of our human relationships, including settings like the business sector. Corporate executives must ensure that their managers refrain from abusing their employees and neglecting their welfare (e.g., in terms of wages and working conditions). Giant corporations should also avoid monopolies that undermine the survival of smaller companies. Developed countries likewise have to renounce unfair trade treaties that hinder the development of poor countries. Employees, small companies, and poor countries in turn should avoid the use of unacceptable practices in defending their welfare and rights.

Moreover, I agree with many that meekness without embittered criticism is crucial to community building on both national and international levels. Specifically, meekness is foundational to mutual respect and authentic dialogue with other cultures, religions, and political views. For instance, in engaging interreligious dialogues, we need to be humble, patient, and gentle in listening to the faith experiences of others, and we need to refrain from violence and control in times of conflict and disagreements. In international conflicts, meekness should challenge the leaders of the powerful countries to refrain from military actions or economic sanctions that would further diminish weaker, emerging nations.

Finally, Crosby insightfully proposes that the demand of meekness can be extended to our relationship with the environment: it points to a stewardship that is in contrast to the violent, abusive dominion of our earth. In this way, a society that upholds meekness would challenge its policymakers to consider other, more environmentally friendly lifestyles, as well as more sustainable forms of energy and other resources.

In conclusion, in light of what we have discussed in many of the commandments in part II, we can say meekness points to a sense of respect toward the other.

NOTES

1. This redaction was probably done prior to the addition of the qualification "in spirit" by Matthew.

2. Neil McEleney notes that some would claim that the beatitude on "meekness" precedes the one on "mourning." Both sequences could go back to the second century. See also note 4.

3. Dennis Hamm points out that the reward/promise of the third beatitude corresponds to Isaiah 61:7 in that they both agree on having the definite article $\tau\grave{\eta}\nu$ ("the") before the noun. Therefore, it is suggested that this verse of Isaiah was the immediate inspiration that led to the quotation of Psalm 37:11. See also William D. Davies and Dale C. Allison Jr., *A Critical and Exegetical Commentary on the Gospel according to Saint Matthew*, vol. 1 (New York: Continuum, 1988), 451.

4. Harrington notes that for this reason some manuscripts place this beatitude immediately after 5:3.

5. However, Luz points out that, within the specific context of Jewish exhortation, $\pi\rho\alpha\tilde{\upsilon}\varsigma$ never means absolute nonviolence or political subordination.

6. Some further argue that Matthew 8:11 suggests that the evangelist was expecting the coming of the Son of Man, who will set up his throne in Israel.

7. Other evidence provided by Davies and Allison and Harrington include the following: First, the term is used without any qualification throughout the gospel (e.g., 6:10); thus, $\gamma\tilde{\eta}\nu$ is not restricted to any particular territory. Second, since the kingdom of Heaven has been spiritualized, the land likewise needs to be interpreted in a similar way.

8. Although this thought was mentioned by Vann more than fifty years ago, it is still applicable to our contemporary world. Some believe, for instance, that technological advancement can eventually eliminate human limitations and transform our humanity totally.

9. Servais Pinckaers, *The Pursuit of Happiness—God's Way: Living the Beatitudes*, trans. Mary Thomas Noble (New York: Alba House, 1998), 57.

10. Clarence Bauman, *The Sermon on the Mount: The Modern Quest for Its Meaning* (Macon, GA: Mercer University Press, 1985), 313.

11. Monika K. Hellwig, "The Blessedness of the Meek, the Merciful, and the Peacemakers," in *New Perspectives on the Beatitudes*, ed. Francis A. Eigo (Villanova, PA: Villanova University Press, 1995), 194.

12. Pinckaers, *The Pursuit of Happiness*, 61.

13. Emmet Fox, *The Sermon on the Mount: A General Introduction to Scientific Christianity in the Form of a Spiritual Key to Matthew V, VI, and VII* (New York: Grosset and Dunlap, 1938), 28, as cited in Bauman, *The Sermon on the Mount* , 312.

14. Hellwig, "The Blessedness of the Meek," 193.

15. For Aquinas, piety differs from the virtue of religion in that the latter worships God from afar.

16. Jean Pierre Camus, *The Spirit of St. Francis de Sales* (Charleston, SC: BiblioBazarre, 2006), 78, as quoted in Catholic Answers, "St. Francis de Sales, Patron Saint of Gentle Evangelists," www.catholic.com/thisrock/2008/0809fea1sb1.asp.

17. Pope Pius XI, *Rerum Omnium Perturbationem*, Encyclical Letter on St. Francis de Sales, January 26, 1923, www.vatican.va/holy_father/pius_xi/encyclicals/documents/hf_p-xi_enc_26011923_rerum-omnium-perturbationem_en.html.

18. Mark D. Jordan, review of *Faith beyond Resentment: Fragments Catholic and Gay*, by James Allison, *Modern Theology* 19, no. 3 (July 2003): 447.

19. See Øyvind Tønnesson, "Mahatma Gandhi, the Missing Laureate," Nobelprize.org, http://nobelprize.org/nobel_prizes/peace/articles/gandhi/.

Chapter Twenty

The Fourth Beatitude in Matthew 5:6

Blessed are those who hunger and thirst for righteousness, for they will be filled.

WHAT DID THE TEXT PROCLAIM?

Matthew 5:6 is the third beatitude shared by both Matthew and Luke, and it is the equivalent of the second beatitude in Luke's version (6:21). However, based on various literary and linguistic differences between the two texts, it is most probable that Matthew inserted "thirst" and "righteousness" in the original beatitude.[1] The insertion of "righteousness" in turn grounds the claim that the fourth beatitude parallels the last beatitude by having the same focus—namely, the theme of righteousness. As noted earlier, for some it becomes a marker for dividing the eight beatitudes into two halves.

On the other hand, according to Harrington, the original macarism alludes to Psalm 107:5, 8, and 9 where God satisfies the hungry and the thirsty. However, Davies and Allison note that in the Old Testament, the images of hunger and thirst point to an active seeking, and not just a longing for God. One pursues God's teaching and the words of the Law just as one desires food and drink (e.g., Isaiah 32:6). Subsequently, the phrase "to hunger and thirst for righteousness" can well be compared to Matthew 6:33, where one seeks God's kingdom and righteousness above all else.

These findings partly explain why Matthew added "thirst" and "righteousness," and foretell the importance of the notion of "righteousness" in the beatitude. The latter deserves our attention here. The notion of "righteousness" (δικαιοσύνη) finds correspondence in Psalm 37 and alludes to a number of verses in Isaiah (e.g., 61:3; 62:1–2). Betz and Stassen claim that it is better rendered as "justice" (especially restorative justice in a covenant community setting) and its use is in conformity to the Jewish understanding. The kingdom of Heaven is the realm of God's righteousness; righteousness is the basis for the interpretation of the Torah and the ethical standard for human conduct. In short, it is the realization of God's goodness in the world and points to "the gift of a right relationship with God."[2] However, there is no absolute agreement among scholars on whether the righteousness results from God's activity or human effort. Based on the view that the Sermon has both an eschatological tone and concerns for the present, I follow the approach of Harrington and Hamm that δικαιοσύνη is best understood *first* as God's justice (Matthew 6:33) and only then as the right conduct of us required by God (e.g., Matthew 5:20).

Matthew's inclusion of δικαιοσύνη in the beatitude has, then, several meanings. First, it clarifies the object of our hunger and thirst.[3] Second, as Betz notes, our hunger and thirst for righteousness is the response to our unrighteous human condition; it refers again to those identified in the first beatitude. Third, as a relational term, it is concerned not just with personal but also with social righteousness.[4] Fourth, it implies the not-yet: the blessed are those who hunger and thirst for righteousness, rather than those who think they have achieved it. Thus, many scholars comment that what is important is to keep up the desire for righteousness and make an effort to achieve it faithfully.

In the second half of verse 6, we see again the use of the future divine passive connotation—it points out that their satisfaction is eschatological in nature and fulfilled by God, as prophesied by Isaiah in 49:10 ("They shall not hunger or thirst"). By referring to the noncanonical work 1 Enoch (48:1), Betz claims that such fulfillment is crucial to apocalyptic literature. But the ways in which the hungry and the thirsty are satisfied by God can be quite diverse, such as through the vision of God or God's glory (Psalm 17:15) and indwelling of righteousness in the world (Isaiah 32:1, 16–17), as Davies and Allison note. A more direct understanding points to the eschatological messianic banquet (Psalm 107:1–9).

In sum, the fourth beatitude calls to our attention the need for God's righteousness. Those who strive for God's righteousness will be satisfied by God, who gives us the eschatological banquet. While the promise is future-oriented, we are called actively to seek God's righteousness, which is a gift. And as we seek first God's justice, we then attain right moral conduct and relationships that have righteousness as the ethical standard.

STRIVING FOR AND DISCERNING GOD'S RIGHTEOUSNESS

By now we are aware of the fact that the notion of righteousness is added to give the fourth beatitude its proper content and object. Many theologians, especially those who seek the social implications of the beatitude, interpret the text narrowly as calling for social justice. Our exploration of the text highlights that we are called to strive first for God's righteousness with effort, and only then do we seek the right conduct required by God as a response to the unrighteous human conditions.[5] To what, then, does God's righteousness refer in today's society, and how do we strive for it?

God's Righteousness or Human Justice?

God's righteousness as revealed in Scripture is very different from our contemporary understanding of justice. As Pinckaers rightly comments, our understanding of justice is never static throughout history. Society's perception of the notion of justice, in particular, has changed since the end of the thirteenth century, "when external changes between men, determined by law, became the special domain of the virtue of justice." He continues, "In order to establish law, justice had to abstract from persons and aim at strict objectivity. Only at this price could there be true justice in such a setting."[6]

Pinckaers then points out that God's righteousness, on the contrary, is built upon personal relationships, first between God and God's people by means of covenant and law, and then between human beings through mutual respect and rightful relationships. As noted above, it is a gift of right relationship with God. In this way, it reveals God's will for us as individuals and as community. It is also the realization of God's goodness in the world. It has God as the source, is manifested in the person of Jesus, and proceeds from our hearts in the form of charity.

However, God's righteousness is not the same as God's mercy and love in the strict sense: the former "stresses the idea of rectitude, uprightness, and the harmonious ordering of those things which are fitting, while love and mercy point more directly to spontaneity, generosity, and abundance in the gift."[7] In other words, there is more than one aspect of God's righteousness. As Pinckaers accurately describes, at times we might be preoccupied with one particular aspect of God's righteousness that calls for the judgment of humankind, and neglect other aspects of our relationship with God. God is thus portrayed as a rigorous judge and vindicator rather than as a merciful and loving God who is eager to make covenant with us.

Finally, more often than not, we fail to distinguish God's righteousness from our own and hence end up striving for a righteousness that is more self-centered than what God desires for each of us and for our community.

The Meaning of Striving

According to Pinckaers, Gregory the Great claimed that we often experience a desire for possessing a particular thing before we actually possess it. Thus, one's hunger and thirst for something is a very fundamental human experience. Moreover, when one strives for something, one commits one's self, so much so that one does not feel inhibited or satisfied with less than necessary; it is an ongoing process that does not end until that desire is fulfilled. One universal experience of such hunger and thirst is our human desire for happiness. As far as Christianity is concerned, the evangelist tells us that the primary object of our hunger and thirst should be God's righteousness. Therefore, striving for God's righteousness means continually and totally orienting one's heart (including emotions, thinking, and behaviors) to do what God's righteousness demands.

Striving for God's Righteousness as a Christian Virtue

The notion of "striving" points us to the virtue of fortitude. According to Aquinas, fortitude is a cardinal virtue and governs the "irascible appetite," i.e., a response awakened in the face of an apparent danger or threat (*ST* I.II. 61.2). It helps overcome the obstacle of "[disinclination] to follow that which is in accordance with reason, on account of some difficulty that presents itself" (*ST* II.II. 123.1). In simple terms, as Vann describes it, fortitude offers us strength to combat our inclination to be lukewarm. Moreover, for Aquinas, fortitude of the soul expresses the determined desire for honoring God's rights and is thus the principal motive for our hunger and thirst for God's justice (*ST* I.II. 69.3 ad 3).

Still, our understanding of the notion of "striving" implies also the need to persevere in our striving, while the understanding of God's righteousness as right relationship with God points us to the virtue of faithful obedience toward God and God's covenant. Therefore, the virtues of perseverance and obedience are also crucial to the fourth beatitude. In fact, Aquinas has already proposed that perseverance, together with patience, magnificence, and magnanimity, are lesser virtues subordinated to fortitude (*ST* II.II. 128).[8]

Furthermore, since God's righteousness implies rightful relationship, first with God and then with others, several Christian virtues come into view. First, our relationship with God is expressed in the virtues found in the first three commandments, such as upholding truthful worship and respecting God's holiness. Second, our rightful human relationship then finds its place in the virtues of justice and charity toward others. Third, the virtue of peacemaking, which we shall discuss later, is particularly needed in restoring broken relationships.

In sum, striving for God's righteousness as a virtue points to a nest of virtues surrounding two key values—fortitude and relationship with God and one another. As we shall see, it naturally correlates with the virtue of the last beatitude.

The Practice of Striving for God's Righteousness

Traditionally, Christian religious acts of justice are understood as a reflection of God's justice. For example, Crosby notes that, based on the teaching of the Gospel, pietistic practices of fasting, prayer, and almsgiving, have been seen by many Christians as concrete expressions of God's righteousness on earth. Fasting makes us more open to experience God's transcendence and thus shapes our vision in a way that we may see the world as God sees it. Prayer (particularly the Lord's Prayer) helps us focus on social transformation; as we pray, we are invited by God to bring God's kingdom on earth and to deliver others from all forms of indebtedness. While justice seeks to correct the suffering caused by unjust economic and political structures of our society, almsgiving can alleviate that suffering while the structures are being transformed.

However, in order to seek and obey God's will, we need to know that our striving is oriented to God's righteousness rather than our own. Ignatius of Loyola, in his *Spiritual Exercises*, thus suggested the practice of "discernment of spirits."

Loyola's classic discussion summarizes all of the earlier Christian treatment on discernment of spirits, including that of Origen, Climacus, and others: reference to good and evil spiritual influences, consolation and desolation, impulses of the senses and affections, inner movements toward or away from God, sadness and joy. Ignatius organizes his treatment into sets of guidelines or "Rules" that accompany various stages of moral or spiritual growth, from the earlier ("The First Week" in *The Spiritual Exercises*), where contrasts between perceived "good" and "evil" choices are bold, stark, and easier to distinguish, to the more advanced stages ("The Second Week"), where the possibility of self-deception is compounded because the "evil spirit" can subtly tempt one under the appearance of the good. At this stage, the discernment process requires attention to the whole development of inner sensitive movements of the soul, from the initial impulse to its likely direction and conclusion. "Only as affectivity is ordered can it in turn become a clue to the influence of God."[9]

Through the practice of discernment one can become clearer about what God's righteousness means to the particular person; hence it gives one a better sense of direction in one's ongoing hunger and thirst for God's justice.

The Exemplars

In the Old Testament there are righteous persons, such as Noah (Genesis 6:9) and Abraham (Genesis 15:6; Romans 4:3), who strive for God's righteousness and live it out faithfully. And it is through them and in their relationships with others that others, especially those in need, experience God's mercy. Still, during his earthly life Jesus teaches us how to respond to God's righteousness by his very own example. For instance, when he asks John the Baptist to baptize him, he says, "Let it be so now; for it is proper for us in this way to fulfill all righteousness" (Matthew 3:15). These words reveal that Jesus comes to fulfill the law, the prophets, and God's will. In fact, Jesus is the embodiment and incarnation of God's righteousness; and his whole life "supremely manifests God's merciful, compassionate justice."[10] Thus, by turning to the earthly life journey of Jesus, we learn the true meaning of God's righteousness.

Still, in our contemporary society, the lives of many Christians, religious and lay alike, can also be concrete demonstrations of what hunger and thirst for God's righteousness mean. Among them is Mother Teresa of Calcutta. Her hunger and thirst for God's righteousness is noted from the very beginning of her vocation to serve the poor: "I was to leave the convent and help the poor while living among them. It was an order. To fail would have been to break the faith."[11] After that time, she continued to hunger and thirst for God's righteousness in her entire life of doing God's will. Although the disclosure of her "secret" life reveals that she was tormented by a crisis of faith for almost half a century, it reminds us that our hunger and thirst for God's righteousness is a lifelong journey, and it demands ongoing discernment of God's will.[12]

Although these exemplars were discerning and responding to God's righteousness on a personal level, the result of their discernments always pointed to the service of others on both interpersonal and social levels. In fact, the practice of discernment may be applicable on the communal and social levels: when the community and society seek to discern and strive for God's righteousness, they bring about change of communal and social practices and modify their ways of proceeding.

The Social, Communal Aspect of Striving for God's Righteousness

Consequently, the virtue recognized in the fourth beatitude confronts us to ask if our society as a whole indeed strives for God's righteousness or otherwise. It also challenges us to discern and reevaluate the values promoted by our society. For instance, is our culture of euthanasia, abortion, and the death penalty a promotion of God's righteousness or our own? Within the Catholic tradition, do we perceive the challenge of others (say ethicists, feminists, and prophets) as an invitation to rediscern whether our moral beliefs are in line with God's righteousness?[13]

In addition, in our diversified society that emphasizes freedom and individualism, we are often tempted to give up or compromise too easily when challenged by other value systems. When we perceive God's righteousness, do we remain steadfast to this vision or do we allow ourselves to be swayed by others? Again, the grace of God is much needed here.

NOTES

1. These differences include the awkward Greek writing and the breaking of the "π" alliteration found among the first four beatitudes (as the Greek word for "thirst" is διψῶντες). See William D. Davies and Dale C. Allison Jr., *A Critical and Exegetical Commentary on the Gospel according to Saint Matthew*, vol. 1 (New York: Continuum, 1988), 451.

2. Dennis Hamm, *The Beatitudes in Context: What Luke and Matthew Meant* (Wilmington, DE: Michael Glazier, 1990), 95. Some scholars thus identify the righteousness in the fourth beatitude as the "gift" aspect of righteousness, while 5:10 stresses the "task" aspect. Others, like Crosby, are worried that the English term "righteousness" may spiritualize δικαιοσύνη with the idea of justification.

3. Davies and Allison add that it makes the Beatitudes in line with the overall theme of "greater righteousness" in the Sermon on the Mount. Moreover, it highlights the Beatitudes' overall correspondence with Isaiah 61.

4. David L. Turner, "Whom Does God Approve? The Context, Structure, Purpose, and Exegesis of Matthew's Beatitudes," *Criswell Theological Review* 6, no. 1 (1992): 40.

5. Therefore, my interpretation here will focus on God's righteousness alone—that is, the "gift" aspect of righteousness. The interpretation of the "task" aspect of righteousness (i.e., as an ethical command) will be discussed in conjunction with the eighth beatitude.

6. Servais Pinckaers, *The Pursuit of Happiness—God's Way: Living the Beatitudes*, trans. Mary Thomas Noble (New York: Alba House, 1998), 98–99.

7. Ibid., 104.

8. The virtue of perseverance will be discussed in chapter 24.

9. Michael J. Buckley, "Discernment of Spirits," in *The New Dictionary of Catholic Spirituality*, ed. Michael Downey (Collegeville, MN: Liturgical Press, 1993), 281.

10. Bernard Häring, *The Beatitudes: Their Personal and Social Implications* (Slough, UK: St. Paul Publications, 1976), 40.

11. See Joan Graff Clucas, *Mother Teresa* (New York: Chelsea House, 1988), 35.

12. See David Van Biema, "Mother Teresa's Crisis of Faith," *Time*, August 23, 2007, www.time.com/time/world/article/0,8599,1655415,00.html.

13. See Mary Ann Hinsdale, "Blessed Are the Persecuted . . . Hungering and Thirsting for Justice: Blessings for Those Breaking Boundaries," in *New Perspectives on the Beatitudes*, ed. Francis A. Eigo (Villanova, PA: Villanova University Press, 1995), 182.

Chapter Twenty-One

The Fifth Beatitude in Matthew 5:7

Blessed are the merciful, for they will receive mercy.

WHAT DID THE TEXT PROCLAIM?

Starting with Matthew 5:7 the remaining four beatitudes are added by the evangelist from his own sources, for no parallels are found in Luke's version. Scholars like Harrington suggest that the first three of these four beatitudes are taken from a tradition that reflects the concerns for greater righteousness (a major theme of the Matthean Sermon). Specifically, the fifth beatitude corresponds to Proverbs 14:21 where those who are kind to the poor will be blessed.

The Greek term for "merciful" (ἐλεήμων) appears only twice in the New Testament—namely, Matthew 5:7 and Hebrews 2:17. And its synonym οἰκτίρμων is found in Luke 6:36 alone.[1] Still, as I will discuss below, the notion of mercy (ἔλεος) occurs rather frequently throughout the gospel. Moreover, the Hebrew equivalent of ἐλεήμων is *hannun*. Betz observes that in the Old Testament and Jewish literature, the practice of mercy often refers to deeds done out of compassion for the unfortunate and helpless, especially in terms of almsgiving (e.g., Tobit 4:5–7). It is a well-known doctrine among the Jewish people and is often praised in the ancient literature.

Despite being a praiseworthy human virtue, many biblical scholars claim, the disposition toward mercy is first understood as an attribute of God (e.g., Exodus 34:6).[2] God has shown mercy to the people (e.g., Psalm 72:13) and, through the words of prophets, wants the Israelites to desire mercy as well (e.g., Micah 6:8). Subsequently, the exercise of mercy becomes one of the most important religious and social duties for the Jewish people.

Within the context of ancient Greece, as Betz notes, mercy was treated with suspicion in Hellenistic philosophical ethics because it was presumed to be the disposition of the uneducated. Nevertheless, Betz and others, like Talbert, are aware of the fact that, in the New Testament, the concept of mercy and its similar sentiments are brought up frequently by Matthew: in the first place, being merciful and compassionate is a proper attitude toward the human condition noted in the first beatitude—the poor, the outcasts, and even outsiders (e.g., 9:10–13). Second, as in the Jewish tradition, to be merciful and compassionate is a fundamental demand by God (e.g., 12:7). Third, mercy is regularly demonstrated by Jesus's words (e.g., 18:23–35) and examples (e.g., 9:27–31). Indeed, the demand for mercy is placed at the center of Jesus's proclamation and challenges the disciples to show mercy to all, including their enemies (5:43–48). Fourth, the particular sentiment of mercy is forgiveness (e.g., 6:12, 14–15). Concrete evidence of this is the parable of the Unforgiving Servant in 18:23–35, where Matthew applies the principle to a narrative context. Fifth, mercy is regarded by Matthew—as well as other New Testament writers—as an expression of righteousness and wisdom (e.g., James 2:13; 3:13–18). Together with faith and justice, mercy is seen as one of the weightier demands of the law (23:23).

On the other hand, Matthew cites Hosea 6:6 twice in his understanding of mercy as a fundamental demand (9:13; 12:7). Here, ἔλεος is used to render the Hebrew term *hesed* ("steadfast, covenantal love of God for the people"). Thus, ἔλεος connotes the idea of loyalty within a relationship, especially loyalty to God. In other words, acts of mercy are concrete expressions of loyalty to God and what God desires of the people. As a result, the polemical tone in Matthew's use of ἔλεος reflects the view that the Pharisees of Matthew's time, on the contrary, failed to remain faithful to God: they failed to act mercifully to others.

Matthew is very aware of the usage of mercy in the Jewish tradition, and yet he rightfully elaborates its meaning, in light of discipleship, for his community.

With regard to the second part of the macarism, the fifth beatitude also employs future divine passive connotation,[3] just as the second, the fourth, and the seventh beatitudes do. Thus, the promise is to be taken eschatologically in that in the final judgment God will show mercy to those who have shown mercy to others (e.g., 2 Timothy 1:18).

As a whole, 5:7 is a rather straightforward macarism that poses very few exegetical problems, partly because the first and second halves of the verse are in exact parallel. Luz thus comments that the beatitude seems to approach the Old Testament's idea that "deeds determine fate" and that there is a correspondence between human and divine behavior. Moreover, for Matthew, mercy is an important Christian virtue that he encourages his community to acquire. The disciples are called by God, who is merciful, to be compassionate and merciful; this is a moral attitude that at the same time demands actions. Jesus's words and examples further challenge them to extend their mercy to all by means of forgiveness. The practice of mercy, compassion, and forgiveness must be built upon the covenantal relationship with God and a response faithful to God's steadfast love.

THE VIRTUE OF MERCY

While the fifth beatitude is straightforward and poses few exegetical problems, we need to ask when and where we encounter these miserable ones and how we show them mercy and compassion.

"Les Misérables"

During my nearly two decades of training as a Jesuit priest, I was privileged to live in different countries, in both the industrialized and the developing world. In Manila, every Sunday during the school year I joined other members of my religious order to serve a large group of children who live in those "smoky mountains" and spend their entire week with their families scavenging for "valuables" from the massive garbage dump at the end of the city. In strife-torn Belfast, Ireland, I attended funerals of those who died in the "war" and visited others who were imprisoned because of their fight for an end to English colonization. In a remote island in the Pacific Ocean, sometimes known as "within the US missile testing range," I worked with a group of islanders whose community was completely abandoned by the outside world and whose environment and natural resources were exploited by the Army. In post–Khmer Rouge Cambodia, I lived day and night with a group of landmine victims who struggled to resume a simple life in spite of their physical disabilities (often limbs lost to the mines) and psychological trauma. In my daily reflection, a simple but all-too-familiar question nagged at me: "Why these unnecessary miseries?"

Indeed, if we really pay attention to those around us, it is not difficult for us to encounter many in our society who are facing all kinds of miseries: poverty, the struggle for freedom, hatred, exploitation, physical/psychological suffering, and so on. Edward Schillebeeckx rightly says that "there is an excess of suffering and evil in our history . . . there is a barbarous excess."[4]

From a religious perspective, each religious tradition has its own interpretation of suffering and responses to those whose lives are marred by misery. Christianity, for instance, rejects the view that suffering is necessarily a result of one's personal sinfulness, even if the argument is occasionally and mistakenly invoked to explain natural calamities. Despite the differences among the faith traditions, Schillebeeckx notes that they all share the same deepest concern that suffering needs to be overcome. For example, during a meeting held by the Federation of Asian Bishops' Conferences, Paul Cardinal Shan Kuo-hsi of Taiwan insisted that the Church's mission of love and service to life is actualized when it is "put into action in concrete forms of service in alleviating suffering."[5] What does this mission of love and service mean in our Christian life in the present day and age? I believe that part of the answer to this question lies in the message of the fifth beatitude—that is, the cultivation of the virtue of mercy.

The Meaning of Mercy

Literally speaking, the English term "mercy" means "the perception of an evil or misery which moves us" and refers to what pertains to misery.[6] Aquinas explained that the term takes its name from *misericordia*, which denotes one's compassionate heart (*miserum cor*) for another's unhappiness. He thus defined it as "the compassion in our heart for another person's misery, a compassion which drives us to do what we can to help him" (*ST* II.II. 30.1).

Keenan, from a different approach, defines it as "the willingness to enter into the chaos of another."[7] From this he offers a theological interpretation of mercy as identifying all the works of God for humanity: creation is God's merciful act that brings order into the chaos of the universe; incarnation is God's entry into the chaos of human existence; and redemption is God's mercy that delivers us from the chaos of slavery to sin. Elsewhere, Keenan further claims that mercy is emphasized by Scripture as the condition for salvation.[8] In short, God, who is mercy, first shows mercy to us and expects mercy from us toward one another.

However, as mentioned above, in ancient times mercy was opposed by some philosophers as a defect of character and an impulsive response rooted in ignorance. It was also considered as a contradiction to justice, for mercy implies unearned help or relief.[9] The latter charge has been a real challenge for both Christians and non-Christians in our contemporary world.

Mercy as a Virtue

In fact, mercy as a virtue is not in opposition to the virtue of justice. Aquinas quoted the words of the early Church Fathers: "Justice and mercy are so united, that the one ought to be mingled with the other; justice without mercy is cruelty; mercy without justice, profusion."[10] Yet Häring reminds us that this view must be understood in light of God's righteousness: God's righteousness precedes and presupposes mercy and is manifested in it. Pinckaers likewise claims that mercy does not oppose justice but is first in the interest of God's justice. Their view echoes what the previous beatitude demands— namely, God's righteousness. Still, Keenan's view best highlights the role of mercy in the promotion of justice. He explains, "Mercy thickens justice by taking into account the chaos of the most marginalized."[11] Specifically, it prompts us to see that justice applies to those who are without justice and at the same time prompts justice to find and assist them to pursue their rights.

Moreover, mercy is inseparable from the Christian theological virtue of charity, for it is actually the active work and immediate effect of charity. Mercy has to be rooted in and regulated by reason (*ST* II.II. 30.3) and is interested first in the conversion of one's heart. Furthermore, the virtue of mercy takes on the virtue of solidarity as well, because we mourn for and take pity on those who experience suffering and misery in their lives.

Finally, as Keenan and others remark, although all Christian traditions recognize the importance of the virtue of mercy, the Catholic tradition distinguishes itself from others by its long tradition of identifying and performing corporal and spiritual works of mercy.

The Works of Mercy in the Catholic Tradition

In the interpretation of the virtuous act of mourning, I identified solidarity as a crucial virtue toward sufferers. However, the virtue of mercy accompanies solidarity and highlights the importance of action to relieve suffering. What are the actions and works of mercy, particularly within the Catholic tradition? Keenan notes that the New Testament provides the foundational guide. First, the parable of the Good Samaritan (Luke 10:25–37) defines "love of neighbor" as the practice of mercy. Second, the Last Judgment in Matthew 25:31–46 demonstrates that the corporal works of mercy need not be something extraordinary; rather, giving food and drink to the hungry and the thirsty, welcoming a stranger, sheltering the homeless, or visiting the sick and the imprisoned is already a Christian act of mercy. These six specific types of merciful acts (together with burying the dead) are later identified by the early Church as the cornerstone of Christian life.

There are, however, also spiritual works of mercy proposed by the Catholic Church, such as giving good counsel and praying for the dead. Likewise, the acts of admonishing the sinner, forgiving the offenses, and bearing wrongs patiently are widely practiced. As a whole, the spiritual works of mercy are primarily recommended for individuals and are often related to the liturgical and sacramental life of the faithful.

In the celebration of the sacrament of reconciliation, for example, we first experience God's mercy and forgiveness and from there we are able to "do likewise" (Matthew 6:12). For instance, the words *Kyrie eleison* ("Lord, have mercy") mark the beginning of the Eucharistic celebration and continue to remind us of our need for God's mercy and our call to bring God's mercy to others.

I agree with Crosby's remark that these liturgical practices highlight the importance of forgiveness as a Christian act of mercy: it allows us to recognize the deprivation and helplessness of the people around us. Thus, mercy demands not just compassion but also the release of people from their enslavement and their debts. It also demands the avoidance of one's negative anger. Lisa Sowle Cahill is convinced that the whole Beatitudes confirms the view that one needs to approach the enemy/evildoer "in a compassionate desire to meet the needs of wrongdoers and victims as well as possible in the circumstances."[12]

The Exemplars

Jesus, being the embodiment of God's greatest act of mercy to humankind (Romans 5:6–8), is the one whom we should ultimately imitate in the cultivation of the virtue. His attitude (e.g., Mark 1:41), words (e.g., Matthew 18:23–35), and deeds (e.g., Matthew 9:27–30) illustrate for us the kind of mercy that God desires. Specifically, Jesus challenges his disciples and the Pharisees to show mercy to all, including one's enemy (e.g., Luke 6:32–36).

From the twelfth century onward, many religious orders, lay associations, and confraternities were founded to carry out various kinds of corporal works of mercy based on the needs of the society of their times and according to their charisms. For instance, the Knights of St. Lazarus were noted for building many hospitals to take care of lepers, the blind, and orphans. Some confraternities were also commissioned to visit prisoners and others. Many of these organizations and institutions continue to serve our society today.

One contemporary example is the birth of the Jesuit Refugee Service (JRS) in 1980 under the mandate of Fr. Pedro Arrupe, then the superior general of the Society of Jesus. It aims at caring for both the spiritual and physical needs of refugees and other forcibly displaced people. Although JRS has been known for emphasizing its unique characteristic of "accompaniment,"[13] it also engages in advocacy and academic research work that tackles the root causes of forced migration on the international level.[14]

These groups and organizations serve not only as concrete models for us but also as channels through which we can practice the virtue of mercy. Unfortunately, although Aquinas claimed that mercy is the greatest virtue among those that relate to our neighbor (*ST* II.II. 30.4), some Christians rightly lament that our contemporary society seems, on the national and international levels, to have become deaf to the call for mercy.

The Social, Communal Aspect of the Virtue of Mercy

The virtue of mercy bears important social and communal implications. I think of two urgent social practices of mercy that need to be *recovered* for our contemporary world. The first is the practice of hospitality toward immigrants. Since the past century, we have witnessed significant international, massive migrations. These migrants are often victims of the interrelated root causes of involuntary emigration, especially natural disasters, economic and political instability, and violence and warfare. We need to draft and implement national and international migration policies that are based on Christian and humanitarian ideas of mercy.

The second is the need for greater amnesty and the abolition of the death penalty. The previous beatitude teaches us to seek first God's justice before human justice. God's justice and mercy in turn urge us to assure social conditions that permit a (normal) person to grow to maturity. Both a life sentence and the death penalty are in principle and in reality contradicting what a merciful society demands. These social and institutional practices do not help eliminate the cycle of violence and vengeance. The Christian virtue of mercy challenges the kind of "eye for an eye" justice and demands us to seek alternative ways that meet the needs of both the victims and the wrongdoers. Finally, amnesty and the abolition of the death penalty are not simply acts of clemency or forgiveness. Rather, they are acts that promote a much-needed reconciliation—which, as we shall see, is essential to the seventh beatitude.

NOTES

1. Davies and Allison believe that the choice of ἐλεήμων over οἰκτίρμων is probably a matter of personal preference—Matthew is noted for having fondness for the ἐλε-root.

2. Their claim is partly supported by strong statistical evidence: in the Septuagint, the word (and its verb, adjective, and noun forms) is predominantly used to describe God and God's actions and only secondarily describes human quality and action. See Jacques Dupont, *Les Béatitudes*, vol. 3 (Paris: J. Gabalda, 1973), 604, as referenced in Dennis Hamm, *The Beatitudes in Context: What Luke and Matthew Meant* (Wilmington, DE: Michael Glazier, 1990), 96.

3. Although NRSV translates ἐλεηθήσονται as "will receive mercy," this Greek term employs a future passive voice and hence literally means "will be mercied."

4. Edward Schillebeeckx, *Christ* (New York: Seabury Press, 1980), 725.

5. Edmund Chia, *Seventh Plenary Assembly: Workshop Discussion Guide: Interreligious Dialogue in Pursuit of Fullness of Life in Asia*, FABC Paper no. 92K, www.ucanews.com/html/fabc-papers/fabc-92k.htm.

6. Servais Pinckaers, *The Pursuit of Happiness—God's Way: Living the Beatitudes*, trans. Mary Thomas Noble (New York: Alba House, 1998), 116.

7. James F. Keenan, *Moral Wisdom: Lessons and Texts from the Catholic Tradition* (Lanham, MD: Rowman & Littlefield, 2004), 72.

8. See James F. Keenan, *The Works of Mercy: The Heart of Catholicism*, 2nd ed. (Lanham, MD: Rowman & Littlefield, 2008), 3.

9. Ibid., 5.

10. Thomas Aquinas, *Catena Aurea: Commentary on the Four Gospels Collected out of the Works of the Fathers*, vol. 1, ed. John Henry Newman (London: Saint Austin Press, 1997), 152.

11. Daniel J. Harrington and James F. Keenan, *Paul and Virtue Ethics: Building Bridges between New Testament Studies and Moral Theology* (Lanham, MD: Rowman & Littlefield, 2010), 206.

12. Lisa Sowle Cahill, "The Ethical Implications of the Sermon on the Mount," *Interpretation* 41, no. 4 (April 1987): 150.

13. See Kevin O'Brien, "Consolation in Action," *Studies in the Spirituality of Jesuits* 37, no. 4 (Winter 2005).

14. See also David Hollenbach, ed., *Driven from Home: Protecting the Rights of Forced Migrants* (Washington, DC: Georgetown University Press, 2010).

Chapter Twenty-Two

The Sixth Beatitude in Matthew 5:8

Blessed are the pure in heart, for they will see God.

WHAT DID THE TEXT PROCLAIM?

Like the fifth beatitude, the sixth in Matthew 5:8 does not have any parallel in Luke and was added by Matthew. Most scholars agree that its explicit Old Testament correspondence is Psalm 24:3–5. The psalm is to be sung during the temple entrance liturgy to describe those who could ascend the hills of the Lord: they are the people who have "clean hands and pure hearts" and therefore are fit for divine worship. Other relevant passages include Psalm 73:1 and Proverbs 22:11, in which God shows goodness to those who have a clean and pure heart. In sum, these references show that the sixth beatitude has a close tie with the Hebrew Bible and points to an ancient tradition.

Historically, as Betz notes, the idea of purity was commonly found in religions in terms of their rituals. First, purification rituals were conducted to remove actual physical impurities. Later, in ancient Greek practices, ritual purity became more closely connected to morality: the internal condition of the person eventually was considered a greater source of impurity than external causes.

How about Matthew's perception of "pure in heart"? Does it also refer to an internal quality? In order to answer this question, we need to turn to the term "heart." In both the Old and New Testament traditions, according to Davies and Allison, the Greek term "heart," or καρδία (and its Hebrew equivalent *leb*), is a comprehensive term. It is at times used interchangeably with the word "soul" (ψυχή)—it can refer to the true self (e.g., Matthew 13:15), the place of emotions (e.g., Acts 14:17), the desire or will (e.g., Proverbs

201

6:18), the intellect (e.g., Mark 2:6), or the inner space where one encounters the deity (e.g., Psalm 27:8). For Matthew, the heart is clearly the source of outward speech and conduct (15:18–19), as well as the realm of inner life (9:4).[1]

On the other hand, the phrase "pure in heart" (καθαρὸς τῇ καρδίᾳ) is understood within the Jewish tradition as "an undivided obedience to God without sin" and is an important virtue.[2] It points both to "singleness of intention" and "to will only God's will" with one's whole being.[3] However, Luz remarks that the phrase is used comprehensively, although its narrow cultic usage is often highlighted. Betz further comments that, in ancient Greek culture, there is a similar and significant idea of "purity of the soul": only those with pure souls can enter "the land of the Blessed."

In the New Testament, as many major scholars point out, the meaning of "pure in heart" can be found especially in the Sermon on the Mount: it means lacking adulterous thoughts and the like (5:27–30), attending to the inner encounter with God and not external piety (6:1–18), and maintaining coherence between interior thought and exterior acts (15:8). In comparison with the Jewish tradition, the New Testament emphasizes more internal than external or cultic purity. Betz adds that this emphasis on interior disposition of the person could imply that those who are "pure in heart" and the "poor in spirit" are synonymous. This does not mean, however, that the macarism overlooks cultic issues completely.

Taken together, I find Harrington best grasps Matthew's thought: "pure in heart" points to neither external purity nor single-heartedness alone but to a sense of *integrity* between one's interior life and external actions.

The second part of the beatitude says that the "pure in heart" will see God. Davies and Allison note that within Judaism seeing God is equivalent to knowing God, and that the knowledge or vision of God is usually associated with the promise of the future (e.g., Isaiah 52:6). There are, however, two contrasting traditions about seeing God: the first focuses on the possibility of physical sight of God in this world (e.g., Exodus 3:6); the second, and dominant, tradition tends to emphasize the blessed goal of acquiring spiritual sight of the world to come (e.g., Psalm 17:15).

However, the use of a future active connotation and the above exploration of Greek and Jewish traditions point to an eschatological understanding of the promise: within the ancient Greek world, only the best could achieve the purity of soul so as to experience a full vision of the most sacred. While only Moses has seen God (e.g., Numbers 12:8), the Jewish hope has been to see God in the *eschaton*.[4]

Finally, regarding the community's conduct, some writers comment that the beatitude challenges the hegemony of the Pharisees and Sadducees, who emphasized cultic preoccupations regarding purity/impurity.[5] The "pure in heart" emphasizes the integrity of one's whole being and understands such an attitude as a fundamental, all-encompassing virtue.

THE VIRTUE OF INTEGRITY

There are rather diverse interpretations on the ethical meaning of the beatitude among contemporary theologians and scholars. Vann interprets it as pointing to the virtue of temperance. Pinckaers turns his entire attention to the meaning of "purity." Others focus on the notion of "heart" or the meaning of "seeing."[6] However, our exegesis indicates that the beatitude emphasizes the integrity of the whole being—the inner self finds parallel expressions in outward actions. The lack of it is sometimes understood as hypocrisy.

Hypocrisy in the Church?

The recent sex scandal crisis within the Catholic Church and the alleged cover-ups by the hierarchy expose hypocrisy. For example, a leading German weekly newsmagazine, under the headline "The Hypocrites: The Catholic Church and Sex," reported a public official's criticism of German bishops for not being truly open and thorough in their investigation.[7] Unfortunately, the lament that the Catholic Church is full of hypocrisy is heard elsewhere.

Hypocrisy points to the hiding of impurity under the cover of external observances. It is "the pretension to qualities which one does not possess, or . . . the putting forward of a false appearance of virtue or religion. . . . Essentially its malice is identical with that of *lying*; in both cases there is *discordance* between what a man has in his mind and the simultaneous manifestation of himself."[8] Reformed theologian Alan Sell similarly suggests that hypocrisy is an attitude in opposition to "honesty" and to "being in accord with one's whole being."[9]

The Meaning of Integrity

Sell therefore identifies honesty and wholeness as the principal meanings of integrity. While these two meanings are rather self-evident in their own regard, integrity as a whole conveys a sense of personal congruence, a correspondence between one's "private" and "public" selves. From a religious perspective, it points to an undivided life commanded by God; hence it opposes hypocrisy that implies a divided heart.[10]

William Werpehowski, from a different perspective, claims that integrity points to a state or condition: "Through a 'spiral' in which will and desire direct practical intelligence and practical intelligence instructs will and desire, a personal subject achieves an integration of self that conforms to the truth of the good as it is given by God, and in charity participates in the divine love."[11]

Integrity as a Virtue

Sell's identification of the two principal meanings of integrity is helpful for our understanding of the virtue. Honesty implies that integrity first points to truthfulness. Many are convinced that the leadership's failure to honor truthfulness from the beginning is an essential cause of the Roman Catholic Church's current crisis in the sex scandal. Therefore, in order to cultivate the virtue of integrity, both individuals and the community's leadership need first to prove their truthfulness.

Wholeness refers to the integration of all aspects, especially one's inner self and external actions. Keenan turns to Aquinas for insights: he notes that prudence "guides the moral agent to living a self-directed life that seeks integration [of natural inclinations]" and in particular, integrates one's appetites and practical reason. Therefore, the virtue of prudence is closely connected to integrity.[12]

A third virtue is vigilance—whether one's interior thought is in tune with the exterior actions can only be known through an ongoing monitoring and evaluation. The disposition of self-evaluation—that is, watchfulness—helps the person not just achieve integrity in a single moment but also form a moral character of integrity.

Finally, from a biblical point of view, Jesus points out that hypocrites, while focusing on external deeds, neglect the virtues of justice, mercy, and faith (Matthew 23:23).

In sum, the virtue of integrity as identified in the sixth beatitude, like that of the sixth commandment, is comprised of two key virtues and yet demands other relevant virtues.

The Practice of Integrity

I find that the role of conscience is crucial for cultivating integrity and its two core virtues, truthfulness and prudence: conscience urges us to act in accordance with what the inner self believes is good and true. It differs from superego in that it calls us to grow rather than acting as a restraint. The Second Vatican Council's *Gaudium et Spes* says,

> In the depths of his [*sic*] conscience, man detects a law which he does not
> impose upon himself, but which holds him to obedience. . . . To obey it is the
> very dignity of man; according to it he will be judged. Conscience is the most
> secret core and sanctuary of a man. . . . In a wonderful manner conscience
> reveals that law which is fulfilled by love of God and neighbor. (#16) [13]

Many contemporary moral theologians, by turning to Aquinas, further
advocate for the primacy of conscience even though our conscience may
err. [14] The practice of integrity in turn points to the need to nurture and follow
an informed conscience. Werpehowski proposes the practice of repentance,
renewal, and perseverance as a means to cultivate the virtue of integrity in
the Christian life: perseverance in repentance and renewal can substantively
contribute to a life of integrity by "shattering illusions about our identity,
making a break with what falsely claims to make it up, and acting in the
world from our suffering and need for the sake of our needy and suffering
neighbors." [15]

Vann claims that the virtue of integrity finds expressions in Christian
liturgy: liturgy is the worship of the whole person—our words and bodily
movements are expressions of the self's total self-offering to God. Moreover,
in the liturgy one experiences integrity on various levels—personal integrity
that is the renewal of the self, cosmic integrity that unites one to all creation.

In Christian spirituality, the practice of the "Prayer of the Heart" by the
Desert Fathers of the fourth century—the recitation of the Lord's Prayer that
slowly integrates into one's breathing and the beating of one's heart—has
been widely adopted as a practice to cultivate an integration of one's inner
life with the external body and action. [16]

Likewise, Christian vigilance calls for the practice of examining our own
life. One growing popular practice is that of daily "examen of conscience" as
suggested by Ignatius in his *Spiritual Exercises*. In this prayer exercise,
sometimes also called "examination of consciousness," one tries to find the
movement of the spirit in one's daily life and through it, to identify the
incongruence between one's inner movements and external actions. Examen
helps us be more sensitive to the longings and sources of our own spirit and
hence become more open to God. Interestingly, as we shall see, both the
examen and the practice of recitation find parallels in oriental religions and
cultures as well.

The Exemplars

In Matthew Jesus denounces the Pharisees and scribes as hypocrites for their
behavior and bad example: their self-righteousness (7:1–5) and their self-
centered and attention-seeking religious acts (such as fasting in public in
6:16) do not match up with what they teach (23:1–33). Jesus, on the contrary,

lived an exemplary life of integrity by doing exactly what he preached about God's kingdom, such as praying to God the Father (14:23) and serving God (20:25–28).

Within the Catholic tradition, the late Pope John Paul II offered his own choice of models of Christian integrity. For example, on one occasion he told an audience that they should cultivate the virtue of integrity as demonstrated in the life of Pope Pius XI.

> Dear brothers and sisters! These are only some parts of the synthetic personality of Pope Pius XI. . . . And here I would invite and encourage you to grow with increasing commitment to the same values of integrity, discipline, dedication to duty, and even more steadfast adherence to Jesus Christ, generous participation in the life of the Church, a strong evangelical witness in society.[17]

Pope Piux XI's pontificate was marked by the emergence of the fascist government and Nazism. His integrity was by and large manifested in his social teaching, which is in tune with the gospel values. In particular, through his writings (e.g., *Quadragesimo anno*) he advocated for social justice and common good, and he spoke against the emerging powers of his time. His Christian integrity had a great impact on the society.

The Social, Communal Aspect of the Virtue of Integrity

The virtue of integrity, in the first place, challenges the leadership of our society and community to reexamine their roles as leaders. Häring rightly noted that the sixth beatitude is very important to our social renewal. When we are truthful to our own vocation in the society as educators, lawyers, or politicians, we contribute to the building up of the society.

Within the Catholic community, many laypeople and clergy, in light of the Church leadership's failure to honor truthfulness from the beginning of the sex scandal, urge the Church not to just apologize and be humble but also to take the courage to change and to be truthful. One pastoral theologian proposes a communicative model of theological reflection—which experiments with the rhetoric of its uncommitted environment and engages in reflections across such boundaries—for Church leaders to maintain integrity as leaders. He explains, "A communicative model of theological reflection provides support and critical facility for our life-long negotiation between pragmatism of organizational leadership and the confessional commitments at the heart of the Christian community's identity."[18]

In the broader society, integrity and truthfulness particularly challenge the unhealthy atmosphere of doing business nowadays. We note from the daily news how corporations, big and small, local and international, cover up the problems of their products.[19] Most advertisements in the mass media often exaggerate their functions, hide the known negative effects of their products, and mislead the possible consumers in their choice-making. Thus, the virtue of integrity ought to call for a conversion in the overall mentality of running business today.

Finally, the social, communal implication of the virtue brings us back to the issue of justice, for one's truthfulness and wholeness affect not only the person's well-being but also that of the community and the society. I note two concrete reflections here. First, integrity demands fairness toward others, especially those who are under one's leadership. Second, leaders who have acquired the virtue of integrity by acting truthfully on their own beliefs inevitably challenge the injustices of their society. El Salvador's Archbishop Óscar Romero defended the poor and called for international intervention, which led to his assassination by the Salvadoran government in 1980. To follow such models, we need the grace of God for the courage to be true to ourselves, to one another, and to God.

NOTES

1. Mark Allan Powell, "Matthew's Beatitudes: Reversals and Rewards of the Kingdom," *Catholic Biblical Quarterly* 58, no. 3 (1996): 472.

2. Hans Dieter Betz, *The Sermon on the Mount*, ed. Adela Yarbro Collins (Minneapolis, MN: Fortress Press, 1995), 134; Ulrich Luz, *Matthew 1–7: A Commentary*, trans. James E. Crouch (Minneapolis: Fortress Press, 2007), 196.

3. Glen H. Stassen, "The Beatitudes as Eschatological Peacemaking Virtues," in *Character Ethics and the New Testament: Moral Dimensions of Scripture*, ed. Robert L. Brawley (Louisville, KY: Westminster John Knox Press, 2007), 252.

4. However, Moses was unable to see God's face (Exodus 33:20).

5. See W. R. Domeris, "Exegesis and Proclamation: 'Blessed Are You . . .' (Matthew 5:1–12)," *Journal of Theology for Southern Africa* 73 (1990): 71; David L. Turner, "Whom Does God Approve? The Context, Structure, Purpose, and Exegesis of Matthew's Beatitudes," *Criswell Theological Review* 6, no. 1 (1992): 40–41.

6. However, they seldom turn their attention to the notion of integrity. See Jim Forest, *The Ladder of the Beatitudes* (Maryknoll, NY: Orbis Books, 1999), 89–103; Michael H. Crosby, *Spirituality of the Beatitudes: Matthew's Vision for the Church in an Unjust World*, rev. ed. (Maryknoll, NY: Orbis, 2005), 140–58.

7. John L. Allen Jr., "Scandal Takes Familiar Trajectory in Germany," *National Catholic Reporter*, March 3, 2010, http://ncronline.org/news/accountability/scandal-takes-familiar-trajectory-germany.

8. *Catholic Encyclopedia*, s.v. "Hypocrisy," www.newadvent.org/cathen/07610a.htm. Italics are mine.

9. Alan P. F. Sell, *Aspects of Christian Integrity* (Calgary: University of Calgary Press, 1990), ix.

10. Stephen L. Carter, *Integrity* (New York: Basic Books, 1996), 8, as cited in Michael Jinkins, "The Integrity of Ministry: Communicative Theology and the Leadership of Congregations," *Journal of Religious Leadership* 8, no. 1 (Spring 2009): 3.

11. William Werpehowski, "Practical Wisdom and the Integrity of Christian Life," *Journal of the Society of Christian Ethics* 27, no. 2 (Fall–Winter 2007): 67.

12. James F. Keenan, "The Virtue of Prudence (IIa IIae, qq. 47–56)," in *The Ethics of Aquinas*, ed. Stephen Pope (Washington, DC: Georgetown University Press, 2002), 259, 265.

13. Vatican II, *Gaudium et Spes*, December 1965, www.vatican.va/archive/hist_councils/ii_vatican_council/documents/vat-ii_cons_19651207_gaudium-et-spes_en.html.

14. James F. Keenan, *Moral Wisdom: Lessons and Texts from the Catholic Tradition* (Lanham, MD: Rowman & Littlefield, 2004), 35.

15. Werpehowski, "Practical Wisdom and the Integrity of Christian Life," 69.

16. See Forest, *The Ladder of the Beatitudes*, 96–97.

17. Pope John Paul II, *Incontro di Giovanni Paolo II con la Popolazione di Desio*, papal speech to the people of Desio, May 21, 1983, http://www.vatican.va/holy_father/john_paul_ii/speeches/1983/may/documents/hf_jp-ii_spe_19830521_popolazione-desio_it.html. The English translation is mine.

18. Jinkins, "The Integrity of Ministry," 7.

19. In 2010 alone, there were serious cases of misconduct and cover-up reported, ranging from former global finance services firm Lehman Brothers Holdings to the car-making giant Toyota Motor Corporation. In November 2011, a class-action suit was filed in the U.S. Central District Court of California against Toyota regarding unintended acceleration and marketing and sales practices. The case is currently pending. In 2011–2012, another multi-billion-dollar company, Olympus Corporation, admitted to misapplication of funds in covering up huge losses.

Chapter Twenty-Three

The Seventh Beatitude in Matthew 5:9

Blessed are the peacemakers, for they will be called children of God.

WHAT DID THE TEXT PROCLAIM?

Matthew 5:9 is the third beatitude added by the evangelist. Scholars note that it finds a parallel in the apocalyptic literature of 2 Enoch 52:11–12 ("Happy is he who establishes peace. Cursed is he who strikes down those who are in peace.") and has similar verbal usage and themes with 5:38–42 (on retaliation). Unfortunately, both 5:9 and its parallel do not carry any qualifications for the peacemakers; consequently, as we shall see, 5:9 is a rather controversial text because of the possible political implications rooted in the meaning of "peacemaking."

According to Betz, the Greek term for "peacemaking," εἰρηνοποιός, is a typical adjective that describes those leaders who establish security and socioeconomic welfare. Within ancient Greek society, peacemaking was highly valued, since the people longed for peace and stability after centuries of wars. Ancient philosophers also understood it as a proper task within families and between individuals.

In Judaism peacemaking has long been considered a virtue. The Hebrew concept of *shalom* ("peace"), as Harrington notes, was fundamental to both the Old Testament and Jewish religions: it points to abundance and all-round right relationships. It is the fullness of God's gift and involves a cosmic dimension in which the Creator intends a cosmic order. Still, one writer points out that the term is parallel to Hebrew *mishpat* ("justice") and is thus closer to the concept of righteousness than to that of tranquility of order.[1] Therefore, war and violence are not completely ruled out by the Jewish tradition.

Betz further notes that, within the New Testament tradition, εἰρηνοποιός occurs only here, while other verbs, such as ποιειν εἰρήνην ("make peace"), are employed more frequently elsewhere (e.g., James 3:18). There are other scriptural references where the same idea of peacemaking is promoted even if the word is not spelled out—for example, the antitheses in the Sermon (e.g., 5:21–48) present instances of peacemaking in the context of family and friendship.

As a whole, both biblical traditions and their corresponding texts tend to envision peacemaking in terms of right (human) relationships.

In light of these relationships, the term implies a positive action and is best applied to someone who seeks to bring peace (i.e., peacemaker) rather than to a pacifist *per se*. Some further suggest that it envisions the notion of reconciliation, which in turn implies forgiveness. In both cases, the pursuit of peace is a requirement for following Jesus, for he is the one who brings peace (Luke 2:14), and God is the principal peacemaker (especially by forgiving sins) and a God of peace (Romans 16:20).

The controversy involving the interpretation of peacemaking is related to the understanding that peace is constitutive of the kingdom of God (Romans 14:17, 19), and peacemaking is a direct consequence (and demand) of righteousness and a function of the kingdom of God.[2] Some suggest that both righteousness and the kingdom require personal pursuit of peace in all aspects of life, including political and economic ones. In this sense, political implications can be expected. However, as seen above, the examples that Matthew provides in the Sermon are concerned with those relationships between individuals instead of between social/political groups. In addition, these and other implications are presented solely as a personal example of the individual disciples. Some thus claim that they are used to help the disciples cultivate the appropriate attitudes with one another, and only then that they apply these attitudes to broader social and political environments. In other words, these implications do not serve as a general guide for political behavior among groups. Peacemaking within a broader political paradigm is at most only a secondary consideration here.

Apart from this controversy, another puzzle regarding this beatitude is the disharmony with 10:34–35, where Jesus claims that he did not come to bring peace but rather the sword. Davies and Allison explain that such a lack of harmony is typical of the evangelist's style (e.g., 16:6 with 23:3) and Matthew simply tries to preserve the tradition and at the same time be creative. Betz adds that Matthew basically affirms the positive values of peacemaking in spite of the hostility experienced by his community: the peacemakers will be rewarded by God.

The promise of the beatitude is that the peacemakers will be called sons (children)[3] of God. Here, the connection between the promise of divine sonship and the exhortation to engage in peacemaking finds parallels in the Old Testament tradition, where sonship and peacemaking were brought together (1 Chronicles 22:9–10).

The phrase "sons of God" occurs only once in Matthew. However, there are various passages in both the Old and New Testaments that indicate who the sons of God are—the righteous ones (e.g., Wisdom 5:1–5; Revelation 21:7). They are called by God. Since it is generally assumed that "called to be something by God" is equivalent to "being that something," the promise can be rephrased as "they will be sons of God."[4] Betz further notes that, for Matthew, those whose conduct is similar to God's own are already sons of God—they are the people of God who address God as "Father" (e.g., 6:9) and are expected to become sons of God and share a likeness to God in the *eschaton.*

The overall eschatological nature of this promise is further supported by the use of future divine passive connotation. However, Betz rightly remarks that Matthew's understanding of divine sonship differs from Paul's in that for Paul the present pronouncement does not exempt the people from facing the last judgment.

In conclusion, the seventh beatitude contains an important ethical message. Peacemaking is a long-established moral virtue valued by both the Greek and the Jewish worlds. It is primarily concerned with interpersonal relationships that demand reconciliation and forgiveness. The pursuit of peace is also demanded by Jesus. Although the notion of peacemaking has posed a couple of interpretative problems with regard to political implications and its seemingly conflicting relationship with violence, Matthew basically affirms the positive values of peacemaking and proposes peacemaking as an appropriate attitude for the followers of Jesus rather than as a purely political agenda. It is much needed in our world, where conflicts are found everywhere.

THE VIRTUE OF PEACEMAKING

An exegesis of the Greek and Hebrew terms for peace shows that peace is paralleled with "justice." Many seem to agree on this point. Some theologians, based on this understanding, further claim that the beatitude suggests a political agenda. However, our study also makes it clear that peace and peacemaking are understood by Matthew to represent appropriate attitudes primarily for personal and communal practices and only subsequently for social change. This reading hardly advocates the establishment of a Christian political party.

Yearning for Peace

Both our personal experiences and historical evidence reveal that our society has been a disturbed one: there are disharmonies and conflicts in almost every aspect of human relationships and social life, especially among cultural/ethnic groups and nations. Some well-known conflicts of the twentieth century include the racial segregation in the United States and the "Troubles" in the north of Ireland. Some of them further developed into warfare, such as the genocide/civil war between the Hutu and Tutsi in Rwanda in the 1990s.

Reflecting on the experience of the Vietnam War, American psychologist Ralph White identifies six causes of conflict (or stumbling blocks) in our human relationships, including self-righteousness and our perception of the other in terms of the "diabolical enemy-image."[5] These stumbling blocks and their subsequent conflicts often lead to hatred, violence, and suffering on both sides. On the global level, they further cause massive death, poverty, migration, fear, and so on. Pinckaers rightly says, "We yearn for external peace, achieved through good relationships with our neighbors, and interior peace which is freedom from anxieties, troubles, and inner conflicts."[6] This yearning for peace, as a result, calls for peacemaking in all aspects and levels of human relationships.

The Meaning of Peace and Peacemaking

Peace is one important blessing of God granted to us through Jesus Christ (e.g., John 14:27). Christians are in turn commanded to bring peace to the world (Luke 10:5). Still, we need to distinguish genuine peace from false peace that some people have mistaken as peace. As Hellwig and others have argued, genuine peace does not mean to compromise, desert, or evade confrontation but rather to acknowledge the inevitability of conflicts. It is only achieved by the transformation of all human relationships and the resolution of conflicts. False peace, however, as Crosby writes, is expressed and obtained through either modeling on a *pax romana* that employs force and dominion to achieve peace or adopting a kind of passivity that accepts all disorder and suffering at any cost in exchange for stability. This misunderstanding of peace further leads some activists to claim that justice and peace are incompatible.

The Second Vatican Council offers a Catholic definition of genuine peace:

> Peace is not merely the absence of war; nor can it be reduced solely to the maintenance of a balance of power between enemies; nor is it brought about by dictatorship. Instead, it is rightly and appropriately called an enterprise of justice. . . . Peace is never attained once and for all, but must be built up ceaselessly.[7]

Peace like war must be waged - Walter Knight

Here, the Council emphasizes and reaffirms that peace is not just Augustine's "tranquility of order" but also the advocacy of the work of justice. Crosby thus claims that peace is a kind of "work" to be "made." Hellwig interprets Christian peacemaking in a similar manner: it is "the recentering of God in one's own life, and in society. . . . [It means] the welcoming of God's order, God's reign . . . [and] living by God's law. . . . [The first step is] to listen to those who have been silenced . . . and restore the means of sustenance and social participation to those who had these things snatched from them."[8]

In brief, the Christian gift of peace, animated by God, is part of the ethical vision of Jesus. In this way, the Christian understanding of peace and peacemaking differs from that of other religions or traditions. However, for all people of good faith, peacemaking is not only an external act but also an inner disposition of the person.

Peacemaking as a Virtue

The above views suggest that genuine peace is built upon justice. Thus, the cultivation of the virtue of peacemaking implies the simultaneous attainment of the virtue of justice. Moreover, since genuine peace is achieved by means of neither force nor passive acceptance of injustice at any cost, the virtues of meekness and fortitude are called into place respectively: meekness insists on patience and the rejection of violence, while fortitude demands active seeking of peace and endurance. In this way, the third and the seventh beatitudes are closely connected to each other.

Still, the virtues implied in the second beatitude, such as solidarity and the virtuous act of mourning, are also relevant to peacemaking, for they motivate us to assist others in achieving peace. Also, in order to avoid the building up of those stumbling blocks to peace, one needs to cultivate humility as well.

Finally, since peacemakers inevitably encounter opponents in the process of making peace, the virtue of mercy (and its particular practice of forgiveness), which leads to transformation of relationships and eventual reconciliation, is crucial to the whole process of peacemaking and restoring rightful relationships.

Thus, we see that the virtue of peacemaking in the seventh beatitude relies heavily on the acquisition of the core virtues in the previous beatitudes.

The Practice of Peacemaking

Various practices and precautions can be identified. First, we need to acquire peace in our own hearts. Pinckaers rightly explains that "we cannot envisage lasting peace . . . without an interior rootedness in peace of conscience . . . [or] to maintain active and stable peace with others if we are in inner conflicts."[9] Second, peacemaking has to be practiced on all levels of human relationships accordingly. Vann and Häring thus insist on the importance of building peace in the family first and only then extending to the community and the larger society. As noted earlier, this framework finds parallel in Confucian teaching. Third, one should not just remove those stumbling blocks but also actively build up right relationships. In so doing, we need to engage in dialogue with and show mutual respect and concern for the other. Crosby, for instance, suggests three stages of creating right relationships based on the practices of the early Christian community (Matthew 18:10–22): affirmation of the other's significance and values, fraternal correction, and communal reconciliation. In fact, most will agree that these three steps are applicable to non-Christian communities as well.

Nevertheless, these practices are often concretely performed in the Christian's liturgical and sacramental life. Within the Catholic tradition, for example, we recognize God's own blessing of peace through the forgiveness of sins granted in the sacrament of reconciliation. During the Eucharistic celebration, we in turn practice forgiveness by communal prayers, especially for our enemies and with those we find difficult in life. The subsequent sign of peace further expresses our willingness to reconcile with and make peace with other members of the community. It is an important liturgical practice of peacemaking, and it unites the faithful of diverse cultural and sociopolitical backgrounds into a single faith community.

The Exemplars

Jesus is the Prince of Peace about whom the Old Testament prophets spoke (e.g., Isaiah 9:6). In Luke's gospel, for instance, Jesus speaks strongly about peace and brings God's peace to us (2:14). Specifically, he does so by forgiving our wrongdoings (23:34). We are called to imitate him in bringing peace in our world (10:5–9).

Within the history of Christianity, Francis of Assisi and Catherine of Siena were known for making peace between the Church and the civil powers of their times. In particular, Francis of Assisi was famous for embracing peace as his lifelong watchword, and a popular prayer of peacemaking is attributed to him: "Lord, make me an instrument of your peace. Where there is hatred, let me sow love; where there is injury, pardon. . . ."[10]

In the twentieth century, there are many international figures who have made great efforts to make peace with their enemies and build peace for their own countries.[11] In the United States, Dorothy Day has been noted for "establish[ing] pacifism and conscientious objection as a legitimate stance for Catholics and for Americans."[12] For decades in South Africa, Nobel Peace Prize recipient Archbishop Desmond Tutu contributed to a peaceful struggle against the unjust system of apartheid by not just persistently criticizing the government but, more importantly, relentlessly urging reconciliation between both sides, especially in chairing the Truth and Reconciliation Commission that has become a model for peacemaking in other similar post-conflict procedures around the world.[13]

Within the Catholic Church, Pope John XXIII is also recognized by some scholars as a promoter of peace. He took bold initiatives to promote peace during his pontificate, as exemplified in documents like *Mater et Magistra* and *Pacem in Terris*. The pope pointed out that a stable world order depends on God's order as established in creation and the nature of human reality in the world, and he offered a radical approach to peacemaking that challenges the established oppressive power. Indeed, the Catholic Church has been well known among other religions for considering peacemaking in the public sphere through its official documents.

The Social, Communal Aspect of the Virtue of Peacemaking

Although the virtue of peacemaking is primarily concerned with the transformation and restoration of right relationships on the interpersonal and communal level, our discussion so far has indicated that it has a strong social implication. In fact, the reality of our contemporary world urges us to go beyond the interpersonal and communal level in the practice of peacemaking. Some theologians and ethicists also argue that since Christ came to bring peace and reconciliation to all people, we too have to bring peace on all levels.

Subsequently, some of these individuals, such as the Mennonite John Howard Yoder, suggest that the analogous practice of peacemaking in the social sector could be nonviolent resistance or nonviolent direct action. They believe that a central norm of Christian life is nonresistant love, which includes nonviolence and pacifism. Stassen, on the other hand, advocates for "just peacemaking," which suggests that nonviolent direct action needs to be accompanied by independent initiatives, such as treaties on nuclear weapon reduction. He argues that the two strategies are not in conflict with one another but actually share certain common features, like being proactive in nature and affirming the dignity of the enemy. In particular, Stassen emphasizes the need for international cooperation and is convinced that nations involved in active international cooperation "make war and have war made against them less frequently."[14] Others further call for national forgiveness as a way to peacemaking in the international realm.

In a similar manner, the Catholic Church turns to taking serious actions on the international scale in the promotion and making of peace:[15] it is not enough to restrain the manner of warfare; rather, there is a need to ban war altogether. Peacemaking is the responsibility of all Christians, and justice is the basis for authentic peacemaking. I believe that each of us can do something to promote peace in our contemporary world.

Last but not least, Carter further extends peacemaking to the cosmic level. He claims that cosmic peace "consists not of exploitation but of all things cosmically in right relation to God" and grounds itself in right relations and justice with all.[16] I am convinced that the extension to make peace with the Earth is not just necessary but also urgent in the twenty-first century.

NOTES

1. See Mark Allan Powell, "Matthew's Beatitudes: Reversals and Rewards of the Kingdom," *Catholic Biblical Quarterly* 58, no. 3 (1996): 474.

2. See Hans Dieter Betz, *The Sermon on the Mount*, ed. Adela Yarbro Collins (Minneapolis, MN: Fortress Press, 1995), 138–39; Ulrich Luz, *Matthew 1–7: A Commentary*, trans. James E. Crouch (Minneapolis: Fortress Press, 2007), 188–89; Powell, "Matthew's Beatitudes," 473–74.

3. Harrington notes that in the Old Testament, being "sons of God" alluded to joining the angels (Genesis 6:1–4). The gender-neutral term "children" might obscure this allusion. Hamm, on the other hand, points out that the inclusive term "children" was available to Matthew, and hence his choice of "sons" might well be tied with the "Son of God" title. I continue to use "sons of God," which is more faithful to the Greek translation. However, such use should not discriminate against women in any way. It is the same with regard to the use of "sonship."

4. William D. Davies and Dale C. Allison Jr., *A Critical and Exegetical Commentary on the Gospel according to Saint Matthew*, vol. 1 (New York: Continuum, 1988), 458.

5. See Ralph K. White, *Nobody Wanted War: Misperception in Vietnam and Other Wars* (New York: Doubleday, 1968), as referenced in Michael H. Crosby, *Spirituality of the Beatitudes: Matthew's Vision for the Church in an Unjust World*, rev. ed. (Maryknoll, NY: Orbis, 2005), 161–62.

6. Servais Pinckaers, *The Pursuit of Happiness—God's Way: Living the Beatitudes*, trans. Mary Thomas Noble (New York: Alba House, 1998), 154.

7. Vatican II, *Gaudium et Spes*, #78, December 1965, www.vatican.va/archive/hist_councils/ii_vatican_council/documents/vat-ii_cons_19651207_gaudium-et-spes_en.html.

8. Monika K. Hellwig, "The Blessedness of the Meek, the Merciful, and the Peacemakers," in *New Perspectives on the Beatitudes*, ed. Francis A. Eigo (Villanova, PA: Villanova University Press, 1995), 199.

9. Pinckaers, *The Pursuit of Happiness*, 158.

10. From the viewpoint of virtue ethics, this prayer suggests several Christian virtues for peacemaking—namely, the theological virtues of faith, hope, and charity, and the virtue of joy.

11. On the interpersonal level of peacemaking, Pope John Paul II is remembered for taking the initiative to forgive and reconcile with the man who attempted to assassinate him in 1981.

12. Mark Zwick and Louise Zwick, *Dorothy Day, Peter Maurin, and the Catholic Worker Movement*, www.cjd.org/paper/pacifism.htm.

13. The Desmond Tutu Peace Center, "About Desmond and Leah Tutu," www.tutu.org/bio-desmond-tutu.php.

14. Glen H. Stassen, "The Sermon on the Mount as Realistic Disclosure of Solid Ground," *Studies in Christian Ethics* 22, no. 1 (2009): 70.

15. Vatican II, *Gaudium et Spes*, ##88–90.

16. Warren Carter, *Matthew and the Margins: A Sociological and Religious Reading* (Maryknoll, NY: Orbis Books, 2000), 136.

Chapter Twenty-Four

The Eighth Beatitude in Matthew 5:10–12

5:10—Blessed are those who are persecuted for righteousness's sake, for theirs is the kingdom of Heaven.

[5:11–12—Blessed are you when people revile you and persecute you and utter all kinds of evil against you falsely on my account. Rejoice and be glad, for your reward is great in heaven, for in the same way they persecuted the prophets who were before you.]

WHAT DID THE TEXT PROCLAIM?

The eighth beatitude is the last of the four beatitudes added by Matthew. Matthew 5:10 has no parallel in Luke and was likely added at a later time.[1] It forms an inclusion with the first beatitude by containing exactly the same promise. Davies and Allison thus suggest that this could imply that the other promises made between these two are basically alternative ways of express-ing the promise of the kingdom of heaven.[2] Harrington also notes that the eighth beatitude echoes the fourth, focusing on righteousness, and prepares us for what is required of the greater righteousness in verse 20. Verse 10 thus plays a special role in the Beatitudes.

Moreover, since verse 10 and verses 11 and 12 share the same subject matter of persecution, they seem to be related in one way or another. Some scholars perceive 5:11–12 as the ninth beatitude, despite the fact that it differs from the rest of the Beatitudes in that it is formulated in the second-person plural and contains many more words.[3] For them, it serves as a bridge between the eight beatitudes and the teaching on love of enemies on the one hand, and as a smooth transition to the "salt and light" saying on the other. It is further argued that Matthew's later addition of 5:10 was simply a numerical consideration—to form a multiple of three and to complete the triadic structure of the Beatitudes. Still, for reasons stated earlier, I stand with the view that 5:11–12 is an expansion of the eighth beatitude (see chapter 14).

Regarding the motif of the persecution of the righteous that is central to these verses, it can be found in many Old Testament passages, such as Wisdom 2:10–20. Betz notes that among these Hebrew texts, the persecution of the prophets was a dominant theme that later became part of the martyrdom ideology. This motif is found in ancient Greek thought, too, where major philosophers are at times portrayed as the prototype of the persecuted righteous man. Nevertheless, Davies and Allison observe that none of the Hebrew passages bestows a blessing on the persecuted. The New Testament tradition, in contrast, poses a possible parallel to the macarism in 1 Peter 3:14, although the beatitude does not invoke the life and death of Jesus as the passage in Peter does.

Davies and Allison further claim that the Greek verb for "persecution," διώκω, may refer to physical violence and/or verbal abuse. The use of perfect passive participle also implies that Matthew is aware that the persecution has begun and continues to the present (e.g., 10:16–33). And the Greek word ἕνεκεν ("on account of") denotes that the righteousness demanded by God prompts the persecution.

This understanding subsequently leads major scholars like Luz to comment that the motif and the description in verses 11–12 mutually interpret each other in various ways. First, the use of the second-person plural in verses 11 and 12 implies that persecution is constitutive of discipleship (for Jesus is now addressing the disciples directly). Second, Matthew's three forms of persecution, when compared to Luke's (6:22), point to a more severe conflict experienced by Matthew's community.[4] Betz, Harrington, and others remark that these forms of persecution find references in both the New Testament (e.g., Acts 5:17–18) and the Jewish tradition. "Revile" is a traditional theme from the wisdom literature and is associated with the persecution of the righteous (e.g., Psalm 69:10). "Persecute" is used peculiarly to imply that persecution could come from within. This in turn hints that Matthew's community was persecuted by the Jews. "Utter all kinds of evil against [someone]" can be viewed as slanders and defamation, which are treated extensively in the Hebrew Bible (e.g., Levi 19:16). It is also a traditional theme of the wisdom literature and is associated with martyrdom (e.g., Proverbs 6:17). The qualification "falsely" might be added to make the hostility more specific.

Third, as Davies and Allison claim, both the words used and the omission of the subject in verse 11 imply that the persecutions are rather general and could be applied to various situations. Still, the verse supplies the concrete description of the persecution; those who experience these kinds of persecution are indeed suffering for righteousness.

Fourth, the phrase "on account of me" states clearly that the proper cause of persecution is Jesus and his teaching. Following Jesus and his teaching is thus the righteous thing for the disciples to do. Here, the deductive reasoning of verse 12 recalls the Old Testament tradition (and theme) that suffering from persecution is part of the prophet's vocation (e.g., Nehemiah 9:26). It also provides a historical verdict for the present persecution as well as the reward granted. The possible agents of persecution are the Pharisees and scribes who are the sons of those who murdered the prophets (Matthew 23:31–36). Betz further notes that persecution for the sake of righteousness is understood within the Jewish tradition as the greatest test for the righteous and produces the highest virtue.

Regarding the promise of the eighth beatitude, we find additional information from the first two parts of verse 12—the receiving of "great" reward. According to Harrington and Betz, the idea of receiving reward from God because of persecution is found in Jewish apocalyptic literature (e.g., 4 Ezra 7:88–100). Nevertheless, Jewish doctrine teaches that reward is a conditional entitlement to be claimed by the qualified person, but it can be claimed only once. When Matthew applies it to the Sermon and the Beatitudes, he implies that those who follow the teaching of Jesus will be guaranteed treasure in Heaven. This guarantee provides the reason for their rejoicing. However, one has to wait for the eschatological coming of the kingdom of God in order to claim the reward, for, as Luz clarifies, the reward is always granted in the last judgment (6:1).

Finally, for Betz and Davies and Allison, the two imperatives χαίρετε and ἀγαλλιᾶσθε ("rejoice" and "be glad") in 5:12 could have a liturgical appeal, and the ὅτι ("for") clause offers an immediate reason for rejoicing: the disciples, like the prophets of the past, would be counted as God's servants and rewarded greatly. This ὅτι clause, though it lacks concrete description of what the great reward is, echoes our understanding of other similar clauses stated in the previous beatitudes. As Betz rightly claims, it actually sums up these promises. In this way, the imperatives likewise point not only to the eschatological future but to the present as well.

In conclusion, 5:10–12 have an important Hebrew foundation: they tell us that those who suffer from various kinds of physical and/or verbal persecution for the sake of righteousness as the prophets did and as the disciples do now, on account of Jesus and his teaching, will be rewarded greatly in the eschatological coming of the kingdom of Heaven. Still, they should rejoice and be glad right now because of the guarantee of this reward. The beatitude sums up the basic thoughts and forms a high point for the ethical teaching of the whole Beatitudes: the attitude of humility identified in the first beatitude reaches its climax in the cultivation of the highest virtue of bearing persecution for righteousness's sake.

BEARING PERSECUTION FOR RIGHTEOUSNESS'S SAKE

Our exegesis reveals that the eighth beatitude focuses on righteousness as the fourth beatitude does. We also saw that persecution and subsequent suffering, though diverse in nature, are the direct effects of seeking righteousness, following Jesus and his teaching, and being prophetic. The evangelist hints that persecution and suffering continue in the present to those who remain faithful to Jesus's mandate and carry on his mission faithfully. This information enriches our interpretation of the last beatitude for the contemporary world.

New Forms of Persecution

In many parts of our present world there are still people who are persecuted for various reasons, ranging from more overt political and religious reasons to simply their fight for justice on behalf of the poor and the suffering. Some of them are physically tortured while others are imprisoned or forced into exile, as seen in countries like China and Myanmar. Even in places where physical persecution is abandoned, the persecuted often suffer from all sorts of unjust treatment, such as censorship and the exclusion of basic human rights. Pinckaers rightly notes that this is also the experience of some contemporary Christians who try to live their Christian life faithfully, such as underground Catholics in mainland China.

While the Church has suffered various kinds of persecution throughout its history, at times it has played the role of persecutor. For instance, the Inquisition acted as a means to censor, silence, and punish those whom it perceived as threats to its doctrinal teaching, as it did in the case of Galileo, whose theory was denounced as antiscriptural and heretical.

In modern times, a number of Christians and theologians continue to experience some forms of persecution (such as marginalization and silencing) by ecclesial authority. Elsewhere, others in the faith community find themselves implicitly or explicitly shunned and excluded because of their sexual orientation or their views on certain nondoctrinal and/or moral issues. Indeed, those who do this to others firmly believe that they are doing what is right and just.

The Meaning of Martyrdom

The unjustly persecuted are best exemplified in the form of martyrdom. The Greek term μαρτυς ("martyr") refers to a witness who is persecuted specifically for his or her testimony. It first appears in Christian literature and points to the disciples' witnessing of their Christian faith with the risk of persecution and even death. Later, the term is used exclusively to refer to those who die for their faith. Aquinas, for example, wrote that martyrdom is an act of the virtue of fortitude, for it "consists essentially in standing firmly to truth and justice against the assaults of persecution" (*ST* II.II. 124.1). Death for Christ's sake is the perfect expression of martyrdom (*ST* II.II. 124.4). Martyrdom was thus understood as one of the defining examples of sainthood in the Church.[5]

Although nowadays we rarely risk our lives in witnessing our Christian faith, one author rightly remarks that we are still called to die to the self in our ordinary lives for the sake of loving God and our neighbors.[6] Both Aquinas's view and this "dying to the self" point to the attainment of certain Christian virtues.

Bearing Persecution for the Sake of Righteousness as a Virtue

The first virtue needed for bearing persecution is evidently fortitude. As one of the four cardinal virtues, it "guard[s] the will against being withdrawn from the good of reason through fear of bodily evil" (*ST* II.II. 123.4). Fortitude allows the person to face and endure the foreseeable persecution without surrender. It also enables one to take on the active, prophetic role.

Still, even more than fortitude, justice is clearly a necessary virtue. We are persecuted because of our hunger and thirst for righteousness on behalf of the poor and the suffering who are victims of social injustice. Our striving for righteousness is thus motivated by the reality of the sufferer and our recognition that we should relieve these victims of their injustice. Still, in our championing justice and righteousness, we are not called to be vengeful. Rather, we are summoned to be imitators of Christ—in this instance, particularly in his meekness. In this way, the eighth beatitude, though relying on fortitude, closely shares those virtues advocated in the first beatitudes.

Finally, we are called to rejoice and be glad not only for the eschatological reward but also in the midst of persecution. We need to learn to rejoice in the midst of trials and in the Lord (Philippians 3:1a, 4:4), rather than rejoicing over physical or material pleasure. This joyfulness, as mentioned in our discussion of the third commandment, points to the virtue of gratitude, which is perceived by some as the "pivotal virtue of moral life."[7] Because our life is filled with God's gifts, the whole Christian life is thus the appropriate response to the benevolence of God.[8] Moreover, gratitude for these persecutions, and not for ordinary happiness, is the root of rejoicing:[9] we become joyful because of gratitude and not vice versa. Our ability to rejoice then builds up further satisfaction and makes us even more thankful. Rejoicing is, therefore, the living out of the practice of gratitude over our suffering for others.

The Practice of Bearing Persecution for a Righteous Cause

As in the practice of mourning, we begin with internal preparation—acquiring a sense of willingness and readiness to bear persecution for a righteous cause. Externally, we practice mortification as a way to prepare ourselves physically and spiritually in facing and enduring possible future persecution. Thus, for Catholics, fasting and abstaining from meat on certain days of the liturgical year, as well as participation in the Stations of the Cross and the Paschal Triduum, are seen as some ordinary and yet helpful practices of experiencing the Lord's suffering and persecution, which in turn make us ready to accept persecution.

Moreover, as is in the practice of meekness, we need to acquire self-control, patience, and forgiveness toward those who persecute us. Here, practices like praying the "Our Father," offering the sign of peace, and receiving the sacrament of reconciliation guide us to experience God's forgiveness and enable us to forgive others, especially our enemies who persecute us in whatever way.

The Exemplars

In the Old Testament, the prophets were above all the objects of persecution, for their prophetic voice challenged Israel's own sociopolitical injustice and unfaithfulness to God (e.g., Jeremiah 26). In the New Testament, we also are aware that Jesus's persecution resulted from his hunger and thirst for God's righteousness; his Passion is "the climax and fulfillment of the protracted suffering of the prophets under persecution."[10] Later on, beginning with the exemplary death of Stephen, the disciples and the Christians were likewise persecuted for the sake of the Lord (Acts 6:8–7:60).

In medieval times, many Christians held firm to their faith even under wrongful persecution by the Church itself. One famous case is Joan of Arc of the fifteenth century. She was first accused of heresy, then imprisoned, and eventually executed. Her death precisely exemplifies the virtues (fortitude, justice, meekness, and gratitude) implied in the joy of this beatitude.

Today in our society, we find Christians who bear persecution and risk their lives because of hungering and thirsting for justice and exercising their prophetic role of challenging society's injustice, as in the case of the six Jesuits and two lay helpers who were murdered by the military government in the city of San Salvador in 1989. Like Archbishop Romero, their exemplary and prophetic role to bring righteousness to the country, despite a possible death threat, is best understood in the following testimony:

> They sought countless ways to unmask the lies that justified the pervasive injustice and the continuing violence. . . . [They] stood for a Church of the poor . . . a prophetic Church like the one that Archbishop Romero symbolizes. . . . [They] knew they were risking their lives. But they understood that that was the price of being human in their time and place; that was the cost of following Christ.[11]

Moreover, many of these models accepted whatever persecution lay ahead, without violence but with faith, and inspired others to do likewise. One such example is Mohandas Gandhi, who taught his supporters to prepare themselves for nonviolent resistance during the famous "salt march." Gandhi's attitude later inspired Martin Luther King Jr.'s 1963 march on Washington, during which he urged his audience to acquire the same willingness and readiness to bear persecution: "We must forever conduct our struggle on the high plane of dignity and discipline. We must not allow our creative protest to degenerate into physical violence. Again and again we must rise to the majestic heights of meeting physical force with soul force."[12]

The Social, Communal Aspect of the Virtue of Bearing Persecution for Righteousness's Sake

These models and their exemplary acts rightly confirm that the last beatitude has an explicit social and communal aspect. The virtue of bearing persecution is definitely other-oriented, for we strive for righteousness and bear persecution on behalf of the unjustly suffering. Moreover, we saw from the previous reflections that much of human poverty, suffering, misery, anger/hatred, and conflict is directly or indirectly caused by structural injustices in our society. Thus, we are called to exercise our prophetic role in challenging these unjust structures and in seeking social change.

This prophetic role in turn calls us to do so courageously by words and deeds on all levels. Unfortunately, in concrete situations, such prophetic voices are often a minority and subsequently are often suppressed or ignored, and their supporters persecuted by the authorities. Like many of the previous beatitudes, the last is a radical call. We greatly need God's grace so as to persevere in our prophetic role and to embrace persecution joyfully.

NOTES

1. Verses 11 and 12, however, parallel Luke 6:22–23.

2. Robert Guelich even claims that the subjects of the first and the eighth beatitudes are synonymous to each other. See his *The Sermon on the Mount* (Waco, TX: Word Books, 1982), 93.

3. There are various suggestions regarding the change from the third-person to the second-person plural: some think that it is a rhetorical design; others propose that it is meant to apply what has been said generally to the concrete situation of the disciples. See Hans Dieter Betz, *The Sermon on the Mount*, ed. Adela Yarbro Collins (Minneapolis, MN: Fortress Press, 1995), 147; Mark Allan Powell, "Matthew's Beatitudes: Reversals and Rewards of the Kingdom," *Catholic Biblical Quarterly* 58, no. 3 (1996), 477–78; and William D. Davies and Dale C. Allison Jr., *A Critical and Exegetical Commentary on the Gospel according to Saint Matthew*, vol. 1 (New York: Continuum, 1988), 461.

4. Yet both Betz and Harrington point out that these persecutions suggest that final conflicts between Jewish Christians and the Jews (such as complete separation) are not yet grasped or implied by the beatitude.

5. Robert Ellsberg, *All Saints* (New York: Crossroad, 1997), 1, as cited in Jim Forest, *The Ladder of the Beatitudes* (Maryknoll, NY: Orbis Books, 1999), 138.

6. See Forest, *The Ladder of the Beatitudes*, 146.

7. Richard M. Gula, *Reason Informed by Faith: Foundations of Catholic Morality* (New York: Paulist Press, 1989), 52. On gratitude as duty and as virtue, see Gilbert C. Meilaender, *The Theory and Practice of Virtue* (Notre Dame, IN: University of Notre Dame Press, 1984), 172.

8. See Mark E. Graham, *Sustainable Agriculture: A Christian Ethic of Gratitude* (Cleveland, OH: Pilgrim Press, 2005), 9–10.

9. See David Steindl-Rast, *Gratefulness, the Heart of Prayer* (Mahwah, NJ: Paulist Press, 1984), 204.

10. Servais Pinckaers, *The Pursuit of Happiness—God's Way: Living the Beatitudes*, trans. Mary Thomas Noble (New York: Alba House, 1998), 170.

11. Dean Brackley, "Remembering the Jesuit Martyrs of El Salvador: Twenty Years On," *Thinking Faith*, November 16, 2009, www.thinkingfaith.org/articles/20091116_1.htm.

12. Martin Luther King Jr., "The 'I Have a Dream' Speech," www.usconstitution.net/dream.html.

Conclusion

A Radical Invitation to All

In part I, I proposed a schema for bridging biblical studies and Christian ethics. It points to the emerging consensus—namely, that exegesis and hermeneutics are inseparable from each other when engaging in Scripture-based ethics. Scripture needs to be treated as "scripted script." I further take virtue ethics as a fitting hermeneutical tool.

In parts II and III, I consolidated this schema by exegeting and interpreting two popular, yet very important scriptural texts from the Hebrew Bible and the New Testament, namely, the Ten Commandments and the Beatitudes, respectively.

Throughout the exegesis of these two texts, I point out that Exodus 20:2–17 and Matthew 5:3–12 are not stand-alone documents but are integral to their corresponding broader units in terms of literary forms and content. Our exegetical findings further confirm that these commandments and the beatitudes are themselves interrelated, although they were treated separately here for clarity's sake.

As far as their contemporary ethical interpretation is concerned, I identified certain core Christian virtues for our daily life. In the case of the Ten Commandments, I admit that the extraction of virtues from the text is unconventional (by today's trend of interpretation), if not innovative, in its own regard: by reading the commandments through the lens of virtue, we understand them not simply as prescribing or prohibiting certain acts but also, and more importantly, as guiding us to be a certain kind of believer and faith community. The virtues implied in the Beatitudes, on the other hand, are at times quite different from what one would expect at first glance. These differences, as explained above, are the result of first carrying out the necessary exegetical task before interpreting the texts.

Regarding the meanings and contents of these virtues, some of them are straightforward and self-evident, such as humility (the first beatitude). Others take on virtues found in other commandments/beatitudes, such as mercy (the fifth beatitude), which takes on solidarity (the second beatitude); or the virtue of respecting God's holiness (the second commandment), which takes on the virtue of upholding true worship (the first commandment). They confirm the interrelatedness within the commandments/beatitudes. This interrelatedness is also found between the commandments and the beatitudes; for example, humility (the first beatitude) and integrity (the sixth beatitude) are also included in the virtues identified in the first, second, third, fourth, sixth, and tenth commandments.

Still, many of the virtues, especially those identified from the Ten Commandments, are actually *clusters of virtues*. Partly because of the complex nature of the concepts presented in the texts, it is difficult to correlate them with simple, stand-alone virtues that we already know. For instance, the virtue of treasuring the sacred temporal space (the third commandment) implies the cultivation of gratitude, patience, humility, trust, hope, and joy. It also takes on the virtues identified in the first and second commandments, namely, upholding true worship and respecting God's holiness.

Moreover, some of these clusters of virtues overlap with each other in one way or another. For example, the virtues of both upholding true worship and respecting God's holiness imply the virtues of faith and religion. Or, taking another example, gratitude, humility, hope, and patience/tranquility are needed in both the virtues of treasuring the sacred temporal space (the third commandment) and satisfaction with contentment (the tenth). Still, it is noteworthy that, especially from the fourth commandment onward, the virtues corresponding to each often call for the cultivation of charity and justice. This is understandable, for charity and justice are crucial to the understanding of "respect" or "valuing" with regard to the other's status, life, marriage, property, liberty, dignity, reputation, and gender difference.

WHAT DO THESE OBSERVATIONS IMPLY IN LIVING OUT A VIRTUOUS CHRISTIAN LIFE?

Epistemologically speaking, I understand these seemingly repetitive and overlapping virtues confirm the view that the commandments and beatitudes are intertwined, not only on the level of textual interpretation but also on the level of ethical implication. In practice, they tell us that the call and invitation to follow these commandments and beatitudes do not mean that one simply chooses to be a humble Christian, a follower of Christ who commits to the corporal work of mercy, or a Christian couple who are chaste and faithful to each other. Rather, to cultivate the virtue identified in a particular commandment or beatitude means also cultivating integrally the virtues identified in the rest of the Ten Commandments or the Beatitudes. Just as we have seen in the case of the Sermon on the Mount, so too the Decalogue and the Beatitudes point to a radical invitation to all who want to live out their Christian lives virtuously based on the teaching of scriptural texts. Indeed, it is most challenging when compared with simply not violating a particular commandment or being a meek person. But with God's grace, exemplary models, and practices, we are able to live a virtuous life daily.

Epilogue

West to East

Renowned Confucian scholar Tu Wei-ming rightly claims that the relevance and impact of the Confucian tradition continues to be felt (though not fully) in many aspects of society in East Asia.[1] I believe, however, that one reason why the tradition's relevance could be felt worldwide is because there is a certain affinity between Christian and Confucian virtues. Rather than make that case here, I shall simply reflect on the Ten Commandments and the Beatitudes to demonstrate that the two fundamental biblical texts for Christian morality actually highlight some of the same moral traits that Confucianism does. By way of concluding my work, then, I will name and describe parallel virtues promoted by texts of the Confucian tradition, especially classical writings of Confucius, Mencius, and Xunzi—the *Analects* (*A*), the *Great Learning* (*GL*), the *Doctrine of the Mean* (*DM*), the book of *Mencius* (*M*), and the writings of Xunzi.[2]

VIRTUE ETHICS AS A SIGNIFICANT COMPONENT OF CONFUCIAN ETHICS

The ultimate goal of Confucian morality (and self-cultivation) is to form a union with the community as well as with Heaven and Earth (*DM* 22). Here the distinctiveness of Confucian ethics consists in two related aspects, namely, *tao* 道 ("the Way") and *te* 德 ("virtue"). The Way functions as a governing perspective and reference point for conforming one's moral life to the will of Heaven.[3] One ethicist thus perceives *tao* as a moral vision and the form of virtues.[4] *Te* is commonly understood as "a kind of moral character trait which is obtained from oneself . . . in the *xing* 性 ('human nature') as a result of personal cultivation."[5]

Those who focus on the *te* aspect of Confucian morality would certainly argue that virtue ethics is the implicit foundation behind Confucian ethics.[6] First, Confucian literature states clearly that ethical education depends on the exemplification of the virtues (*GL* 1). It also bequeaths a large and complex virtue-related ethical vocabulary (e.g., *A* 9:29). Second, self-cultivation is an end in itself and results in the attainment of the cardinal virtue of *jen* 仁 ("humanity/benevolence"). Third, Confucian ethics also considers the four important goods of virtue, which are practices and habits, character and dispositions, exemplars, and communal identity. Fourth, Confucians stress certain key virtues as the ancient philosophers did, like *jen*, *yi* 義 ("righteousness"), and *li* 禮 ("ritual propriety").

As a whole, although Western philosophy and Confucianism may disagree on certain issues regarding virtue, I believe that it is appropriate to approach Confucian ethics from the perspective of virtue ethics, at least on the "thin" level.[7]

CONFUCIAN RECEPTION OF THE VIRTUES OF THE DECALOGUE

In this section I follow the outline of the Decalogue and offer ten teachings from Confucian ethics that highlight evident similarities to the Decalogue.

Revering (*jing* 敬) Heaven

For Confucians, Heaven (*tien* 天) is understood as a source for self-transformation and at times functions as "a religious authority or absolute often theistic in its portrayal."[8] The basic attitude toward *tien* is respect and fear (*A* 3:12; 16:8). Confucius suggested that living a virtuous life is the best prayer to Heaven and other deities (*A* 7:35). Moreover, we need to trust in Heaven, which alone understands us completely (*A* 14:35).

In *A Discussion of Rites,* Xunzi claimed that *tien*, being the basis of life, is the proper object in the practice of ritual propriety. Sincere generosity, reverent formality, and respectful reverence are therefore the proper attitude in performing rites.[9] However, Confucian ritual does not view Heaven as a person or establish any personal relationship with it.

Respecting Heaven's Holiness

Confucius made it clear that the best way to respect gods is to give them reverence and yet keep a distance from them (e.g., *A* 6:22). Still, on a few occasions Confucius called upon and swore to Heaven and even expressed his deep emotions to it as Jesus did during his Passion and death on the cross (*A* 6:28; 11:9; cf. Matthew 26:39; 27:46). Xunzi, on the other hand, stressed that what makes Heaven different from us is its holiness. Based on this distinction, he taught that we should not attempt to interfere or compete with Heaven's work, to "play God," or to curse Heaven. Rather, we simply obey what Heaven dictates.

Treasuring the Sacred Temporal Space

The attitudes of Confucian figures toward rites reflect a certain similarity with Christian aspects of treasuring the sacred temporal space. First, Confucius acknowledged that all that we have depends on Heaven (e.g., *A* 12:5). Ceremonies and sacrificial rites are wonderful ways to express our gratitude to Heaven, provided that they are done qualitatively and sincerely (*A* 3:4, 17). Second, for Xunzi rites are means of providing satisfaction to our senses and hence bring us joy. They are in accordance with the Way, and hence we should take appropriate time to carry them out. Third, rituals allow us to express emotions and care for others just as Christian works of mercy do. Finally, regular celebrations and rites by the community are beneficial.

Filial Piety (*xiao* 孝)

Filial piety toward parents is probably the most well-known Confucian virtue in the West.[10] The rationale for *xiao* is that parents are the immediate root of our lives. *Xiao* grounds the growth of the Way and cultivates our character (*A* 1:2; *DM* 20:7). The *Analects* illustrates the characteristics of filial piety, some of which are similar to our earlier exposition of the fourth commandment. It calls for adult children (2:5) to follow the rules of propriety with reverence and respect (2:7), to maintain attentiveness toward parents and solidarity with them and their feelings and emotions (4:21), to meet them with eagerness and joy (2:8), to offer them readiness and availability (2:6; 4:19), and to exercise gentleness and patience when correcting their mistakes (4:18). Finally, *xiao* continues even after one's parents have died (e.g., 1:11).

Mencius, from a different perspective, highlighted what is unfilial, such as "the neglect of parents through laziness . . . through indulgence in games . . . and fondness for drinking" (*M* 4B:30). Among them, having no heir is the most serious failure (*M* 4A:26).

Respect for Life

Mencius claimed that human life is an important (but not an absolute) good (*M* 6A:10). Like Confucius, he also brought up the issues of war, killing, the death penalty (e.g., *A* 12:19; *M* 7B:4; 1B:7–8), and, specifically, the two aspects of the virtue of respect for life. Confucius was very aware of anger, hatred, and jealousy and hence taught that *chün tzu* 君子 (the gentleman) would learn to refrain from revenge even toward unrighteousness (*DM* 10:3). Xunzi further pointed out that hatred would lead us to obsession of the mind. Nonetheless, Confucius insisted that avoiding aggressiveness and resentment alone does not make a person *jen*; rather, we need to do good as well (*A* 14:1). This points to the promotion of the well-being of others: we should teach others, with respect and without negligence, to stand on their own feet just as we wish the same for ourselves (*A* 6:30; *GL* 10:16).

Reciprocity (*shu* 恕)

Like other ancient societies, the Chinese perceived marriage as foundational to the building of an ordered society. Specifically, as an androcentric society, they expected the wife to obey her husband and acquire specific virtues in relation to her actions, speech, appearance, and skills. Thus, Mencius emphasized the living out of one's marriage according to those prescribed distinctions and reciprocal functions between husband and wife (*M* 3A:4). He also seemed to suggest that obedience is the basic virtue for married women (*M* 3B:2). Nevertheless, Mencius's emphasis on the distinction between husband and wife needs to be understood through the Confucian idea of mutual responsibility between two parties in a relationship and through the virtue of reciprocity that is actually the Golden Rule (*A* 15:24).

For Xunzi, marital relationships, like other human relationships, must be guided by the virtue of ritual propriety. It is by means of *li* that all our (sexual) desires are trained and satisfied.

Valuing the Property and Liberty of Others

Poverty was a pervasive reality during Confucius's time, and slavery and theft were prevalent (*A* 12:18). Surprisingly, none of the three thinkers talked about respect for others' property or liberty much, even though their emphasis on righteousness would seem to fit. Nevertheless, Confucius perceived stealing as a result of our disordered desires, especially those found in the leadership (*A* 12:18). Coveting and the actual act of stealing are thus inseparable. Mencius, on the other hand, employed stealing as an analogy to express his view on unrighteous actions (*M* 3B:8). Xunzi further suggested that *li* helps us cultivate the virtue of respect for others' property and liberty by taming the desire to take possession of what belongs to others.

Valuing the Reputation and Dignity of Others

In the *Analects* 13:18, Confucius said that it is justified for father and son to cover up each other's crimes. This controversial text gives the impression that he values one's reputation or familial relationship more than truthfulness and justice. Some defend Confucius, saying that he was concerned about familial responsibilities by asking whether giving evidence against one's own father/son is a sensible thing for a son/father to do in the first place. [11] For Confucius, who definitely had an appreciation for a sense of justice, "legal justice is considered secondary to parental loyalty." [12]

Elsewhere Confucius advised that we should speak cautiously and with sincerity (*A* 4:24; 16:10). When he claimed that *chün tzu* would encourage and help others realize their own goods, Confucius implied the use of good words by the gentleman as well (*A* 12:16).

Appropriate Interaction with Women

Confucius has long been charged with misogyny and sexism for his famous saying that "the women and the small men . . . are difficult to deal with" (*A* 17:25). However, it is argued that Confucius was only making reference to concubines or female servants. He was simply complaining about "their ignorance of appropriate forms of social interaction" that are required by the society. [13] Confucius also never implied that women could not achieve self-cultivation. Moreover, the oppression of women was actually influenced by other traditions. [14] Therefore, the least we can say is that Confucian thinkers were not per se sexists nor did they perceive women as objects of lust.

Contentment and Simplicity

Confucius hinted that coveting is a characteristic of the "small man," who in contrast to *chün tzu* seeks fulfillment of appetite and comfort, desires material goods, and is preoccupied with profit (e.g., *A* 4:16). Xunzi alone explicitly discussed human desires. He insisted that desires lead one to obsession and delude our mind. They need to be tamed and satisfied by means of rites.

Regarding contentment, Confucius is revered for living it truthfully: he said that being able to regularly try out what has been learned or being visited by a friend who comes from afar is already a delight and a source of contentment (*A* 1:1). A lifestyle as simple as eating coarse rice and drinking plain water can equally bring contentment and joy (e.g., *A* 7:16).

CONFUCIAN RECEPTION OF THE VIRTUES OF THE BEATITUDES

Here I would like to highlight a congruency between the virtues outlined under the Christian beatitudes and Confucian ethics. As in the previous section, I will follow the set order of the eight beatitudes in Matthew.

Humility

The *Doctrine of the Mean* is often seen as an excellent commentary on the virtue of humility (e.g., 13:4).[15] It portrays the humble person as one who "in a quiet and modest manner . . . goes about the great task of self-realization."[16] In the *Analects*, we find other texts that advocate the cultivation of humility (e.g., 6:15). Moreover, Xunzi's formulation of filial piety highlights a significant aspect of humility:[17] *xiao* is the proper response toward one's parents, who make fullness of life possible. Filial piety thus attends to one's origin. It reveals and expresses one's fundamental stance of dependency toward the origin of one's life, to whom one can never fully repay the debt incurred. One thus has to humble oneself before one's origin.

Solidarity

We find in the *Analects* a few narratives of mourning, such as Confucius's grief over the death of his beloved disciple (11:9, 10). Here Confucius called for empathy with the sufferer (7:9). Mencius also commented that sensitivity and compassion toward the sufferer is an innate response of humankind (*M* 2A:6). Xunzi, on the other hand, claimed that mourning has a multilevel, sociocommunal, and practical purpose: it accommodates the emotions involved and extends the honor due, distinguishes the duties owed to different related people, and represents the ultimate principle of harmony and unity within a community.

Finally, although *chün tzu* alone fully understands the mystery of suffering and accepts it willingly, it is still the moral responsibility of each person to accompany and help others understand and ease their suffering.[18]

Meekness

Confucius and Mencius talked about how the inferior and the superior should cultivate gentleness proper to their status. Regarding the poor and the oppressed, there exists a strong inclination toward anger and vengeance; they have difficulty in refraining from revenge toward unrighteousness (*A* 14:10; *DM* 10:3). Confucius thus not only talked about meekness but also lived it out—being benign, upright, courteous, temperate, and complaisant (*A* 1:10). He understood such a person would accept what happened to him without anger or revenge (*A* 6:3).

For the powerful and the rich, Confucius commented that it is not enough for them not to be arrogant (*A* 1:15). Rather, they should imitate *chün tzu*, who shows forbearance and gentleness in teaching those who are inferior (*DM* 10:3). Mencius, by commending the virtuous acts of sage King Shun, likewise pointed out that meekness is a virtue of the benevolent and the powerful (*M* 5A:3).

Obedience to and Discernment of the Mandate of Heaven

Confucian thinkers acknowledged the existence of the Mandate of Heaven and conceived it as a moral imperative, a specific personal mission, and an abiding commitment and responsibility.[19] Confucius thus warned against disobeying the Mandate of Heaven (*A* 3:13). Instead, one must take time and effort to know and understand it (*A* 2:4; 20:3).

Mencius's view on one's response to the Mandate of Heaven was comparable to the Western understanding of the discernment of spirits: the acceptance of one's destiny should be conditional. One needs to discern carefully and only accept what is proper to one's destiny, which means following the Way alone (*M* 7A:2).

Curiously, Confucius did not believe that one should strive for something that is unattainable.[20]

Benevolence (*jen* 仁) and Kindness (*en* 恩)

Jen, as a specific virtue of benevolence, is often compared to the Christian virtue of charity (*M* 7B:1).[21] For Mencius, benevolence comes from human nature: it emerges from the heart of compassion and reaches out to the natural world (e.g., 2A:6, 1A:7). It is practiced differently according to the status of its objects, for instance, family members (7A:45).

With *en* the texts point to mercy and compassion to the least advantaged people in the society who are deprived of even the most basic human relationships (1B:5). Therefore, it is an important virtue of the leader and, like righteousness, is a guiding principle in government (e.g., 1A:1; 3A:3). Consequently, Mencius strongly advocated for a benevolent government that commits itself to the welfare of its people (e.g., 7A:14).

Loyalty/Conscientiousness (*chung* 忠)

Chung 忠 renders a virtue close to that of integrity: it refers to one's action being loyal to one's own heart and conscience. [22] Confucius was aware of the lack of integrity in many common people and hence compared them to small and cowardly men (*DM* 7; *A*, 17:12). It is thus very important to act in accordance with what one believes and vice versa (e.g., *DM* 13:4).

Confucius also advocated the examination of the self as Christian spirituality does. In the *Analects*, we learn that his disciple practiced self-examination frequently (1:4). It is a practice recommended for all. One scholar thus concludes that the entire process of self-cultivation implies the virtue of integrity, for self-cultivation is aimed at "attaining authenticity . . . through conscientious study, critical self-examination, continual effort, and a willingness to change oneself." [23]

Peacemaking

Confucius, like the ancient Greek philosophers, was concerned about the establishment of a well-ordered society that is based on good government. He rejected the idea of warfare as an effective means to this end. Rather, he perceived self-cultivation as the means to achieve peace and was convinced that peacemaking should begin with one's inner self (*A* 14:42, *GL* 0.4). Mencius further understood waging war and its related behaviors as a grave crime that should be punished (*M* 4A:14; 7B:4). Instead, one should acquire the virtues of benevolence and righteousness to achieve peace (*M* 7B:4). Xunzi again stressed that *li* is crucial for establishing order and peace. However, he did not reject the possibility of war for the sake of righteousness—it is a right thing to do when it is done out of love. In each instance, all three stress self-cultivation as the ground for good order.

Righteousness (*yi* 義)

Yi is often translated into righteousness or dutifulness. However, it should not be totally equated with fairness or justice understood in a Western philosophical context. [24] For Confucius, *yi* is frequently paired up with the vice of excessive concern for profit—to denote fair distribution of wealth and the lack of greed (e.g., *A* 16:10). It also renders other meanings, such as the importance of doing what is right (*DM* 20:5). [25] Here, one repays evil with justice (*A* 14:34). Thus, some scholars liken him with the prophets of the Old Testament. [26]

Mencius similarly argued that profit cannot be the measurement for choosing or determining what is right (*M* 1A:1). He further connected the virtue of righteousness with the emotions of *xiu* 羞 ("shame") and *wu* 惡

("dislike") to illustrate the psychological reason for choosing righteousness: one will not allow oneself to be disgraced by committing an unrighteous act (*M* 2A:6; 6A:6).

Courage (*yong* 勇)

Confucius named *yong* 勇 as one of the three virtues that express one's inner moral force, and through which one attains the Way (*DM* 20:8). He also clarified that courage must be accompanied by *yi* and practiced for the sake of righteousness (*A* 17:23). Thus, sacrificing one's life for what is right is a courageous act (*A* 14:12).[27] Mencius made a similar claim (*M* 2A:2), and in his famous analogy of choosing bear's palm over fish when one cannot have both, he further stressed that we should choose righteousness over life (*M* 6A:10).

In sum, the rigorous views of Confucius and Mencius about upholding righteousness run parallel to the Christian practice of martyrdom. Like the prophets of the Old Testament, they appealed to the authority of Heaven and fearlessly criticized those unrighteous rulers and the prestigious (*M* 7B:34). Finally, I agree with Lee Yearley that *jing* 敬, being the appropriate virtue and gratuitous response to Heaven, can be compared to the Christian virtue of gratitude.[28]

NOTES

1. Tu Wei-ming, "The Implications of the Rise of 'Confucian' East Asia," *Daedalus* 129, no. 1 (Winter 2000): 204–7.

2. The *Analects*, widely accepted as the most reliable source of Confucius's doctrines, is a collection of sayings by the Master and his disciples. The *Great Learning* (a short text attributed to Confucius) and the *Doctrine of the Mean* (a discourse attributed to Confucius's grandson) are two texts relevant to transmission of the teachings of Confucius. See Confucius, *Confucian Analects, the Great Learning, and the Doctrine of the Mean*, trans. James Legge (New York: Dover Publications, 1971); *The Analects*, trans. D. C. Lau (Middlesex, UK: Penguin Classics, 1979); Mencius, *Mencius*, trans. D. C. Lau (London: Penguin Classics, 1970); Xunzi, *Basic Writings*, trans. Burton Watson (New York: Columbia University Press, 1963).

3. Tu Wei-ming, *Humanity and Self-cultivation: Essays in Confucian Thought* (Berkeley, CA: Asian Humanities Press, 1979), 37.

4. James T. Bretzke, "The *Tao* of Confucian Virtue Ethics," *International Philosophical Quarterly* 35 (1995): 34.

5. Liu Yu-li, *The Unity of Rule and Virtue* (Singapore: Eastern Universities Press, 2004), 37.

6. See Chan, Yiu-sing Luke, "Why Scripture Scholars and Theological Ethicists Need One Another: Exegeting and Interpreting the Beatitudes as a 'Scripted Script' for Ethical Living," (PhD diss., Boston College, 2010); Liu, *The Unity of Rule and Virtue*, 44–49; Edmund D. Pellegrino and David C. Thomasma, *The Christian Virtues in Medical Practice* (Washington, DC: Georgetown University Press, 1996), 14; Tu Wei-ming, "Confucianism," in *Our Religions*, ed. Arvind Sharma (New York: HarperOne, 1993), 141, 186.

7. Bryan Van Norden, *Virtue Ethics and Consequentialism in Early Chinese Philosophy* (New York: Cambridge University Press, 2007), 16–21.

8. Rodney Leon Taylor, *The Religious Dimensions of Confucianism* (Albany, NY: SUNY Press, 1990), 2.

9. See also Lee H. Yearley, "Virtues and Religious Virtues in the Confucian Tradition," in *Confucian Spirituality*, vol. 1, ed. Tu Wei-ming and Mary Evelyn Tucker (New York: Cross-road Publishing Company, 2003), 143.

10. Some commentators, unfortunately, interpret Confucius's teaching on filial piety as a kind of blind obedience.

11. 張連康, 廿一世紀的當家思想—論語, 下冊 (台北: 漢康圖書出版社, 1999), 765–68.

12. Erin M. Cline, "Two Senses of Justice: Confucianism, Rawls, and Comparative Political Philosophy," *Dao* 6 (2007): 370.

13. Sandra A. Wawrytko, "Kongzi as Feminist: Confucian Self-cultivation in a Contemporary Context," *Journal of Chinese Philosophy* 27, no. 2 (June 2000): 174–76.

14. Li Chen-yang, "The Confucian Concept of Jen and the Feminist Ethics of Care: A Comparative Study," *Hypatia* 9, no. 1 (Winter 1994): 70, 83.

15. Donald Corcoran, "Benedictine Humility and Confucian 'Sincerity,'" in *Purity of Heart and Contemplation: A Monastic Dialogue between Christian and Asian Traditions*, ed. Bruno Barnhart and Joseph Wong (New York: Continuum, 2001), 233.

16. Tu Wei-ming, *Centrality and Commonality: An Essay on Confucian Righteousness* (Albany, NY: SUNY Press, 1989), 89.

17. Yearley, "Virtues and Religious Virtues in the Confucian Tradition," 143–44.

18. Taylor, *The Religious Dimensions of Confucianism*, 130.

19. William Theodore de Bary, "The Prophetic Voice in the Confucian Noble Man," *Ching Feng* 33, nos. 1–2 (April 1990): 5.

20. However, *Analects* 14:38 could lead one to mistakenly view Confucius as a stubborn person who strives for what is impossible. See 張連康, 857–58.

21. Julia Ching notes that in the pre-Confucian era, *jen* was understood as a virtue of the superior showing kindness toward the inferior. Confucius later transformed it into a general virtue—humanity—although it is also understood as a specific virtue. See Julia Ching, *Confucianism and Christianity: A Comparative Study* (Tokyo: Kodansha International, 1977), 93.

22. Ching, 94. In contemporary usage, *chung* often refers to the loyalty of the inferior to the superior.

23. W. Theodore de Bary, *Learning for One's Self: Essays on the Individual in Neo-Confucian Thought* (New York: Columbia University Press, 1991), as cited in Mary Evelyn Bucker, introduction to *Confucian Spirituality*, vol. 1, ed. Tu Wei-ming and Mary Evelyn Tucker (New York: Crossroad Publishing Company, 2003), 6.

24. R. P. Peerenboom, "Confucian Justice: Achieving a Human Society," *International Philosophical Quarterly* 30 (1990): 17–32, as cited in Bretzke, "The *Tao* of Confucian Virtue Ethics," 31n21.

25. Cline, "Two Senses of Justice," 370.

26. Yeo Khiok-khng, *What Has Jerusalem to Do with Beijing? Biblical Interpretation from a Chinese Perspective* (Harrisburg, PA: Trinity Press International, 1998), 122, 124.

27. Confucius also suggested that one should sacrifice one's life for benevolence's sake (*A* 15:9).

28. Yearley, "Virtues and Religious Virtues in the Confucian Tradition," 143.

Table 1

The Numbering of the Ten Commandments by Various Traditions

Exodus 20 Verse(s)	Septuagint, Orthodox Christians	Philo	Jewish Talmud	Augustine	Roman Catholics (CCC)	Lutherans (LC)	Reformed Christians (ICR)
2	—	—	I	—	I (2–5)	—	(I)
3	I	I	II	I		I	I
4–6	II	II				(—)	II
7	III	III	III	II	II	II	III
8–11	IV	IV	IV	III	III	III	IV
12	V	V	V	IV	IV	IV	V
13	VI	VII*	VI	V	V	V	VI
14	VII	VI	VII	VI	VI	VI	VII
15	VIII	VIII	VIII	VII	VII	VII	VIII
16	IX	IX	IX	VIII	VIII	VIII	IX
17a (neighbor's house...)	X	X	X	X (Deut 5:21b)	X (Deut 5:21b)	IX	X
17b (neighbor's wife...)				IX (Deut 5:21a)	IX (Deut 5:21a)	X	
17c (male/female slaves...)				X (Deut 5:21c)	X (Deut 5:21c)	IX	

* Philo reversed the order of the commandments against killing and adultery (see chapter 3).

Glossary of Chinese Terms

English pinyin	Chinese character	English translation
chung	忠	loyalty/conscientiousness
chün tzu	君子	the gentleman/superior person/noble man
en	恩	kindness
jen	仁	humanity/benevolence
jing	敬	respectful reverence
li	禮	ritual propriety
shu	恕	reciprocity
tao	道	the Way
te	德	virtue
tien	天	Heaven
wu	惡	dislike
xiao	孝	filial piety
xing	性	human nature
xiu	羞	shame
yi	義	righteousness/dutifulness
yong	勇	courage

Index